S0-BBI-270

the Unofficial Guide™ to Online Genealogy

Pamela Rice Hahn

IDG Books Worldwide, Inc.
An International Data Group Company
Foster City, CA • Chicago, IL • Indianapolis, IN • New York, NY

IDG Books Worldwide, Inc.
An International Data Group Company
919 E. Hillsdale Boulevard
Suite 400
Foster City, CA 94404

For general information on IDG Books Worldwide's books in the U.S., please call our Consumer Customer Service department at 800-762-2974. For reseller information, including discounts and previous sales, please call our Reseller Customer Service department at 800-434-3422.

ISBN: 0-02-863867-0

Manufactured in the United States of America

10 9 8 7 6 5 4 3 2 1

First edition

Acknowledgments

Special thanks to David Hebert, Sheree Bykofsky, Brice Gosnell, Tracy Boggier, Kitty Wilson Jarrett, Cynthia Kitchel, Kris Fehr, Matthew Helm, John M. Scroggins, Tim Stowell, Andrew Rice, Ann Rice, Lara Sutton, Taylor Sutton, Charlie Sutton, my parents, Katie Bonvillian, Laura Bonvillian, Susan Albrecht, Keith Giddeon, Eric Ehlers, Kathan Michele, Tony Rice, Jodi Cornelius, Michael Ostlund, Robert Marcum, Kelly Milner Halls, and Troy More; and to Mary Jo, Roberta, Joy, Linda, and everyone else at the St. Marys Community Library. I also want to thank Myrt of DearMYRTLE.com and all the other genealogists who unselfishly donate their time to contribute to and maintain genealogy-related Web sites; their generosity benefits us all. Their encouragement and support (and, in some cases, willingness to be quoted in this book) helped give me the confidence to write www.genealogytips.com.

Contents

The *Unofficial Guide* Reader's Bill of Rights

We Give You More Than the Official Line

Welcome to the *Unofficial Guide* series of Lifestyles titles—books that deliver critical, unbiased information that other books can't or won't reveal—*the inside scoop*. Our goal is to provide you with the *most accessible, useful* information and advice possible. The recommendations we offer in these pages are not influenced by the corporate line of any organization or industry; we give you the hard facts, whether those institutions like them or not. If something is ill advised or will cause a loss of time and/or money, we'll give you ample warning. And if it's a worthwhile option, we'll let you know that, too.

Armed and Ready

Our hand-picked authors confidently and critically report on a wide range of topics that matter to smart readers like you. Our authors are passionate about their subjects, but have distanced themselves enough from them to help you become armed and protected, and help you make educated decisions as

xv

you go through the process. It is our intent that, from having read this book, you will avoid the pitfalls everyone else falls into and get it right the first time.

Don't be fooled by cheap imitations; this is the genuine-article *Unofficial Guide* series from IDG Books Worldwide, Inc. You may be familiar with our proven track record of the travel *Unofficial Guides*, which have more than three million copies in print. Each year thousands of travelers—new and old—are armed with a brand-new, fully updated edition of the flagship *Unofficial Guide to Walt Disney World*, by Bob Sehlinger. It is our intention here to provide you with the same level of objective authority that Mr. Sehlinger does in his brainchild.

The *Unofficial* Panel of Experts

Every word in the Lifestyle *Unofficial Guides* is intensively inspected by a team of three top professionals in their fields. These experts review the manuscript for factual accuracy, comprehensiveness, and an insider's determination as to whether the manuscript fulfills the credo in this Reader's Bill of Rights. In other words, our panel ensures that you are, in fact, getting "the inside scoop."

Our Pledge

The authors, the editorial staff, and the Unofficial Panel of Experts assembled for *Unofficial Guides* are determined to lay out the most valuable alternatives available for our readers. This dictum means that our writers must be explicit, prescriptive, and above all, direct. We strive to be thorough and complete, but our goal is not necessarily to have the "most" or "all" of the information on a topic; this is not, after all, an encyclopedia. Our objective is to help you narrow down your options to the best of what is available, unbiased by affiliation with any industry or organization.

In each *Unofficial Guide* we give you

- Comprehensive coverage of necessary and vital information
- Authoritative, rigidly fact-checked data
- The most up-to-date insights into trends
- Savvy, sophisticated writing that's also readable
- Sensible, applicable facts and secrets that only an insider knows

Special Features

Every book in the series offers the following six special sidebars in the margins that are devised to help you get things done cheaply, efficiently, and smartly:

1. **Timesaver**   Tips and shortcuts that save you time.

2. **Moneysaver**   Tips and shortcuts that save you money.

3. **Watch Out!**   More serious cautions and warnings.

4. **Bright Idea**   General tips and shortcuts to help you find an easier or a smarter way to do something.

5. **Quote**   Statements from real people that are intended to be prescriptive and valuable to you.

6. **Unofficially...**   An insider's fact or anecdote.

We also recognize your need to have quick information at your fingertips, and have thus provided the following comprehensive sections at the back of the book:

1. **Glossary**   Definitions of complicated terminology and jargon
2. **Resource Guide**   Lists of relevant agencies, associations, institutions, Web sites, etc.
3. **Recommended Reading**   Suggested titles that can help you get more in-depth information on related topics
4. **Abbreviations and Acronyms Found in Genealogy**   Information on abbreviations common in genealogy research
5. **Index**

Letters, Comments, and Questions from Readers

We strive to continually improve the *Unofficial Guide* series, and input from our readers is a valuable way for us to do that.

Many of those who have used the *Unofficial Guide* travel books write to the authors to ask questions, make comments, or share their own discoveries and lessons. For Lifestyle *Unofficial Guides*, we would also appreciate all such correspondence—both positive and critical—and we will make our best efforts to incorporate appropriate readers' feedback and comments in revised editions of this work.

Where to write to us:

Unofficial Guides
Lifestyle Guides
IDG Books Worldwide, Inc.
909 Third Ave.
New York, NY 10022
Attention: Readers' Comments

About the Author

Pamela Rice Hahn says her interest in genealogy began with what she considers her writer's curiosity—a desire to learn more about the history behind the hand-pieced quilts that were stitched by her maternal grandmothers and other family stories and artifacts; it evolved from there. In addition to *The Unofficial Guide to Online Genealogy*, Pam is also the lead author of *Teach Yourself Grammar and Style in 24 Hours* (Sams/Macmillan General Reference, June 2000), *Master the Grill the Lazy Way* (Alpha Books/ Macmillan General Reference, June 1999), and *How to Use Microsoft Access 2* (Sams/Macmillan Computer Publishing, July 1999). She has served as editor for a local community-action commission newsletter, *The AMCAC News*, as well as for a number of computer-related and business newsletters. In addition, she has taught business and sales training seminars; her most recent speaking engagements have been about writing opportunities on the Internet. Pam has published several hundred bylined and ghostwritten business, general interest, technical, and humorous articles that have appeared in *Glamour, Country Living, Business*

Venture, Current Notes, and other national publications. In addition, she works as a technical editor and writer for Macmillan Computer Publishing, Sybex, Osborne, Quessing, and DDC.

Pam is publisher and editor-in-chief for the online magazine *The Blue Rose Bouquet* at www.blueroses.com, and she maintains several other Web sites, among them her personal site at www.ricehahn.com as well as www.ricehahn.com/grill, www.genealogytips.com, The Ultimate Chronic Illness Resource Directory at www.ricehahn.com/resource, and, along with Keith Giddeon, the Authors on the Undernet chat channel pages at www.blueroses.com/authors.

Pam is the 1997 winner of The Manny Award for Nonfiction from the MidWest Writers Workshop.

The *Unofficial Guide* Panel of Experts

The *Unofficial Guide* editorial team recognizes that you've purchased this book with the expectation of getting the most authoritative, carefully inspected information currently available. Toward that end, on each and every title in this series, we have selected a minimum of two "official" experts comprising the Unofficial Panel who painstakingly review the manuscripts to ensure the following: factual accuracy of all data; inclusion of the most up-to-date and relevant information; and that, from an insider's perspective, the author has armed you with all the necessary facts you need— but that the institutions don't want you to know.

For *The Unofficial Guide to Online Genealogy*, we are proud to introduce the following panel of experts:

> **Matthew Helm**   Mr. Helm is the executive vice president and chief technology officer for FamilyToolbox.net. He is also the publisher of the *Journal of Online Genealogy*, and the creator and maintainer of Helm's Genealogy Toolbox and a variety of other Web sites. Mr.

Helm is the coauthor of *Genealogy Online For Dummies, Family Tree Maker For Dummies*, and two upcoming books, *Tracing Your Roots Online* and *Get Your Degree Online*. He is also on the board of directors of GENTECH, a nonprofit organization promoting the use of technology in genealogy, and a member of the Association of Professional Genealogists.

John M. Scroggins   During his 35-year career with the U.S. National Archives and Records Administration (NARA), Mr. Scroggins created and later directed the regional archives program, managed microfilming operations and audiovisual and cartographic records, and worked on the requirements for several automated systems, including NARA's NAIL system. After retiring from NARA, he worked briefly for Ancestry.com as director of electronic records. He has received the Federation of Genealogical Societies Award of Merit for his efforts to bring the federal government's historical and genealogical records to the people and to build and strengthen archival outreach programs.

Mr. Scroggins holds a bachelor's degree in history from Jamestown College and a master's degree in public administration from The American University, and is a member of the Academy of Certified Archivists, the Society of American Archivists, and several genealogical societies.

Tim Stowell   Active in online genealogy for 4 years, Mr. Stowell currently coordinates 13 county and two state sites for the USGenWeb

Project. In his 23 years of doing genealogy research, Mr. Stowell has worked with marriage, obituary, newspaper, and census records either in original form, electronic form, or microfilm. He's also done research for himself and others at the National Archives in East Point, Georgia, and the State Archives in Atlanta and Nashville. A native of Newnan, Georgia, Mr. Stowell corresponds with several dozen people from all over the United States and the world on a monthly basis.

Introduction

Introduction

Whether you are curious about how to discover your roots, or are already a seasoned genealogist facing an overwhelming stack of inherited family papers, or just embarking on tracing your ancestors, be thankful for the Internet.

Not that many years ago, you probably never would have imagined accessing the great libraries of the world from the comfort of your own home—at least not without amassing huge telephone bills and needing to have language interpreters standing by. No one would have believed that you could sit at your own desk and research the Civil War era (or any era, for that matter) without ever touching a piece of paper.

The Internet has changed our lives. Now, all those things are possible, and if you're reading this introduction, you'd probably like to learn how to do them. In this book, we've taken the guesswork out of the process.

Simplifying the Process

Genealogy research isn't easy. Add trying to find things on the Internet, and it can be a daunting task. That's why we'll show you how to find the resources you need to research your lineage—and we'll do so in a way that will make your work as painless as possible.

Even if you're not familiar with genealogy, we've broken down everything you need to know and presented it in an easy-to-learn fashion.

Unofficially...
genealogy:
An account of one's descent from an ancestor who did not particularly care to trace his own.

Human curiosity about the past isn't a recent phenomenon. "Who are your people?" may be the way some now phrase the question, but the desire to know the answer to that question is a historical one—of biblical proportions; that's why you read about so many of those *begats*. That's how the Gospels establish that Jesus is a descendant of David—Matthew and Luke tell who begat whom in much the same way you'll be doing your genealogy documentation. Although Matthew starts from the past and works forward, you'll want to start your genealogical work with yourself and work backward, and we'll tell you why.

Working Your Way through the Book

Because you'll spend a lot of your research time gathering proof, in Chapter 1 we'll start off by explaining some of the basics about the types of documents you'll be using. You'll learn the relevance of primary and secondary records and how to go about getting copies of the ones you need for your files.

In Chapter 2, you'll learn how to set up your office, including the basics of what computer equipment you need—not only for organizing your research, but for getting online as well.

Chapter 3 covers ways to organize your research and records so that you begin to form good work habits. So that you can see the names of those who make up your family tree at a glance, we'll teach you how to begin your research, using family group sheets and pedigree charts. We'll show you ways of organizing your information so that you don't have to depend on your memory. Someday somebody else may need to make sense of your research or want to consult the same resources; in order to do so, you (or he or she) need to be able to find resources again; therefore, you'll want to keep your research as organized as possible. You'll also learn about some of the genealogy software programs that are available. In Chapter 4 you'll learn more about using forms, plus information about the different numbering systems unique to genealogy.

Chapter 5 covers email—an explanation of the features of email and a description of the software options, how to check your email directly on the Web, and how to choose a Web-based email service. We'll demystify some of the terminology surrounding the Internet and give you tips and suggestions for using an email program and subscribing to newsgroups and mailing lists so that you can benefit from the genealogy assistance they provide.

Throughout the book, but primarily in Chapter 6, we introduce you to Web sites that help you access many of the records you'll need for your research; some require a fee, membership, or donation, and others are free. The book's companion Web site, www.genealogytips.com, includes links to even more Web sites—some with case study examples about how others organize their work so that you can continue to learn from others.

Unlike others books, which simply list URLs (uniform resource locators—the addresses that send your browser to the Web page you want to view), this book provides details on specific Web sites and resources that you can consult for specific tasks. Whenever possible, when we show a URL, we show the title for that page or other descriptive information; that is usually sufficient to find the page. You can search that title in the site index if it's been moved somewhere else on a Web site or use it to do a search engine or directory phrase search. Search engines such as Profusion (www.profusion.com) and HotBot (www.hotbot.com) let you search on a phrase. Others, like AltaVista (www.altavista.com), treat anything you place in quotation marks as a phrase. You'll learn more about this and how to perform efficient online search engine and directory searches when you move on to Chapter 7.

By Chapter 8, you'll be ready to start doing research in earnest. We'll tell you about which records you'll need to gather (starting with yourself) to go about unpuzzling your past. To help you continue to develop good research habits, we'll also teach you about the importance of citing your sources, giving you instructions on how to do basic citations, where to go online for more information, and the books you can buy to find out even more ways to correctly document your research.

In Chapters 9 and 10, you'll learn about gathering information about the rest of your family, including how to go about finding relatives online. Chapter 11 explains how to preserve your family's history by conducting interviews with family members. We'll tell you how to conduct effective interviews and give you suggestions on what questions to ask, including some pointers on how to go about asking sensitive questions. In this chapter you'll also learn about newspaper records and family memorabilia, as well as some of the options available for maintaining and preserving those items.

In Chapter 12, we provide links with explanations about where you can go online to find specific information about such things as the major genealogy libraries in the United States, local Family History Centers (maintained by the Church of Jesus Christ of Latter-day Saints [LDS]) where you can access a great deal of genealogical data, and other online and onsite locations for information compilations.

After you've completed your research on your immediate family, you are ready to move backward in time. In Chapter 13, you'll discover the importance of census records and the meaning of Soundex and how it can help you track down spelling variations in names as you search census records. (You'll also learn why those census records are so important.) You'll find out how to consult the Social Security Death Index (SSDI). We'll also show you how to use city directories and find immigrant information through such things as ship passenger lists. We'll cover the importance of church and courthouse records, plus military and other records.

Chapter 14 provides information about putting your personal Web page online and about efficient Web page design.

Get ready to have some fun in Chapter 15. After you learn about the realities of viruses (and how you can protect yourself against them), we provide information on how you can debunk urban and family legends. We'll teach you how to exchange files online efficiently and point you toward some free online file storage space. Then you'll be ready to learn how to plan an online family reunion. We'll teach you how to gather your family in an online

> **66**
> Latter-day Saints believe that they can perform ordinances such as baptism for their deceased ancestors, linking families together spiritually, enabling them to be together in heaven eternally. Therefore, it is important for Latter-day Saints to research their genealogy so they can be familiar with the people for whom they perform these ordinances.
> —Eric J. Ehlers, genealogist and LDS member
> **99**

chat and tell you about other extras that you can use to provide an inexpensive and easy way to get together with other family members who have Internet access.

We'll wrap things up with the appendixes, with the first one providing one of the most comprehensive genealogy glossaries and guides to abbreviations and acronyms available anywhere. We'll also recommend other books that you can consult for specialized areas of research.

Revolutionary Realities

The PC and Internet revolutions are in full swing. Almost every second of every day, somebody buys a new home computer. Most of those new computer owners make their way onto the Internet.

People like you are turning the Internet genealogy community into a thriving oasis of volunteer-driven pages and resources. Much of what you need for your research is already online. More is being added every day—much of it by people who do volunteer work for such organizations as the Tombstone Project (now known as The USGenWeb Tombstone Transcription Project, at www.rootsweb. com/~cemetery), a group that compiles cemetery records and posts them in a central location.

Because everyone's research takes a slightly different direction, we'll give you information on the basics and beyond, and then, on the companion Web site for this book, www.genealogytips.com, we'll point you toward other online tutorials and resources that can provide additional help. Think of doing your genealogy research as going on a treasure hunt, where one clue leads to another.

We'll provide information on state archives and libraries (and where to find them), and we'll point you to the sites that can help you find out whether there are Web sites maintained for the counties and towns in which you need to do your research.

When you're ready to broaden your scope even further, you'll learn how to consult such resources as the USGenWeb Project (www.usgenweb.org) for nationwide genealogy research. We even provide online information for vital records and other resources for many countries around the world.

The Internet provides countless benefits for those whose busy schedules means it's essential that their genealogy research be done in the most efficient way possible, and sometimes at odd hours. (It's easier to keep things fun if they don't become tedious chores, after all.)

The Web also really shines when it comes to helping those whose disabilities limit the amount of time they can spend away from home doing research. Even when records aren't just a keystroke away, there are volunteer organizations and helpful online assistance sites that are.

Recent technological changes also mean that document duplication, which used to take hours, can now be done at the touch of a button for those who have a scanner (covered in Chapter 2) and the necessary software to run it. Likewise, by digitizing records and saving the images to an electronic medium, such as a CD, you can now easily preserve precious photographic records. In different points in the book and on the Web site, we'll discuss those possibilities as well as information about preserving old newspapers and other family memorabilia.

Throughout the book we refer to the book's companion site, www.genealogytips.com. At this site we list links to Web sites that provide additional

xxxii THE UNOFFICIAL GUIDE TO ONLINE GENEALOGY

information on the topics discussed in each chapter. Think of this site as your own private set of instant genealogical bookmarks. The site provides everything you need to continue on your genealogical journey. Other links at the site will help you for years to come.

Not for Beginners Only

Beginning and seasoned genealogists alike will benefit from the facts compiled on these pages. Even if you're an old hand at using the Internet, you can streamline the work you do online by following the tips and suggestions in this book.

As happens in so many areas of life where so-called experts are involved, you may encounter some snobbery when it comes to contacting someone involved in genealogical research; for some, genealogy is like a social club in which it takes years to prove your worth. Thank goodness those people are few and far between. More than likely, you'll contact others who are happy to help—by answering questions or providing directions about where you can find the answers you need. Hopefully, after you've read this book, you'll appreciate that there's no reason to feel intimidated in your quest or because of your questions.

Genealogy is an adventure. Some call it an addiction. Whatever you decide to call it, this book provides lots of ways to not only make your research more efficient, but to keep it fun.

Get ready to embark on the most exciting adventure of your life—discovering the story of your life. Tracing your ancestors will help you acquire a better sense and appreciation of who you are. Turn the page and let your adventure begin!

Getting Started on Your Genealogical Journey

PART I

GET THE SCOOP ON...
Establishing your genealogy goals ▪ What you
can find online ▪ How the Internet can make
your research easier ▪ Finding primary and
secondary source information ▪ The importance
of citing your sources

Beginning Your Genealogical Journey

G enealogy involves searching for, recording, and verifying all the information that proves your family's lineage—your descent from those ancestors who make up your pedigree. In the past, in addition to a great deal of dedication, conducting research into your family history involved a lot of traveling. You had to spend time on trips to the library, courthouse, church archives, newspaper archives—anywhere you might find documents that could shed light on your family's history. You also had to spend a lot of time on the phone, trying to track down sources of information. As long as the search remained in the United States, things weren't so bad; but when you started to look outside the country, the task got more difficult.

The Internet has made my genealogical searches a lot easier, and I'll show you how it can make yours easier, too. Thousands of genealogy sites are available online. Because many people like you have

Unofficially...
People have always been interested in their ancestors. Biblical and other ancient accounts of family lineages indicate that an awareness of family history was just as important to people long ago as it is now.

made their research available on personal Web pages, their efforts might ease your search. More and more government offices are making historical information easier to find by publishing it on the Web. On top of that, a great number of commercial genealogy sites have made information available for a fee.

Now that a lot of information is easier to find, more and more people are getting involved in genealogical research. They come from all walks of life—men and women, professionals and students, teenagers and grandparents. Each has his or her own reason for pursuing genealogy. Whatever your reason, you're sure to find a rich history and interesting stories while you research your family.

But researching a genealogy isn't all roses. You're bound to hit some rough spots, where source information doesn't exist or research trails hit a dead end. It can be very frustrating work, but identifying your family's place in history is a rewarding gift to yourself and to subsequent generations. Be proud that you've decided to do this, and don't give up. If a trail is cold, it doesn't hurt to leave it alone for a while. Often, information turns up when you don't expect it, and you can go back and fill in the blanks later.

Using the Internet

As more people have become interested in genealogy, the Internet has begun to revolutionize the way research is done. The following are some of the advantages of this trend:

- *Information*   More and more data is becoming available.

- *Access*   In many cases you can communicate instantaneously with other researchers.

- *Fast answers*   You get the kind of immediate gratification that may help maintain interest longer.

- *Shortcuts*   Other people may have done a lot of your research for you.

On the downside, because of the questionable quality of some online data and the risk of encountering scam artists, if you use the Internet to do research, you must be diligent in verifying your findings thoroughly. I cover this in more detail in Chapter 3 and elsewhere throughout the book.

You can connect to the Internet in a variety of ways. I'll cover computer and other technological issues in Chapter 2, to give you an idea of what you'll need for genealogical research.

Many people now use the WebTV interface, which allows you to view Internet Web pages on a television. If you have such a system, you will be able to do a fair bit of your genealogical research using it. You should note, however, that WebTV won't allow you to use a great deal of the resources that are available when you search through a regular computer's browser. WebTV is not a personal computer, and you cannot run software on it. That means that you may not be able to download some information. For example, Adobe Acrobat files are saved in a format known as .pdf, which stands for portable document file. The Adobe Acrobat Reader program displays .pdf files on a computer screen, but it doesn't work with WebTV. If you want to take advantage of some of the documents that are available in .pdf format, you'll have to use a computer.

66
You know you're hooked on genealogy when you've researched your family tree back to Adam and Eve and still want to continue looking further.
—Raymond Keith, genealogist
99

What's out there

Some records you'll need in your genealogical search can still be found only in archives, attics, courthouses, old churches, or town halls. But according to USGenWeb (www.usgenweb.com), approximately 3,300 counties in the United States have records available online, and that number increases daily.

It's not just the counties that are getting in on the act, either. Because of the increased interest in online genealogy, big business has a presence in the world of genealogy as well. On the Web, the thousands of genealogy sites you come across fall into four main categories:

- Commercial sites, which charge a membership fee or promote software and other products
- Free sites, which are provided by volunteers
- Government sites, which provide resources through municipal, state, or federal government departments
- Hybrid sites, which combine aspects of the other three (such as free services provided by commercial sites that promote products)

You'll learn more about the different types of sites in Chapter 6.

This book contains many pointers to Web sites that may help you with your genealogy research. I've also created a companion Web site for this book, www.genealogytips.com, where I provide links to all the Web addresses (commonly called *URLs*, for *uniform resource locators*) mentioned in this book. In choosing sites to include in the book, and in creating the companion Web site, I asked several questions:

- Have the sites been helpful to me personally in my work?
- Are they recommended by Web sites that regularly rate the popularity of genealogy sites?
- Which of the rated sites best represent the types of services that are available on the Web?
- Which sites turn up in Web searches?
- What is the quality of the navigation at the site (that is, how easy is it to follow links and find information within the site)?
- Which of these Web sites will appeal to the most people?

I don't mention Web sites in this book and on the book's companion Web site according to some type of formal "page hits" rating system. I have tried to weigh how beneficial each site would be, and take into consideration its likelihood of being one that has had or would have longevity. One factor that's hard to predict is whether a Web site that is online today will be there when you're ready to check that page tomorrow. The Internet is an ever-evolving environment. For example, during the writing of this book, one of the major free sites (RootsWeb Genealogical Data Cooperative) was purchased by a commercial site (Ancestry.com).

Determining your research objective

People begin genealogical quests for many different reasons. You may be interested in history, or you might want to research your family's medical history to find out about diseases or other illnesses that have affected your relatives. You might even be hoping to find a family connection to someone famous.

Bright Idea
The Escapees RV Club has message boards devoted to genealogy, the Internet, and other pursuits on its Web site, at www.escapees. com/webx. If you own an RV, circle the wagons and post to the genealogy board; you'll help make it an active message board and meet others who share your interests.

Determining your main objective(s) will help you decide on the type of research to do. If you are interested in your family's medical history, for example, you will look mostly at medical records and death certificates, but if you are interested in trying to get into the Daughters of the American Revolution (DAR) or another society, you will look more at service and military pension records.

The type of end product you want will also determine the kind of research you do. Consider the following:

- Do you want a simple family tree? If so, your focus will mainly be on significant dates, such as births, marriages, and deaths.

- Do you want an album to present to your children or your grandchildren? In this case, your focus will be on a combination of significant dates and special mementos, such as documents and photos.

- Do you plan to produce a book? If so, you'll want to dig around for all of the above, as well as for stories that will interest the reader.

Your research objectives may change, of course, as you go more deeply into your project. If you focus on your main purposes for doing this work as you go along, you won't lose momentum by getting hung up in tangential material.

Where to start

After you've identified your research objectives, start with yourself. I'll cover this idea in more depth in Chapter 8, but for now, know that the trick is to figure out what kind of information you need to gather. You need to start by collecting and recording, in a structured manner, whatever you can about yourself. After that, you can move on to your siblings and parents, and then your grandparents, and (if the information is readily available) your great-grandparents. If you do this before going on to anything else, you'll have a firm foundation for later work. It's much better to start your research with a focused, rather than a willy-nilly, approach.

Don't be in a rush to gather a stack of documents pertaining to dates and places of births, marriages, deaths, military service, or church affiliation. Although all these records will be useful to you eventually, understanding how they will be useful will help you to better organize your quest. Granted, when it comes to genealogy, the according-to-Hoyle police aren't going to show up at your door with a warrant to inspect your records to verify that you're complying with the standards. But you'll save yourself a lot of grief later if you learn some of the basic concepts now.

The two terms you'll probably encounter most often during your foray into genealogy are *primary source* and *secondary source*. As you'll soon discover, a primary source document can sometimes contain secondary source information, and vice versa. You'll better understand what I mean as you work your way through the next sections of this chapter.

Primary sources

A *primary source* is an unbiased, objective record of an event made at or near the time the described event happened. Primary sources, according to the Library of Congress Web site (www.loc.gov), are "actual records that have survived from the past, such as letters, photographs, articles of clothing." Primary sources are considered the most reliable source of information about the past. Ideally, you

Timesaver
You may be able to do a quick online search on a surname and find that a great-grandparent's ancestry has already been traced back several generations. You'll need to confirm the information you find, of course.

want information that was recorded by someone who didn't have a personal interest in the event. A few examples of primary sources are birth certificates, marriage certificates, and census records. You will encounter many different forms of primary sources as a family historian.

Timesaver
Contact family members and tell them to hang on to all family documents—including certificates, family Bibles, photographs, and other items of historical and family value. Getting this information from within the family is often much easier than having to track down names and places on your own.

In the United States and every Canadian province except Québec, the official government records of births, marriages, and deaths are called *vital records.* (In other countries and Québec, official government records are called *civil registration.*) Primary source records include the following:

- Census records (state or federal)
- Church records (primarily for baptism and marriage)
- Courthouse records (such as birth records, court proceedings—both civil and criminal—deeds, death records, naturalization records, probates, or wills)
- Divorce decrees
- Driver's licenses
- Military records
- Passports
- Ships' passenger lists

In some instances, you can use a primary source as a secondary reference. A marriage certificate, for example, is a primary source about a marriage that includes information such as the date and the participants. It may also list the participants' dates of birth, but it shouldn't be used as a primary reference for that; to ensure that you have the most accurate birth information, use the marriage certificate as a secondary source, a pointer to find a primary source.

The Library of Congress (www.loc.gov) defines *secondary sources* as "accounts of the past created by people writing about events sometime after they happened." Examples are history books, personal memoirs, and other things written after the fact. Because of their distance from the actual event, they're considered secondary. (You'll learn more about secondary sources later in the chapter.)

You sometimes need to verify even primary sources. You might find that self-interest has clouded a record; for example, people have lied about their ages in moments of vanity. You may stumble across young men in your family who lied about their ages in order to fight for their country; although Social Security applications and other documents are considered primary records, someone may have had a reason for not telling the truth. On top of all this, the people who record information aren't infallible. Mistakes happened in the past just as they do today. If conflicting records turn up, you might have to find a third source to verify information.

Where to find vital records

In the United States, the county in which the family lived generally serves as the main repository of vital records for that family, so always record the county of residence in your notes. In most New England states, however, vital records are primarily recorded and maintained at the town level. Yet other states have taken the initiative to centralize these records and handle them at the state level.

Records in other countries may be stored centrally or at the relevant state or province area. For example, Scottish birth, marriage, and death records

Watch Out!
Conflicting information can turn up on both primary and secondary source documents. When such discrepancies occur, always track down additional sources to verify the information.

are kept in Edinburgh, and records for England and Wales are kept in London.

You can find information on where and how to obtain vital records in the United States (by state and county) and its territories at www.vitalrec.com. This site is a good example of the free resources you'll find provided by volunteers. It gives information about the various state offices you may need to contact, including the prices of some certificates. The site also provides some information for foreign vital records. Links to foreign vital records can be found at www.vitalrec.com/links2.html.

The U.S. National Archives and Records Administration (www.nara.gov) in Washington, DC, maintains federal records from all three branches of the U.S. Government. See Chapter 6 for information on U.S. National Archives genealogy page and archive sites.

Death certificates

A death certificate is considered a primary source if a doctor, coroner, or medical examiner signed the document and wrote the date, place, and cause of death on it. Other information on the certificate, such as the date and place of birth of the deceased person or the names of his or her parents, is secondary information; it is only as reliable as the informant named on the certificate. Even if you can consider the informant a reliable source, confusion or grief at the time of death may have caused an error in the reporting. Such recording is done from memory, and the informant may have misunderstood what information was requested (for example, whose mother's maiden name is needed: the deceased's or her mother's?). The possibility exists, too, that the person recording the information could have transcribed it incorrectly.

Census records

The U.S. Federal Census has been conducted since 1790. Every 10 years, when the year ends in a zero, the federal government performs a census. In the beginning, very little information was asked; the number of questions has grown in subsequent censuses.

Today's census has continued to evolve. You're probably familiar with the long form/short form census now conducted by the government; this approach generates far less paperwork than if everyone were required to complete a long form with a lot of questions. The long form is distributed to random households, with each household representing a certain portion of the population, much the way TV polls are considered to represent the population as a whole.

Census records are sealed for 72 years after the census is conducted. The government can use the information statistically, but individual information cannot be released until after that time period has passed. This ensures that personal information remains confidential for 72 years after the census has been conducted. I'll provide much more information on census records in Chapter 13.

Military records

Military records exist in a variety of forms, and can act as a great source for genealogists. Whereas military service records may not yield much data, military pension records often contain a great deal of information about soldiers and other military personnel. At the very least, military records can

Bright Idea
If you love solving a mystery, check out Laura Heidekrueger's article "Dissecting Death Certificates for Your Family's Health History," at www.daddezio.com/genealogy/research/grs-il1d.html.

usually point you in a direction where you can uncover more data.

Archives exist for career soldiers, volunteer soldiers, minority soldiers (or "colored soldiers," a historical phrase that means something specific to genealogists and therefore to search engines), navy personnel, and others in the military service. I'll cover military records in greater detail in Chapter 13.

Federal land records

Federal land records are available through the U.S. National Archives (www.nara.gov), where you can search for information about ancestors who purchased land from the federal government in one of the 30 "public land" states (primarily from Ohio west).

Federal land records list only the first transfer of the land; the National Archives does not have information on any transfers of the title after the land was purchased from the government. I'll give you more information about land records in Chapter 13.

Secondary sources

As you know, secondary sources are records created after an event or for which the account was supplied by somebody who was not an eyewitness to the event. Published works such as county histories, genealogies or indexes, and abstracts of original records are considered secondary sources.

Primary records are the most reliable sources of information, but secondary sources can provide valuable clues and shortcuts to other information. For example, almost everything you will find on the Internet is a secondary source. When you view something onscreen, it's a representation of a record, not the actual record itself or even a certified copy of that record. It's been transcribed, so there's a step between the actual record and what you're viewing; this means there's a possibility for error. Even so, you can use the dates and places in these sources as evidence of where to search for more supporting information.

Family Bibles

Many families record important events—dates of births, marriages, and deaths—in the family Bible. Such records are usually reliable; however, it's still a good idea to be cautious about such information, especially if it appears that all the information was recorded at one time rather than as the events occurred. Dates are also sometimes altered, often to mask that a conception took place before a wedding date.

Because many jurisdictions haven't always reliably maintained vital records, the information found in family Bibles is sometimes the only record available. Many state libraries and historical societies keep indexes of data transcribed from Bibles. You can visit Web sites for state or local libraries to see if that information is available in the area you want to research.

Cemetery and tombstone records

Cemetery and tombstone records are another way to confirm ancestors' dates and causes of death. You might want to visit cemeteries themselves at some point, but you can start doing much of your preliminary research online. (Remember that the companion Web site for this book, www.genealogytips.com, provides links to all the URLs mentioned in this book. You'll find links to cemetery and tombstone record sites on the Chapter 6 page of that site.)

Bright Idea
In Chapter 9, you'll learn why you should honor your family's pack rats. Family memorabilia can be an important part of your genealogical research.

Church records

Church records are a valuable resource, especially in areas where early courthouse records have been destroyed by fire or other disasters. Records maintained vary from denomination to denomination and church to church. Some are kept in a national or state repository; others are found on closet shelves of the current church secretary.

If you know your ancestor's religious affiliation, you might check to see what records are available at the appropriate churches in your area. You can also do an online search for "church records" and the denomination and area you need. You might find that records (or information about how to obtain those records) are maintained by a denomination online. (See Chapter 7 for information on how to conduct Web searches.)

Other organizations' records

If one of your ancestors belonged to a fraternal organization or service club, you can research that organization at its Web site as well as find information (or somewhere to write for information) about whether it has membership records archives available for research.

Keeping informed

You can keep abreast of new Web sites, products, product updates, and other news about genealogy by subscribing to some (or all) of the free newsletters available online. The newsletters mentioned in Chapters 5 and 6 are sent by email. You can find information about how to subscribe to Web sites' newsletters at www.genealogytips.com, on the Chapter 5 page.

Many families publish their own online newsletters, and many sites have family forums, where specific surname forums also exist. Historical societies also publish journals and other periodicals that may help in your search. This is an excellent way of keeping informed about areas that interest you.

Get it or put it in writing

I cannot stress this enough: *Write everything down!*

Pretend you're on a soap opera and likely to get amnesia every other day. You'll need a record about every separate piece of paper, research fragment, or photograph. That record should include the following:

- The source of the information
- When you got the information
- Where you got the information
- Who has the original and where it is
- Any anecdotes related to the information

For photographs, you should record who is in the photo, who has the original and negative, and the event or location and date of the photograph.

Write down other useful information about the items you find, and confirm spellings. For example, for years I thought everybody called my mom's great-aunt "Aunt Cow." I always thought, "What a strange name for a tiny wisp of a lady." I only recently found out that they were calling her by a nickname short for "Callie." The shortened version should have rhymed with "Al," but because of the family's Midwestern twang, it ended up sounding like the name of an animal instead. Can you imagine someone a century from now trying to track down the "Cow" in one of my photographs?

Timesaver
It's okay to include cross-references in your citations, as long as they are easy to follow. For example, you could keep a numbered listing of family names, alphabetized by first names, and refer to that when naming people who appear in numerous photographs in your collection.

Your main concern should be getting all the vital pieces of information about a source. You should always write down who told you what, when they told you, and where each piece of information came from. Take good preliminary notes, and you can always write the citation in perfect form later, when you reduce those notes to your final format, whether it's a record in your notebook or typed into a computer program. (Just don't forget to do so.)

Cite Your Sources: A Manual for Documenting Family Histories and Genealogical Records by Richard Lackey (University Press of Mississippi, 1986) was once the authority on how to document sources; however, because it also covers online research, Elizabeth Shown Mills's newer book, *Evidence! Citation and Analysis for the Family Historian* (Genealogical Publishing Company, 1997), is now a popular choice.

Citation style models for genealogy are based on the recommendations of *The Chicago Manual of Style: The Essential Guide for Writers, Editors, and Publishers* (University of Chicago Press, 1993). Genealogy requires some additional models not addressed in that book, especially when it comes to National Archives citation styles, other government documents, and church and family records. Some important things to keep in mind as you cite your sources are the following:

- *Full citation*   Your initial reference to a source should contain all important elements.

- *Later citations*   Subsequent mention of a source can be referenced to the full citation and only needs to contain enough information to identify the original citation.

Unofficially...
Maternal refers to those relating to the mother's side of the family; *paternal* refers to the father's side.

- *Bibliographic entries*   You should begin with the broadest component and move to the most specific element.

- *Bibliographic entries with an emphasis on location* These entries are used with a number of records from a collection of records, citing first the place (geographic location) and then, in descending order of importance, showing specific records or record groups.

- *Bibliographic entries with an emphasis on person* You use these entries when only one record to a single individual is cited to the source; you list first the surname and then the given name.

- *Footnotes or endnotes*   This is left to your preference.

  The following are some examples of citations:

- *Taped lecture:*

  Full citation:

  1. Pamela Rice Hahn, "Refining 'Online' Searches," (lecture, annual conference, *Unofficial Guide to Online Genealogy* [*UGOG*], Smalltown, Ohio, September 2000); audiocassette recording available as UGOG H-0001 (Winnipeg, Canada: Lurquer Recordings, 2000).

  Later citation:

  1. Hahn, "Refining 'Online' Searches," *UGOG* lecture, 2000.

- *Bibliographic entry, person:*

  Hahn, Pamela Rice. "Refining 'Online' Searches." Lecture, annual conference, *The Unofficial Guide to Online Genealogy* [*UGOG*], Smalltown, Ohio, September 2000. Audiocassette recording, UGOG H-0001. Winnipeg, Canada: Lurquer Recordings, 2000.

Timesaver
The University of Colorado at Colorado Springs Department of History has a Web page devoted exclusively to examples of how to cite online sources, at web.uccs.edu/ ~history/toolbox/ citeguide.htm.

- *Web site:*

  Full citation:

  1. The American Museum of Photography, The American Photography Museum, Inc., online (www.photographymuseum.com/index.html), Photographs by Shotaro Shimomura data downloaded 30 September 2000.

  Later citation:

  1. The American Museum of Photography, The American Photography Museum, Inc., online (www.photographymuseum.com/index.html).

- *Bibliographic entry:*

  Photography, The American Museum of, The American Photography Museum, Inc. Online (www.photographymuseum.com/index.html). Shimomura data downloaded 30 September 2000.

Learning how to evaluate the accuracy and reliability of records and sources will be one of the most important skills you acquire in your genealogical work. Citing sources is one way you can do that. Eventually you'll notice that patterns emerge. Aunt Bertha may not have been as good at getting spellings correct as was Granny Smith. When you know that, you'll better know when and where to proceed with caution. You'll always want to verify your information, but it will be helpful to know that you may have to try alternate spellings to verify anything that comes from Aunt Bertha.

There's no such thing as "just for me"

Even if you decide that your venture into genealogy is going to be an informal hobby, the information you gather today will be of immeasurable value to generations in the future. You know that Aunt Trudy hates her real name; however, unless you mention it somewhere in your documentation, those who consult your photo labels won't know that the legal name found on all of Trudy's vital records is Gertrude.

In documenting everything, you'll make things easier on yourself. And although you may not be around to hear them, future generations will thank you for your diligence and thoughtfulness. After all, preserving a sense of family is as important as recording a family's history. Vitality is more valuable than just vital statistics.

Just the facts

- Primary sources or vital records are your most important means to document events, and secondary sources can give you clues to finding other primary source information.

- Important records are being added to the World Wide Web at an astounding rate by individuals, government agencies, and businesses.

- If you take good notes now, you can always do your official documentation later.

- You only need full or complete source citations when you first record the information; after that, it's okay to use a shorter citation that contains enough information to point back to the full citation (and subsequently to your original source).

GET THE SCOOP ON...
Creating a hassle-free workspace ▪ Finding a
computer that's right for you ▪ Getting online
▪ Choosing additional equipment

Online and Off: The Right Tools for the Job

Chapter 2

Before the advent of computers, a home genealogy office could look like the government warehouses you see in movies, with stacks of dusty boxes and imposing rows of filing cabinets lining every wall. Although you'll still need to have a place to store documents and other mementos, doing genealogy online today means that you can store much of your information on a computer and have room for other equipment that will make your job easier.

You may choose to set aside an entire room in your house to use as an office, but you don't have to. Your home office can be as elaborate or as simple as you want it to be—even as basic as keeping additional supplies in a plastic storage box you can slide under the bed and pull out only when you need it. You might even want to consider using a small suitcase. This option certainly makes taking your research on the road a lot simpler: You'll have one bag already packed!

You don't have to have every tool that I'm about to mention. You don't *need* all these things, but you will probably *want* them. In this chapter I'll help you make the choices that will best fit both your needs and your budget.

Setting up your workspace

Whether you consider your computer area your workspace or call it your home office, these elements will make it a pleasant place to be:

- A computer desk
- A comfortable office chair
- An ergonomic keyboard (one especially designed to reduce wrist strain while typing)
- A bookcase and a filing cabinet nearby for your computer manuals, family records, and reference materials
- A convenient storage area for extra paper and printer supplies
- Adequate lighting
- (Optional) An air purifier (No one can give a peak performance in a stuffy room, so why force it? Breathe and work easier instead.)

You should keep the following items within easy reach:

- Three-hole punch
- Paper cutter
- Plastic stackable drawers to hold forms and different types of paper
- Postage scale
- Ruler
- Scissors
- Stapler

Bright Idea
If you like to color-code your work, have a variety of writing instruments available. Office supplies fanatics (like me) recommend having every kind of colored pencil, pen, dry-erase marker, transparency marker, highlighter, and calligraphy pen imaginable. (That doesn't mean I can always find the one I want, though!)

- Long-arm stapler
- Tape dispenser

You'll also want a number of notebooks to organize your research. In addition to a primary three-ring notebook containing my current research, I have a series of research notepads, most of which are spiral notebooks. I have a small one that fits in my purse and larger ones that I carry in an attaché. I like having a different notebook for different tasks—interviews, historical research, and so on. I number these notebooks and indicate the appropriate number on my research log.

Several years ago I began using three-ring notebooks with built-in hangers that you can store as hanging folders in filing cabinet drawers. The spine of each notebook has a holder where you can insert a label. Check with an office supplies store for other organizational ideas. You can order supplies from home, too—check www.genealogytips.com (the Chapter 2 page) for links to office supplies companies. To learn more about using notebooks effectively, see Chapter 3.

Determining your computer needs

Of course, a big consideration in setting up an office will be the equipment you use to get online. In the most basic terms, you'll need a computer, a printer, and a way to connect to the Internet.

As mentioned in Chapter 1, WebTV allows you to surf the Internet using a television. It allows you to view Web pages, and that's about it. You cannot install software on it or use it for other purposes. If you plan to do a lot of research, you're better off doing it on a computer.

The computer you decide on will be your main tool for online research activities. If you already

> ❝
> When doing research at a public library or archive, I bring along a complete index of every name in my computer database. (Yes, all 9,000 of them!) I couldn't possibly bring every family group sheet, since they are housed in sixty-three 4" note-books.—Myrt :), DearMYRTLE daily genealogy columnist, www.DearMYRTLE.com
> ❞

have one, that's fine. This chapter will help you determine whether it will meet your genealogy research needs. You need a good system to ensure that you're getting the best performance from software; you want to complete the task at hand quickly, without having to wait for the computer to catch up.

In the following section, you'll learn about important computer components that affect the speed, performance, and utility of your system. When you understand the important things to look for, you can purchase a package deal or even have someone build a computer for you.

Macs tend to be a little more expensive than PCs, and there isn't as much genealogy software available for that platform. For those reasons, this book focuses on PCs. Some people prefer to use a Mac at home if they use one at the office, so that it's easier to transfer work back and forth. Don't think that you need a PC; many genealogists use Macs and wouldn't think of using anything else. It boils down to personal preference; however, if you don't have a computer system yet, price may be a big deciding factor for you.

If you don't own a computer, buy the best system you can afford. Some of the things you should note about your existing system or one you're planning on purchasing include the following:

- The speed of the processor
- The speed of the motherboard
- The amount of RAM installed
- The size of the hard drive
- The monitor size
- The video card (that is, graphics card) memory size

- The speed of the modem
- Backup systems and storage devices
- Surge protection and uninterruptible power supplies (UPSs)
- The type of printer

The following sections cover all these items, giving you an idea of what to look for in each one.

The processor

The processor is the heart of the computer. Some people may still refer to it as a *central processing unit (CPU)*, but the majority of users now simply call it a processor.

A variety of processors are available; you have probably heard of Intel and AMD, two of the biggest sellers. Intel produces the Pentium III and other chips, and AMD produces the K-6. Both chips do basically the same thing: process information.

For genealogy research, as for most other work, the most important aspect of the processor is its speed. The processor speed indicates how fast the computer can process information; the faster it is, the faster programs will run.

You can get an idea about the speeds currently available in new systems by taking a look at newspaper ads or the Web for computer systems. The higher-priced systems contain the faster chips, and the discounted or clearance models show the lower end of the spectrum. Quite often, even the discounted models will be fine for your purposes.

Those who test software or do technical writing update their computers frequently. Regardless of how hard anyone tries to remain up to date, however, there's no such thing as waiting for the best deal or the biggest and brightest anymore. Technology

Timesaver
You can find the latest news and specs for Apple's Macintosh computers and operating system at www.apple.com. The Microsoft site for the Windows operating system can be found via the All Products link at www. microsoft.com. These links and others are available at www. genealogytips. com.

moves too fast. Technological advancement is estimated to be doubling every 18 months. Many experts now recommend that a user upgrade his or her computer system at least every two years.

You don't necessarily have to upgrade your system every couple years, but working on an older computer costs you in productivity. Access times on the Internet can be sluggish as your computer gets bogged down processing the data and tries to catch up. You may have a very fast modem, but that's immaterial when your computer can't keep up with the data it's receiving.

Having a faster processor means that you'll have less difficulty when trying to run more than one program, so your productivity level will increase. Computer people call this *multitasking*. For example, you can run a Web browser and a genealogy software program at the same time, so you can shift back and forth without having to close the programs. RAM, as you'll learn soon, is also an important consideration when it comes to multitasking.

The motherboard
The motherboard is the main circuit board inside a computer. It contains the processor, bus, memory sockets, expansion slots, and other components. The bus allows the computer to exchange information between its parts. The slower the speed of the bus, the longer it will take to process your information and get it on the screen.

RAM
The amount of memory also affects the speed of a computer. RAM, which stands for *random-access memory*, provides a computer with the resources necessary to run several programs at once. Think of RAM as the computer's brain power. The processor

Unofficially...
To give you an idea of how fast computers change, the system I'm using to write this book is less than 6 months old. Since I got it, the available speed has almost doubled!

speed is how fast the computer thinks, and the RAM is what it thinks with.

RAM is relatively easy and inexpensive to upgrade, and it's widely available for most computer systems. Some users even install their own. If you don't want to mess with opening up the case, you can take your computer to a local computer store to have it done.

The other components described in this chapter take a little more work to upgrade and might be more expensive. If you have an older computer, you might be able to upgrade the RAM with a small investment and end up with a computer that will work well for you for a few more years. If you're looking at a new computer, you can always put more RAM in later if you find that what's there is not enough.

Fortunately, software retailers tell you how much RAM you'll need to run a particular program. Knowing what you'll want to do with the computer will help you decide the minimum requirements you'll need. I talk more about genealogy programs in Chapter 3.

The hard drive
The hard drives on newer computers are measured in gigabytes. Like RAM and processing speed, the bigger the hard drive, the better. Programs are a lot fancier than they used to be, and they take up a great deal of hard drive space. They get bigger with each new release, and that doesn't show any sign of changing anytime soon.

With only a little bit of research, you can find the current standards by checking the Web sites of major computer retailers or by reading the ads in the Sunday paper. You can get a good idea what's

> 66
> If computers were fashion, you'd need a new one every 15 minutes just to keep up.
> —David L. Hebert, www.lurquer.com
> 99

Watch Out!
Many operating systems use spare hard drive space for virtual memory, which allows the computer to store information temporarily on the hard drive until it's needed again later. If your hard drive is very full, the computer won't be able to store as much, so it will run more slowly.

currently available by looking at the package deals in ads. The newer (and more expensive) packages show the high end of what's out there, and the slightly less expensive, discounted packages show the middle of the road. This will give you an idea of what to look for in a new system, or what you should upgrade in your old one.

The monitor

Monitor prices have dropped significantly in the past several years, and you'll probably find that if you're considering a new system, a 17-inch monitor will only cost you a little more than a 15-inch one. A larger monitor allows for more screen "real estate." If you plan to run several programs at once, a larger monitor lets you stagger your windows so you can view more than one of them at a time. Even if you don't plan to run several programs at once, a larger viewing area makes everything onscreen a little bit larger, saving you some eyestrain. Remember that if you opt for the larger monitor, you'll need to have enough room for it on your desk.

Video RAM

A computer uses a video card to send information to the monitor. Video RAM is different from RAM; it sits on the video card instead of on the motherboard. The more RAM you have on the video card, the faster it will be able to display graphics, videos, Web pages, and everything else that's shown on the monitor.

Your need for video memory depends on the size of your monitor, the number of colors you choose to view, and the resolution at which you set the monitor. To some degree, the number of programs you are viewing at once also plays a role. Your need for video memory also depends on the intended uses for your computer. If the kids plan to use the computer as a 3D gaming machine when you're not using it, you'll probably want to get something with plenty of video RAM. If you're using the computer primarily as an office machine, you can get by with a lot less.

You should check with a retailer to see if the video memory in the machine you're considering buying can be upgraded or if you'll have to purchase an entirely new video card should you need to upgrade.

Even though my system is only six months old, I find that I'm going to need a bigger video card soon. It's not unusual for me to be running several browsers (see the section on browsers later in this chapter), an email client, and one or two chat programs, and also have several documents open in my word processing or genealogy research programs. When I add a graphics-editing program to that mix, I sometimes notice a decrease in performance, such as stray lines that remain on the screen because it doesn't refresh (that is, redraw the images onscreen) properly.

The modem

Computers use modems to transmit information over either phone or data lines. You'll need one if you plan to access the Internet.

Most computers now come with dial-up modems, which can be used to connect to the Internet or to send and receive faxes. These modems use a telephone line.

If you're using a standard Internet service provider (ISP) dial-up connection, I cannot overemphasize the importance of having a reliable phone line. If you don't yet have a computer, ask your

Unofficially...
If you have a 17-inch monitor set to 1024 × 768 resolution and 16.7 million colors, you should consider at least an 8MB card. I have a 17-inch monitor on my system and a 16MB video card, and now wish I'd have sprung for the 32MB one.

Bright Idea
Even if you don't have a computer yet, you don't have to fret about all the Web sites mentioned in this book. You can usually access the Internet at the local library. That's a great place to begin your online adventure.

neighbors if they've experienced any problems with their online connections. Otherwise, put your computer through a number of online paces yourself. Connect to the Internet, and test to see how long it takes to load Web pages.

Test your system under as many different weather conditions as possible to ensure that your connection is dependable. The weather may not seem important; you're inside a safe and warm (or air-conditioned, cool) room, after all. But in some areas, especially rural areas where phone equipment may be dated to begin with, moisture can wreak havoc with modem transmission. Phone line static is your enemy. In any endeavor, the last thing you need is an additional hassle that's beyond your control. If you find that static or line noise is disrupting your Internet service, contact the phone company's service department to determine how to correct the problem.

Dial-up modems used to be the only option available, but depending on where you live, you may be able to find higher-speed alternatives. Cable modems can operate at up to 100 times faster than dial-up modems. Asynchronous Digital Subscriber Line (ADSL) modems offer download results comparable to those of cable modems, but they have slower upload speeds (for when you're sending files out over the Internet). However, ADSL upload speeds are still considerably faster than those using dial-up modems, and the average user doesn't upload large files very often. If you're looking for a high-speed connection and these options are available in your area, either one should easily meet your needs.

If you want to use any of the faster modem technologies that are available, you'll need to have an Ethernet card installed in your computer, to network computers together. If you don't want to tackle that task, you may want to purchase one with your computer or have one installed by your favorite computer store.

File backups and sharing options

Computers are convenient and can do amazing things for your productivity, but remember that nothing is infallible. Like the old saying about putting all your eggs in one basket goes, you should never leave the only copy of a data file on your computer.

Backing up your data means making copies of your files so that you can retrieve them later should something disastrous happen. A few short years ago, floppy disks were really the only alternative. You can still use floppies, but they don't hold very much data. Personally, I don't like them. I've lost more data due to faulty floppies than I have in hard drive crashes. If you're serious about your data, you should probably investigate some of the other options that are available.

If you're investing in a new computer system, you might consider buying one with a CD-R (compact disc–recordable) drive. Prices of CD-R drives have dropped, and they are often the most practical way to back up files for your own archives or to share with others. You can purchase blank CDs, which each hold 600MB to 650MB of data, depending on your CD-R drive. Almost everyone has a CD-ROM drive on his or her system, so even if Uncle Max can't record CDs to share with you, he'll still be able to use any CDs that you send to him.

Bright Idea
If you're worried about tying up the phone line or missing important incoming calls while you're doing online research, consider getting a second phone line. If it's available in your area, voicemail from your telephone company is another alternative.

Moneysaver
Consider getting
a refurbished
computer. Most
refurbished sys-
tems come with
the same soft-
ware and warranty
as new units, but
they cost
less money. For
information
on where you
can find one,
see www.
genealogytips.
com.

CD-RW (compact disc–recordable rewritable) drives are slightly more expensive than CD-R drives, and a blank CD-RW disc costs a little more than a CD-R, too. The nice thing is that CD-RW discs can be erased and reused up to 1,000 times. You can also use regular CD-R discs in a CD-RW drive.

A text file is usually small enough to fit on a floppy disk. Larger files may not. A CD-R can hold around the equivalent of 450 floppy disks, but that's not the only option available. Some people use a Zip drive for larger files (but fewer people have those on their systems, so they're not as "transferable"). When you start taking digital photographs or scanning in family photos, your archive storage or file sharing needs will increase dramatically.

Most newer CD-R or CD-RW drive models also allow you to copy directly from one CD to another. For example, I have a DVD-ROM drive and a CD-RW drive. After I make a CD archive, I can easily make a backup of my original to share with other family members. I put the original in the DVD/CD drive and record the backup in the CD-RW drive. Check with your computer vendor to determine the cost of having both types of drives on your system.

You can find links to CD-R and CD-RW drive manufacturers online at www.genealogytips.com.

UPSs and surge protectors

Steady and stable electrical current is a computer user's best friend. Sensitive equipment such as a computer requires a consistent supply of power of the correct specifications in order to operate. A power surge or other disruption while a computer is writing data to the hard drive can cause a great deal of physical damage to a hard drive, and it can cause you to lose the data that was being written at the time. It's the leading cause of a scrambled hard drive, whose only cure is usually to reformat and start over, which means you lose all your data. If you have very important data on the hard drive and no backup, you can hire a company that will attempt to recover data from badly damaged disks, even those damaged by fire. But it's a very expensive option and may not work in all situations. To prevent your computer from having these problems in the first place, you can hook up a UPS between your computer system and an electrical outlet.

A UPS acts like a buffer by regulating the power that goes to your computer equipment so that your computer is oblivious to surges, spikes, and brownouts. When the power goes out completely, a UPS switches to its battery backup system, which gives you enough time to properly shut down your computer and go sit with a candle in a corner somewhere, tapping your foot and performing other impatient gestures while you wait for the power to come back on. Options available on UPSs include phone line protection and multiple power jacks. You can find links to UPS manufacturers at www.genealogytips.com, on the Chapter 2 page.

A surge protector guards against electrical fluctuations causing damage to a computer. Most UPS units have a surge protector built in; however, not all equipment can be run through a UPS. Mine doesn't allow me to plug my laser printer into it. Therefore, I use a separate surge protector for the printer.

Printers
Your choice of printer will depend on whether you plan to do color or high-quality printouts. Not long ago, the print quality of inkjet printers was far below

Watch Out!
If you use a UPS and the power goes out, don't rely on the battery supply to keep working. A UPS is designed only to have enough power to allow you to save your data and shut down the computer before you lose any of your data. Consult the UPS's documentation to see how long you have.

what you could get with a laser printer. That's no longer the case. Both offer high-resolution printouts. A standard laser printer, which limits you to black-and-white or grayscale pages, gets you speedy print-outs. Although a laser printer might be a fairly expensive initial investment, it may actually cost you less per page than an inkjet if you do a lot of printing.

On the other hand, if in addition to printing your family tree research, you want the capability of getting color printouts of some of the Web pages you visit, plan to create your own greeting cards, or would like the ability to do photo-quality printouts of digitized images (whether achieved from using a digital camera or by scanning in existing family photos), then an inkjet printer is probably the kind you'll want to get. You can get a good color inkjet printer for $90–$140. (Color laser printers are available, but most are priced too high for home user budgets.)

Keep these things in mind when you're choosing a printer:

Moneysaver
Try to find a color inkjet printer that lets you swap the color cartridge for a black one when you're only printing text. That way you can save your more expensive colored ink.

- Initial cost of the printer
- Laser cartridge or ink cartridge costs
- Text quality
- Graphics quality
- Printer speed (These speeds vary quite a bit. A laser printer can print several pages in the time it takes an inkjet printer to do just one.)
- Image permanence (Will the toner or ink degrade over time? If you're archiving information, you won't want your printouts to fade.)
- Volume capacity (Most printers are rated as to their duty cycle—that is, the printer's daily page capacity or how many pages you can expect the printer to print in its lifetime.)

You can find links to popular printer manufacturers at www.genealogytips.com, on the Chapter 2 page.

Adapting an older system

If you want to stick your toe in the water before you dive in and just don't feel you can justify the costs involved with a new computer, by all means start with a less expensive, older model. Or if you already have a computer system, before you spend a lot of money on an entirely new system, you might want to update specific components. For example, a new modem is relatively inexpensive, and an old one will cripple you more than older software and a slower processor. A new, faster modem will give you a speedier Internet connection, which means Web pages will load faster for you. The faster the pages load, the more research you'll be able to get done.

The best computer for you depends on your individual needs. As long as the machine is able to do the things you ask it to do, you should be okay.

Given the software you are likely to want to run, you should consider these options the minimum requirements:

- 266MHz processor
- 32MB RAM
- 56Kbps modem

Later, after you've determined that online genealogy is worth an investment, you can splurge on a new computer and give your old system to the kids or let your spouse use it to play solitaire.

Getting online

When you've decided to pursue your genealogy search online, you'll need to have a connection to the Internet.

Bright Idea
ZDNet offers Quick Start Guides that provide tips on installing new computer equipment as well as tips about printers, scanners, digital cameras, and more, at www.zdnet.com.

If you're only using the services of your ISP for personal research, a single ISP connection should be sufficient. Many people use a backup account with another ISP for a number of reasons:

- They divide their time between two or more locations and need local dial-up connectivity at each.

- They telecommute to work from home and cannot afford to be without a connection, so keep a second account as an emergency backup.

- More than one family member is often online at the same time, so it's easiest to have a general family account and a personal one.

If you haven't already chosen an ISP, consider the following points before you sign up with one:

- What are the rates? Do you want to get an unlimited connection, or do you want a plan that allows you a certain number of hours per month? Depending on how much you plan to use it, you may find it cheaper to opt for a number of hours per month. If you plan to be online a lot, be sure to confirm your ISP's definition of an "unlimited" connection. Some charge more if you're online beyond a set number of hours during what they consider "prime time." Also, some ISPs offer an annual flat rate that's usually a little cheaper than the monthly fee. I pay my ISP fees annually rather than by the month; the resulting discount gives me the equivalent of two months of free service.

- Is there a local dial-up number? You'll want to find an ISP that has a local access number you can dial to connect to the Internet so that you don't end up paying long-distance charges every time you're online.

- Does the ISP offer national or international options, such as a toll-free number? You may have to pay extra for such a service, but it can be invaluable if you travel frequently.

- Does the ISP support your modem speed? Some ISPs can only handle connections at 28.8Kbps, either because of their hardware or problems with your local phone lines. Whatever the cause, it's considerably slower than the 56Kbps most modern modems can handle. Even if you have a 56Kbps modem, you will suffer slow connection speeds if your ISP is set up to handle only 28.8Kbps connections. These speeds can differ from area to area, so ask about your specific city or town.

- Will your telephone lines support the modem speed? Some older telephone lines do not handle data very well. You might find that your 56Kbps modem can't connect at any faster than 14.4Kbps.

- Does the ISP provide high-speed options such as ADSL or cable modem connections? Check the yellow pages in your phone book. The tech support people for those systems can answer any questions you might have about the different modem requirements. Be sure to check the monthly connection costs, too. Your connection fees are an ongoing expense, so you want to make sure they fit within your budget.

- Do you get to choose your account information, or is it assigned? Some ISPs won't let you choose your login name if they use a specific system for generating logins. Because your login name is usually your email address, this may be a concern for you. If you can't choose

Moneysaver
If you're away from home, you don't have to dial long distance to check your email. Web sites such as Mail2Web (www.mail2web. com) let you access an email account through a Web interface.

your login name, ask if the ISP can provide you with an *email alias*—an email address that gets forwarded to your main email account.

- Does the ISP provide Web space? Most ISPs offer a 2MB or 5MB storage area for user pages. If you want to create a Web site but don't plan to go to the expense of getting your own domain, you may want to make sure your ISP has space available.

- Does the ISP provide software? Some ISPs provide Netscape Navigator or Internet Explorer already configured to connect to their servers, and some provide *proprietary software*—that is, software that is designed to work only with their servers. Other ISPs provide no software at all, requiring you to obtain it.

- If the ISP provides software, will you be able to use your own instead? If the ISP uses proprietary software, you may not be able to use your own software.

- Does the ISP have adequate technical support? Find out if the ISP offers a 24-hour technical support line, and investigate other options such as email support and online help guides. If you are new to computers, you may need to talk to technical support a few times to get your software working properly.

- Will the ISP support large email messages and attachments? Some ISPs truncate—that is, cut off—email messages if they exceed a certain size. You may find yourself sending large files by email; if the ISP does not allow large messages, you may suffer delays while trying to find other file transfer options.

Bright Idea
Find out if there are a lot of busy signals or lengthy waits to speak to an ISP representative by calling the ISP a few times before signing up for its services.

- Does the ISP offer newsgroups? Although there are a few free newsgroup servers available, they tend to be very slow. Find out if the ISP offers a good variety of newsgroups in the subject areas you'd like to research.

- Does the ISP offer a free trial period? Many national ISPs provide a free trial period so that you can evaluate their service; local ISPs may also offer special promotions.

Links to national ISPs are available at www.genealogytips.com, on the Chapter 2 page.

Using the Web to find an ISP

If you're having trouble coming up with an ISP and can access the Web from the library or a friend's house, consider trying the following online resources:

- The List (thelist.internet.com) lets you search by U.S. area code (or country code for ISPs located outside the United States).

- CNET (webservices.cnet.com/html/aisles/ Internet_Access.asp) allows you to search by area code and connection type—dial-up, cable, or ADSL.

- Computer Currents (www.currents.net/ resources/ispsearch/index.html) provides a comprehensive search form, with many options for connection types, including high-speed options.

Because these sites contain different data, you should try all three. Searching for "finding an ISP" at a search engine may also provide additional resources.

Dial-up settings

After you choose an ISP, you have to tell your computer how to connect to it. Many times, this is simply a matter of installing the software provided by the ISP—running the program on a floppy disk or CD, and waiting for it to install.

You might have to configure the computer yourself, in which case the ISP will give you instructions on how to set up a dial-up connection for your computer.

Browser options

A *Web browser* is a program that lets you view Web pages. Choosing a browser is like making a Ford/Chevy decision—you're going to use what you're most comfortable using. The differences between the available browsers really aren't that great, and the ultimate choice in a Web browser ends up being personal preference.

You may come across some sites that contain codes which aren't recognized by all browsers; in such cases, the Web site will usually state the best browser to use for that site.

When you're choosing a browser, look for the most recent version that's available. The Internet is always evolving, and so is the software that lets you view it. New technology is constantly being adapted, and older versions won't display some things (for example, JavaScript and plug-ins). Older browser versions may not support those innovations, and you won't be able to view pages that use them.

Be careful, however; don't accidentally download a beta version of a browser. Software developers often release early versions of programs to provide an opportunity to learn about any bugs or glitches in the program (and give the developers a chance to

fix them). The final version contains the full program, without the bugs discovered in the beta
release.

Microsoft Internet Explorer

Windows machines often come with Microsoft
Internet Explorer installed. To use it, you simply
double-click the Internet icon on the desktop, or
click on Start | Programs | Internet Explorer. You
may have to run the Setup Wizard the first time you
use Internet Explorer.

If the program is not located on your hard drive,
you can download it free from www.microsoft.com.
The full version of Internet Explorer includes
email, newsgroup, and Web design tools you can use
to design your own Web site.

Internet Explorer allows you to save sites in a
favorites folder (which you can easily subdivide into
folders for different categories), so that you can
return to a site again without having to perform a
search.

Internet Explorer offers strong encryption,
which means that online transactions are safer when
used with a secure site, such as sites that offer online
banking. The current version also offers a content
advisor that allows you to specify which Web pages
can be viewed by your children when they're surfing
online.

Netscape Communicator

Netscape Communicator offers most of the features
included with Internet Explorer, including email,
newsgroup, and Web design software. It also offers
strong encryption.

Netscape allows users to save the location of sites
using bookmarks. You can download Netscape from

Bright Idea
Having trouble
downloading a
Web browser?
Both Internet
Explorer and
Netscape allow
you to order CDs
of the most cur-
rent version.

www.netscape.com, either as a standalone Web browser (Netscape Navigator) or as a complete software package, including the Internet support tools (Netscape Communicator). Like Internet Explorer, Netscape is free.

Opera

Although Opera isn't free and does not run on a Mac, it offers many of the same features as Internet Explorer and Netscape; in addition, it's a much smaller program, so it usually runs faster on slow machines and laptops.

You can obtain a shareware version of Opera at www.Opera.com. After a 30-day evaluation period, you can choose to purchase the product for $35 or remove it from your hard drive.

Opera offers some unique features that aren't available with the other browsers, such as the ability to toggle the loading of images. Other browsers can be set to display or not display images; to change this setting, you need to access the Preferences in Netscape or Internet Options in Internet Explorer. Opera, however, allows you to toggle images with the click of a button. You can choose to view all images, no images, or only the images that have already been downloaded.

Opera has a similar toggle feature for colors; if you find that a site is hard to read because of the colors or background images, you can switch it to conventional white-on-black simply by clicking a button.

Opera also offers security and a simple email interface that allows you to send email messages by clicking on an email link.

One thing that sets Opera apart from other Web browsers is the way it handles multiple sites. Both Internet Explorer and Netscape only allow one Web page to be viewed at a time—a second Web site requires a new browser window. Opera allows you to connect to more than one site, by using multiple windows within the program, which makes it easy to organize sites when you're doing research.

Other browsers
Many other shareware and freeware Web browsers are available, each with different features. You can find more information on other browsers by visiting the following sites:

- The Ultimate Collection of Winsock Software, www.tucows.com

- Stroud's Consummate Winsock Applications, www.cwsapps.com

- CNET Download.com, download.cnet.com

Browser hints and shortcuts
Despite the differences in browsers, a few tricks apply across the board to Web browsers:

- *Right-clicking your way to freedom*   By using the right mouse button on a link instead of the left, you can access most of the functions you'll want to perform. (Macs only have one mouse button, so this section applies to Windows users only.) Clicking on a link with the left mouse button indicates that you want to load that page; right-clicking provides more options in a popup menu. The following are some of the options available by right-clicking:

    Back or Go Back   If you've followed the wrong link or just want to get back where you were, you can either click the Back button on the Web browser or right-click

Timesaver
If you face any difficulties using the browser you choose, check the browser's online help section for additional information.

anywhere onscreen and choose Back from the popup menu to view the last page you loaded.

Reload or Refresh If you want to reload the same page you're viewing now, you can right-click and select Reload or Refresh, depending on the browser, to tell the browser to request the page again from the server.

Copy You can select Copy from the popup menu to copy selected text or images.

New Window If you want to load a link, but don't want to lose the page you're currently viewing, you can right-click it to select Open in new window. This loads the new page while leaving the original open.

Save Image If you want to save a picture from a Web page, right-click on it to bring up the popup menu. You can choose to view the picture in a new window or save it to your hard drive (Save Picture As).

Copy Location Instead of following a link, you can right-click on it and select the Copy Location option. That copies the URL to your computer's Clipboard so that you can paste it later. This is a great shortcut if you're compiling a list of sites into an email message or a document.

Add Bookmark Known as a favorite in Internet Explorer, a bookmark saves the site location so that you can visit it later. Selecting this option in the popup menu saves the location. Browsers use bookmarks in different ways, so check the browser's help file if you have any questions.

- *Keyboard Navigation*   Some users find using a mouse cumbersome. Even if you don't mind reaching for the mouse, you may find that some of the following keyboard shortcuts save time:

  Reload   You can reload a page on a PC by pushing the Control and R keys at the same time. On a Mac, push the Command and R keys at the same time.

  Back or Go Back   You can move to the previous page by pushing the Alt and left-arrow keys at the same time.

  Forward or Go Forward   If you've already gone backward and want to go forward again, press the Alt and right-arrow keys at the same time.

  Stop Page from Loading   Pushing the Escape key will stop the current action.

  Help   In almost all Windows programs, you can bring up the help screen if you push F1.

  Page Up and Page Down   You can use the Page Up and Page Down keys to navigate throughout a Web page. Pushing the Spacebar has the same effect as pushing the Page Down key, which can provide easy keyboard navigation when you're reading.

  Close   You can close a browser window by pushing the Control and W keys at the same time. Pressing Alt and F4 at the same time also closes a Windows application.

- *Plug-ins*   Some Web sites use plug-ins, or small programs that help browsers display Web content. There are a few plug-ins you may want to

Unofficially...
If you're not a techie type and know that you'll be intimidated by any kind of tweaks to your computer, your best bet is to buy one from a vendor that provides reliable tech support. Many include it for free during the first year and at a low charge thereafter.

download, as many Web sites take advantage of the technology available. All of the following are available for both the PC and Mac:

RealPlayer   Allows you to listen to audio and video broadcasts over the Internet and provides support for MP3 music files, WAV audio files, and other sound formats: www.real.com.

Shockwave   Used by many sites for animation and other graphical presentations: www.shockwave.com.

Apple QuickTime   Allows you to see and hear video and audio broadcasts recorded in Apple's QuickTime format: www.quicktime.com.

Adobe Acrobat Reader   Allows you to view documents published as .pdf (portable document format) files from a browser window or as files downloaded to the hard drive: www.adobe.com.

Additional equipment considerations

Unofficially...
You can find statistics and other information regarding browser popularity and usage at the BrowserWatch Web site, at browserwatch. internet.com.

Outfitting an office doesn't end when you have a computer. Some other equipment you might want to consider includes the following:

- 35mm or digital camera
- Notebook computer (if you plan to travel to do a lot of your research or to take with you to the library)
- Photocopier
- Tape recorder (with a warning indicator that tells you when you reach the end of a tape)
- Transcription machine
- Tripod

- Voice recognition software
- Video camera (such as a digital camcorder, which is likely to include a feature that lets you take still shots)

Before you add additional hardware or other equipment to your electronic arsenal, be sure to do your homework. Start by brainstorming. Make a list of why you think you need the equipment. You might determine that you're better off hiring someone to do the additional work for you. For example, you don't necessarily need to go to the expense of buying a scanner that will scan slides (35mm transparencies) if you have only five of them to do. Likewise, you probably won't need a separate photocopying machine if you have a scanner connected to your computer equipment. Many scanners come with the software necessary to use your scanner as a copier by sending scans directly to the printer, without saving a copy to the hard drive.

One advantage of working with a digital image is that even if it's a scan of an existing image, you'll be able to see details that aren't otherwise visible in the photograph because you can blow it up. The technology that was once only for show in detective movies is now available on your home PC.

You can use a scanner with a computer to archive and preserve family photos and other records. Before you make a decision about whether to include a scanner among your electronic tools, see the links at www.genealogytips.com, on the Chapter 2 page. These Web sites provide the answers and instructions you'll need on how to go about getting the best scans.

When considering a scanner, first you need to decide what you'll be using it for. Will you be

> 66
> It is my firm conviction that you can obtain better images from poor negatives, prints, and slides with your scanner than the best photo darkroom!—Michael J. Sullivan, professional photographer, www.hsdesign. com/scanning/ salvaging/ salvaging.html
> 99

Moneysaver
If you don't think you'll use a scanner enough to justify the expense, you'll probably be better off having that work done at a local copy center.

scanning only photographs, or do you need the ability to scan slides and transparencies, too? Do you plan to scan pages from a book? If so, you'll need a flatbed scanner so that you can lay the book on the scanner plate. Do you plan to use it to scan legal-sized documents? Then you'll need a larger surface scanning area to accommodate those 14-inch-long pages. Do you plan to use a scanner in lieu of a photocopier? Do you need optical character recognition (OCR) to scan text and convert it to a format for use with a word processor rather than simply taking a photographic image of the text?

Manufacturers make scanner models to fit almost any needs you might have. Do your research so that you make sure that the one you get fits all your needs. Make a list of your anticipated or known scanner usage needs. Weigh those needs against the price to purchase a scanner that fulfills them all.

Just the facts

- Establishing a home office or work area will help keep you organized and keep all your important paperwork in one convenient place.

- Many genealogists find it helpful to keep all their to-do lists, notes, and logs in a master notebook.

- You'll be spending a lot of time working on and at your computer, so you need to carefully consider which features are important to you.

- You can save time and money by scanning your documents at home.

Managing Information

PART II

GET THE SCOOP ON...
Planning your work and organizing your files
▪ Choosing genealogy software ▪ Publishing
research on the Web ▪ Using software to
document nontraditional lifestyles

Charting Your Course and Following It

Chapter 3

G enealogy research may be the only thing that generates more paper than law school: The proliferation of paper can be astounding. If you're not on top of the game, all the paper can quickly overwhelm you.

With a little foresight, you can easily overcome the paperwork challenge. Getting a handle on organizing your information will help you in a lot of ways. Not only will you be able to access your information quickly, but you'll find it easier to remember what you have. It complements your mental filing system, too.

Because you're reading an online genealogy book, it makes sense that you'll eventually want to enter all your information into the computer. To do so, you'll need to find out what you'd like in a computer program, and in this chapter you'll get a feel for what's out there.

Think organization

What good does all your hard work do you if you can't find the document you need when you need it? It's important to plan your research and other genealogical work using good record-keeping habits. By following a few simple steps, outlined in this chapter, you can make your research a lot easier.

The only wrong way to organize your paperwork is to skip doing it in some way or another. Throughout this chapter, I offer suggestions on how you can go about maintaining your files. It's up to you to decide which method will best fit your style. If you're not sure about what that style is, there's no reason to fret. If you start out using notebooks and decide that method doesn't work for you, switch to using a system of file folders, or vice versa.

Creating a "Swiss army knife" notebook

In much the same way that a Swiss Army knife is designed to meet every need, your notebooks are one of the most important tools you'll use to organize almost everything related to your research. Some authorities recommend discarding some of your preliminary paper records after you've entered that information into your genealogy program. Even if you keep backups of all your computer data, I believe you should retain your initial paper records as well. You may miss entering something, or you may later want to verify the accuracy of some of the information. If you hang on to all your original records, you'll have your original starting point right there. It can save you from having to find information all over again. If you don't have the space to store the paperwork you've compiled, an alternative would be to donate it to another family member after you get your records stored on the computer.

66
You want your notes on particular events, persons, books, and so forth to be as detailed as possible—including who, what, where, when, why, and how. And most important, always cite the source of your information.
—Matthew L. Helm and April Leigh Helm, authors of *Genealogy Online For Dummies*, 2nd Edition
99

Being online will make your job easier, but you have some work ahead of you. And when you're faced with the vast number of records waiting to be filed, combined with the amount of work you've yet to do on your family history research, it can seem overwhelming. In a way, you're writing the book about your family. Your task is similar to one faced by a character in one of my favorite books, *Bird by Bird: Some Instructions on Writing and Life* by Anne Lamott (Anchor Books/Doubleday, 1995). The title of the book comes from advice Anne's father gave her brother when he was working on a school report on birds. Overwhelmed by what he needed to get done, almost in tears, her brother asked his dad how he was ever going to finish it. His dad told him, "Bird by bird."

I recommend that you establish a primary three-ring notebook, divided into three sections:

- *Your "direct-line research"* This is the pedigree chart that starts with you and fans out to all your direct ancestors.

- *Individual pages of notes* These will later be filed in chronological order, after you've indicated cross-reference notations on them.

- *Guidelines* This serves as the user's manual for the work you've compiled, which you'll learn more about at the end of Chapter 15. It explains how you've set up your notebook and filed your paperwork.

As you'll learn in Chapter 4, you'll be dealing with a number of forms, each of which serves a different, valuable purpose. Throughout the book, I sometimes recommend additional forms. The primary forms you'll use include the following:

- *The pedigree chart*   Your at-a-glance information on each relative

- *The family group record and family group record continuation sheet*   The detailed record for each household (that is, family) on your pedigree chart

- *The family group record notes page*   The notes you'll need to complete the citations

- *The research calendar*   Your chronological record on when you conducted what research

- *The research extract*   Extended notes on research conducted at a given location

- *Birth/christening research extract*   A synopsis of birth records research

- *Marriage register research extract*   A summation of marriage records research

- *Death register research extract*   An abstract of death records research

- *Contact log*   A record of whom you contact, when you made contact, the reason for the contact, and how that contact was made

Despite what many experts recommend, when I complete forms and charts for my notebook, I prefer to use ink. However, I do sometimes like to use the chart in this notebook to "pencil in" the possibilities—my best guesses on unknown dates or to-do notes I want to keep in front of me on the chart. If you use colored ink, make certain that it will show up in photocopies. Black ink is always a safe bet because some copiers are set to ignore shades of blue, and anything in that color may not copy at all. Also, never use a highlighter to mark information on documents you may need to photocopy; the highlighter may cause that area to come out black and unread-able with some photocopiers.

Place a check mark beside each date you have verified and for which you have documentation. You likely won't be able to remember which dates you've verified unless you do so.

Create one research log page for each document you need to find. Put those log pages directly behind your pedigree chart.

Create a "tickler file" in your notebook. (It's called that because it "tickles" your memory.) Maintain one page per month, for at least the next year. On these pages you can jot down reminders to yourself that you need to transfer to your calendar. You can indicate such things as the dates for follow-up correspondence, a promised Web site update, and completion of things on your to-do lists.

Next, use index tabs to create sections in your notebook for each surname that you're researching. To begin with, you'll have one for your current last name (surname). If you're female and married and have taken your husband's name, you'll have one for your father's surname (your maiden surname). You'll also have one each for your mother's maiden surname, your father's mother's maiden surname, and your mother's mother's maiden surname. The number of names you'll be researching literally grows exponentially as you go back each subsequent generation. In fact, later on in your research, you'll probably need to create a separate notebook for each surname.

Within each surname section of your notebook, organize photocopies of your family group sheets, with the most recent generation first and the oldest generation on which you've done research last.

Bright Idea
You can create a Web site research log and record the Web sites that have been particularly help-ful to you in your research. To save time, you can add each site to your bookmark or favorites file as you research, and then record the URLs later.

Watch Out!
Don't assume that an ancestor's wife took her husband's name. Sometimes the opposite occurs—the husband takes hers—or both partners take a new name. This is why you should create a separate notebook for each surname. Documenting out-of-the-ordinary circumstances like this can keep you on track as you continue to research your lineage.

By maintaining family sections, you can keep all your main research notes in a notebook that you can take with you on the road. You need to keep your notebook up to date so that you can tell at a glance which documents you need or what information you're still looking for. Put your name and contact information in a prominent place in the notebook, in case you lose it.

Later in this chapter, I'll talk about computer programs for storing data and organizing your research.

Establishing a filing system

For the genealogist, this will never be a paperless society. Your computer can only maintain so much information. Sure, you can digitize documents by scanning them. But whether you do so using optical character recognition (OCR) technology to produce a word processing document or creating a photocopy-style or photographic-quality reproduction of the original, you'll still need to store the originals somewhere.

You need to devise a system that you know will work for you and stick with it. If you have to modify the system later, that's no problem, but try to keep on top of it. It is frustrating to face stacks or bags or boxes of papers that need to be filed in their proper places.

I envy those who can stick with the "handle each piece of paperwork once" organizational rule. That never seems to work for me. However, rather than stack documents on my desktop, I do have "to be filed" and "read, then file" folders. The secret is to devise a system that is simple enough to serve your needs (so you don't spend more time on your filing and cataloging details than you do on your research), yet comprehensive enough to handle all the paperwork that's part of your project.

Be careful not to get stuck in a rut. As you become more involved in your research, you'll know more about your needs. Having to revamp your filing system doesn't mean that you started out doing things wrong; it means you've learned a more sensible, tailored way to handle things.

Another great way to organize your data is to use a hanging file folder for each surname you're researching, so that you can place several file folders of information in each hanging file. Label each hanging folder with the surname; each file folder within a hanging folder should be labeled in a "surname, first name" format and then filed alphabetically by first name within the hanging file. This creates a handy way to grab the folders for a surname to take with you to another location, such as when you need to make photocopies of the records contained in the folders.

You'll eventually have a folder to correspond with each family group sheet you create. The first sheet of paper within each of those folders should be a log of the documents contained within the folder. This system will allow you to keep the records within the folder in chronological order as you find them. Simply assign each find a folder-specific number, and enter that number and the document description on your log. The log then serves as a makeshift table of contents for the folder. Later, you'll be able to consult that table of contents log page to see if you have a specific document within the folder, rather than shuffle through the papers to do so.

It's practical to keep the original family group sheet for which the folder was created within that

Bright Idea
If you prefer to store your paperwork in a filing cabinet rather than use notebooks, try keeping things organized by stapling your family group sheet inside the file folder, to the left. On the right, use pronged metal fasteners to hold pages in place as you add them, with the newest pages on top.

folder. Keep a photocopy of it in your notebook. This way you can enter information on the sheet when you're away from your files doing research and later update the group sheet in the folder. Just keep in mind that you want the copies in both locations—the folder and the notebook—to be up to date. Your original is the one you want to keep tidy; should the photocopy in your notebook get covered in reference notes you've made to yourself to record elsewhere (shame, shame—instead of on the appropriate research log), you can eventually throw it out and replace it with a fresh copy of the original.

Later, as your records grow, you may need to switch some of your standard hanging file folders with some of those designed to hold catalogs; you can find such hanging folders that will accommodate a paper depth of an inch or more.

Many find it helpful to color-code files. For example, you could use blue hanging folders for information related to your paternal ancestors and red for the maternal ones. Using colored labels on the file folders within each hanging folder is another possibility.

I include links to online articles that are devoted to research organization on the Chapter 3 page at www.genealogytips.com.

Optimizing your research notes

Your research notes not only need to cover the subject you're researching, but also, in order to be effective, they need to be organized so that you can find them when you need them. Some things that will help are to do the following:

- Maintain one research log for each family group sheet.

- Limit research notes to one family per sheet of paper, cross-referenced to the appropriate family group sheet.

- Handle notes on a given research notes sheet so that they can continue from session to session (to save paper); establish the means to indicate on that sheet whether you've transcribed and filed your notes.

- If you dictate notes into a microcassette or other recorder, indicate the tape number, date, and research topic on your research log; provide a space to indicate when you've transcribed and filed those notes.

- Transcribe and then post your notes as soon as possible after you take them, while they are fresh in your mind.

- If your handwriting is legible, consider simply filing photocopies of your notes; each time you recopy your notes, the chances of introducing errors increase.

- Keep an index sheet for any photo albums you maintain, and record where the originals or negatives are located.

The Web has some online tutorials that offer many more suggestions on how to keep organized. They can be found at www.genealogytips.com, on the page for Chapter 3. Myrt of DearMYRTLE fame also has a monthly organizational strategy, which she presents as a 12-step program. I've provided links to all 12 months at www.genealogytips.com, on the Chapter 3 page.

Archiving your ancestors

Until recently, people would often hire someone to film their records to preserve and store them on

Watch Out!
Prevent your paper records and photographs from yellowing and becoming brittle. Verify that the archival filing materials you use consist of acid-free papers, acid-free page holders, and tape and craft glue that are safe to use for preserving your research and supplies.

microfilm. Around 3,000 images could be archived on a roll of microfilm, which was generally then stored in a safety deposit box.

Today, you can use a scanner to digitize records and save those images on other storage devices, such as a CD, in addition to your hard drive. Using a camcorder is another way to preserve records; most newer units let you capture individual images as bitmaps or other files, which you can transfer to a computer. You'll have the digital tape, and you can also record anything moved to the computer on another archival medium, such as a CD.

One thing hasn't changed, despite technological innovations: It's a good idea to keep a copy of all your work offsite. Some people choose to store CDs in safety deposit boxes, and others make copies for other relatives. It's inexpensive to do this, and it insures your work against fire, flood, or other disasters.

It's a good idea to set specific dates on a calendar to make CD or other backups. You already check your smoke detector batteries twice a year, when the time changes to Daylight Saving Time and then back. Backing up your work should be a regular part of your routine as well. I back up my data at least once a month, and more often if I've done a lot of data entry. Some people like to do a backup after entering a predetermined number of records, such as 200. Find an interval that works for you, and stick with it.

Organizing your work on the computer

If you want to use the computer to hold your information, you'll need to choose a program to use. A few different programs are available, each with advantages and disadvantages.

Each genealogy program organizes data slightly differently. This means that you might not be able to open a database file from one program in a different program. However, you can exchange genealogy databases using a file format called GEDCOM, which stands for genealogical data communications. In a GEDCOM file, all the information is stored in a specific way so that other programs will be able to read it. GEDCOM files are widely available on the Internet, and you might find that after you've verified the information it contains, you can just import part of someone else's GEDCOM to fill in some of your blanks.

Genealogy database programs allow you to export (that is, extract) or import (that is, insert) data using GEDCOM files. Sometimes, different programs extract the information slightly differently. Some computer programs will make a GEDCOM file compatible with the software you choose. If you find that you need this type of software, look at the links at www.genealogytips.com, on the Chapter 3 page.

When choosing a program, the best thing to do is figure out which features are important to you and which ones you'll be able to use the most. Then you can look for the software that gives you those things.

You may find that one of the popular commercial programs will suit you the best. If you don't like those, you can always try some of the shareware programs that are available. There's no harm in trying different programs before you make a final decision; in fact, that's probably the wisest way to make a decision.

Ask the following questions when you're looking into genealogy software:

- Will the program let you store the kinds of information you want to store? Some programs are rigid in their interface, whereas others let you add additional fields. (Remember that if you use a lot of additional fields, your GEDCOM file may end up being slightly different in appearance from what you're used to seeing.)

- What kinds of reports will you want to produce? Will you want to print a full family tree? Will you want to produce a copy to send to a publisher? Do you intend to prepare data to present on a Web site?

- How important are the available features? Will you ever really need to print out a family calendar? Does the software have additional features, such as research tracking, that may save you time? Balance the features you'll use against the ones you won't to determine whether the program is worthwhile.

- How important is price? Will your budget allow you to spend money for a commercial program and pay for frequent upgrades? You might find in the commercial programs additional features that are worth the money.

- Do you have the computer resources to handle the program? Some programs are very large and require a fairly fast computer. Make sure you find a program that fits the limits of your system.

- Is the program easy to use? If you don't understand computers very well, you'll probably want to go with a program with a good graphical user interface (GUI)—one that has tabs and visual icons for the tasks you'll want to perform.

- Which program makes you feel the most comfortable? You'll probably be spending a lot of time with it, so don't decide to use something you really don't like.

Like any other type of software, genealogy programs come in all shapes, sizes, and price ranges. I provide links to a number of software choices on the Chapter 3 page at www.genealogytips.com. The following sections describe some of the most popular genealogy programs.

Family Tree Maker
www.familytreemaker.com

Family Tree Maker (FTM) is brought to you by the people at Genealogy.com. It's a big download, so if you don't have a very fast Internet connection, you might have to stick around for a while. If you don't want to download the program, you can order the program on CD from the FTM Web site. Check with the site for the current price of the program.

FTM helps you organize information, and it goes a step further. FTM lets you include photographs, images, and captions, giving you a great deal of control over the way the final printout looks. It also has drag-and-drop features that make it easy to use.

FTM offers data CDs that have a great deal of genealogical information on them, which you can use with the software. You don't have to buy them, unless you want the convenience of having those copies on hand or are unable to visit a genealogy library or Family History Center (see Chapter 12) to research that information. You can also find much

Moneysaver
Before you invest money in a genealogy software program, try one of the free ones available online. You'll be able to transfer the data you entered if you decide to upgrade to a full-featured program later.

of the same data on the Internet.

You can use FTM to create reports, such as tree reports, family group sheets, maps, calendars, and time lines. You can also modify these reports with pictures and captions.

Personal Ancestral File
www.familysearch.org/go_to_dist_center.asp

Personal Ancestral File (PAF) is distributed free by the Church of Jesus Christ of Latter-day Saints. It is available from the Software Downloads—Free link on the site. If you want to order a CD instead of downloading the program, follow the Software Products link.

One of the nice features of PAF is that it gives you the ability to publish information directly to the Web. Instead of having to export information to a GEDCOM file, you can have PAF save the information directly to a Web site. If you think you'll want to publish your information on the Web and update your site often, you might find that PAF will save you a few steps. (Publishing to the Web is covered later in this chapter.)

PAF is a great choice for researchers that should meet most genealogists' needs. It can generate family group sheets and other forms and GEDCOM files. Special features include Print to File, which saves a document in rich text format (RTF), complete with index marks and scrapbook and slide show options that let you include video and MIDI sound files. You might find that it's not as easy to use as other programs, but the fact that it's free is a bonus.

The Master Genealogist
www.whollygenes.com

The Master Genealogist is made by Wholly Genes Software, and is available in both Silver and Gold editions. The Gold edition includes reference tools and other information that may be of interest. The Silver edition is a streamlined, less expensive edition; some of the customized reporting options are not available in the Silver version.

The Master Genealogist comes with multimedia support, allowing you to customize reports and include pictures and other information. It offers other unique features, such as the ability to search for duplicate names, even based on phonetic comparisons.

You can use The Master Genealogist to import information directly from many other file formats, so it may reduce the need to use GEDCOM files when transferring data, which saves you an extra step. You can also save files in different formats, including a number of word processing file formats.

Reunion
www.leisterpro.com

Reunion creates a variety of charts and reports, and it allows you to include pictures and other information in reports. It is developed by Leister Productions, and is available only for the Mac.

A free demo with limited features is available at www.leisterpro.com. This demo version doesn't allow you to import or export, and you can enter only a limited number of names. If you want the full version, you need to order it from Leister Productions or contact one of the vendors listed at Leister's site.

With Reunion, you can add your own fields to insert customized information, keep track of your research, and take advantage of features such as entering a default century to cut down on data-entry time. You can also use Reunion to publish

Moneysaver
Take advantage of free trial periods. By trying out programs before you buy them, you'll save both time and money.

information directly to the Web.
Publishing to the Web

If you choose a software program that doesn't offer the convenience of directly publishing information to a Web site, you need to convert your data into a GEDCOM file. You do this by exporting the information, and you need to consult your software help for directions on exactly how to do this in the program you're using.

When you have a GEDCOM file, you need to prepare it for the Web. A variety of GEDCOM converters are available, some of which are free and some of which are offered as shareware. Two popular and easy-to-use programs are Gedpage (www.frontiernet. net/~rjacob/gedpage.htm) and GED4WEB (www. ged4web.com). Links for those and other programs are provided at www.genealogytips.com, on the Chapter 3 page. Both programs publish data on the Web. The results are a bit different with each one, though. Because they're shareware, you can try them before you decide whether to purchase either one.

The program you choose will take the data from your GEDCOM file and convert the data to hypertext markup language (HTML) format. After you convert GEDCOM files, you will have a set of fully functional Web pages with a surnames list, person index, and pedigree information. All these will be linked together accordingly. All you need to do is transfer the files to a Web site; you'll learn more about this in Chapter 14.

You might decide to publish your information by creating a text file containing the information you want to publish. Then, it's just a simple matter of pasting the file into a basic HTML editor. Your information won't be automatically cross-referenced and linked, but if your objective is to get the material on a page so that people can read it, this works just fine. Chapter 14 contains information about creating personal Web pages.

Dealing with special circumstances

When choosing software programs, be aware that they aren't very flexible when it comes to recording information on family members who don't fit in a distinct male or female category or who are in same-sex unions.

In the following cases, you should record information according to the sex and legal name somebody was born with:

- *Known name change*   A person may adopt a new name without going through formal or legal means to change that name—for example when converting to a religion, or when, as in the case of many flower children in the 1960s, choosing to go by a new name (such as Peaceful Harmony Butterfly).

- *Sexual reassignment*   A person, referred to as transsexual or transgendered, may go through hormonal therapy and surgery to assume or correct his or her sex; this often also involves a legal name change.

- *Transvestite*   A person may wear clothes that are meant for the opposite sex.

In the same manner that you record a nickname as an aka, which stands for *also known as* (such as in the case of Aunt Trudy, who never lets anyone call her Gertrude), most genealogists agree that you also put known sexual identity issue explanations in

Unofficially...
Medical records
are private. You
won't be able to
obtain such infor-
mation unless
your relative
willingly supplies
you with copies.

the aka category.

If, after you enter the sex the person was born with, you learn the date and place when and where any surgery took place, you can enter that information, too—along with any documentation you may have.

There may be other times when you just don't know someone's gender information and it would be awkward or impossible to obtain it. This may involve an ancestor for whom you've only been able to find a name and no other information, such as in a mention in an obituary. It could also involve an estranged relative's child for whom at this point you have a name only. Some suggestions on how you can record such information include the following:

- For gender-neutral names such as Pat or Kelly, list the sex according to that which is most commonly associated with the name.

- When you're uncomfortable speculating about somebody's sexual preference or sex, if you're maintaining paper records or if your program allows it, use "unknown."

Most states do not provide legal recognition of same-sex marriages. In the case of a lesbian union, record each person under her maiden name and cross-reference that information to each other. Similarly, gay male partners should be listed by their legal names at birth and cross-referenced to one another.

Just the facts

- Keep track of all your activity, and keep everything up to date.

- It's important to develop good habits when you begin your research, while everything is still manageable.

■ You can use genealogy software programs to help organize your research; try different programs so that you can identify the features that will be most useful to you.

■ You can use a GEDCOM-to-HTML converter if your software program doesn't publish information directly to a Web site.

■ You can get around software programs that don't accommodate nontraditional lifestyles or name changes by documenting legal name and sex at birth, and use aka and unknown to make further notations.

GET THE SCOOP ON...
Organizing your research with forms ▪ Keeping
your ancestors straight ▪ Formal ways to
present your genealogy ▪ The various numbering
systems you can use

Chapter 4

Optimal Record-Keeping Maintenance

When you were a kid, did anyone ever offer to pay you a penny a day and double your pay each day if you'd work for him? Your first reaction was probably to say, "No way!" You thought he was trying to rip you off. That is, until you did the math.

Ancestors double, too. They don't do it on a daily basis, but they do so each generation back. When you factor in additional marriages and stepchildren, things become even more complex. That's why researching genealogies produces a lot of data. When you begin your search, it's relatively easy to keep everything straight, sometimes even using simple charts to show the progression of your family. When you start going further back in history, however, the data can become large and unwieldy. You begin to understand just how many people have gone before you.

In Chapter 3 you learned how to set up a system to manage all the information you'll uncover. In this chapter you'll learn about the forms you need to get your search organized and strategies that will make your job easier: You'll learn that you can make your research manageable.

In this chapter you'll also learn about the most popular forms of presenting genealogical information. Genealogical reports can move in two directions—up and down. When you're starting your research, you'll want to keep track of your ancestors as you move backward through time; this is called the *ancestral numbering system.* When you're done, however, you'll want to approach things differently: You'll want to start at an ancestor and then list all the people stemming from him or her, so you'll be moving forward through time; this is called a *descendant numbering system.* At some point you're bound to come across all these ways of presenting information. Understanding them now will save you time later.

Forms and their functions

I can't overemphasize my belief in the importance of forms to help you organize your research. One of the quickest, easiest ways to get an idea of how research forms can help is to visit the Lineages genealogy Web site (www.lineages.com). Although it's not the biggest site, it's one of the few that will send out a group of forms automatically by email. From the Lineages home page, follow the link to the First Steps section. There you can request Lineages's free toolkit, which includes a pedigree chart, a family group record, and a research calendar—all in printable format. Within moments of requesting that information, you'll receive an email message with a file attached.

Timesaver
You'll need Adobe Acrobat Reader to read documents you find online that are in .pdf format, including those in the Lineages toolkit. If you don't have Acrobat Reader installed on your computer, go to the Adobe Web site (www.adobe.com) to download the program free of charge.

If you're using WebTV to access the Internet, you'll need to send the files to a computer in order to view them; Adobe Acrobat doesn't yet work with WebTV. If you're using a computer with Acrobat installed, follow these steps to save, open, view, and print the files in the Lineages toolkit:

1. In your email client, find the message with Lineages' Genealogy Toolkit in the Subject line.

2. Either open the email or highlight it to select it.

3. From the File menu, choose Save Attachments. Follow the prompts to set the file path (including the hard drive and folder) where you want to save the document, which is named InetPubwwwrootmultimediaPDFBasic.pdf.

4. Open and run Adobe Acrobat Reader by either double-clicking on the program icon on your desktop or by choosing Start | Adobe Acrobat | Acrobat Reader.

5. From the Acrobat Reader File menu, choose Open.

6. Find and then choose InetPubwwwrootmultimediaPDFBasic.pdf, and click Open.

7. To print the documents, choose File | Print. Select the print range: all 12 pages, the current page, or the page range you want.

You might eventually want to design your own forms because you can print, but not edit, pages that are a part of a PDF document. You might find that you prefer forms offered elsewhere, or that you prefer to use a genealogy program to generate your forms after you've input the appropriate data into

Watch Out!
You can open files directly in your email client (that is, email program) via the Save As or Open options or by double-clicking on the attachment, but do so with caution. Always check files for viruses. See Chapter 15 for more information.

the program. However, because the forms that come with the Lineages toolkit are representative of the ones you'll want to use to track your research, they can help you devise your plan for organizing the family statistics you gather. They can also help you become familiar with some of the terms you'll encounter as you begin that research. The following are the forms in the Lineages genealogy toolkit:

Unofficially...
A number of tutorials on organizational methods are available online, with more added almost every day. Links to many of them are available at www.genealogytips.com, on the Chapter 4 page. You can also search for some at the genealogy search engines mentioned in Chapter 6.

- *Pedigree chart*   This is like a snapshot of your whole ancestry. The pedigree chart allows for cursory information on each relative: birth date and place, marriage date and place, and death date and place.

- *Family group record*   This is a detailed record of one household. Ideally, each family on the pedigree chart should have a corresponding family group record; you may also want to prepare family group records for your ancestors' siblings.

- *Family group record continuation sheet*   Use this form when more than three children are in a family. It provides space for another six children.

- *Family group record notes page*   This page provides space for you to include information on the source of information for each fact mentioned on the family group record.

- *Research calendar*   You use this form for brief notes on your family history research at a given site. It also provides space for you to record what you looked at, when you looked at it, and what you found. Here you can keep track of the sources of any documents or clues you've found.

- *Research extract*   This page is for expanded notes on research done at a given site.

- *Birth/christening research extract*   This form provides space for information on seven children. You may prefer to have a separate research extract for each child; if so, you can adapt this form or create your own.

- *Marriage register research extract*   This form provides space for information on seven marriages; if you want to create a form for each marriage, you can adapt this form or create your own.

- *Death register research extract*   This form provides space to record the source and the location of the source for death records, plus information on the descendant's description and relationships.

- *Contact log*   You can use this form to keep a running log of who you contacted (and his or her address, phone, and email information), the subject discussed, the date of the contact, and the results of that contact.

Using predesigned forms makes your job easy. For example, completing the pedigree chart mentioned earlier is simply a matter of filling in the blanks. You'll first want to do one for yourself. Your name and other information go in space 1, your father in space 2, and your mother in space 3. In the appropriate spot in the upper-right corner, number this as Chart 1.

Because you will eventually prepare other charts, the form provides a space in the upper-left portion of the page to indicate whether "No. 1 on this chart" appears on another chart; if so, you indicate that it

Bright Idea
The Lineages genealogy toolkit and other sources recommend that you complete forms in pencil so that you can easily erase any mistakes. I prefer to use ink because that forces me to make a notation about any corrections. I draw a line through incorrect information, and then I initial and date the correction.

"is the same as No. X on Chart No. Y," with X and Y being the appropriate numbers.

If your research goes beyond your great-great-grandparents, you'll need to make a continuation chart. To do this, you fill in the next available chart number where it says "Cont. on Chart no." below the space for your great-grandparents' names (8, 9, 10, 11, 12, 13, 14, and 15). Mark the new chart with that number; on that chart, below where it says Pedigree Chart, complete the "No. 1 on this chart…" line information.

Using charts like these can help keep your research organized. Making the extra effort to record your research details as you do the research makes your work easier in the long run. Even if you purchase genealogy software and use it to compile much of your data to create your pedigree chart and other forms, at some point you'll probably have to take notes in longhand when you're out in the field.

You can find links to sites where you can purchase printed forms or find forms online at www.genealogytips.com, on the Chapter 4 page.

Genealogical numbering methods

When it comes to genealogical data, one thing is certain: You need to be able to make sense of everything. Through the years, genealogists have addressed this by devising numbering systems, which assign numbers to the people in a genealogy. Not only does this allow genealogists to keep data organized, but it also provides a common reference point so that a particular genealogy will make sense to other people.

Some people start with manual or software numbering systems, tie their sources and files into it, and later find that they want to use software that won't handle the numbering system, or they find software that will handle the numbers but doesn't have all the other desired features. Many people have learned this the hard way, when they've had to change software programs because the one they were using was discontinued.

You could create your own database, but that will work best only if you're starting from scratch and can manipulate the database program to extract information in a particular format. If you ever want to exchange your data with other genealogists, they'll need to be able to use your data file. Unless you're a database programmer, you're probably better off choosing a genealogy program like the ones covered in Chapter 3.

Whether you use a computer program to manage your genealogies or not, you need to learn about numbering systems. You will probably encounter data presented in a variety of formats, and it's an excellent idea to have a handle on how they work. That way, you'll be able to find the information you want quickly, instead of trying to figure out what everything means. The ahnentafel system, covered in the next section, is used to number ancestors for research purposes. After you learn about that, you'll learn about descendant numbering systems, which you use after your data is compiled.

Ancestral numbering: The ahnentafel system

The ahnentafel system is a method for organizing and keeping track of your ancestors; *ahnentafel* means "family table" in German. It is very popular among genealogists and is widely used to arrange

Timesaver Computer programs can save you a lot of time by implementing numbering systems for incomplete genealogies; the program automatically renumbers individuals as needed when new data is added.

Bright Idea
You need to consider compatibility issues regarding which numbering system you prefer or use when choosing a genealogy software package. See Chapter 3 for information on some of the available genealogy software.

data. This method of numbering ancestors was first developed in 1676 by Spanish genealogist Jerome de Sosa. It became popular after Stephan Kekule von Stradonitz used it in 1896, when he included it in the Ahnentafel Atlas. Hence, the system is often referred to as the Sosa-Stradonitz System.

People like the ahnentafel system because it's very easy to use. If you're doing a genealogy about yourself, the ahnentafel system starts with you. When you're organizing your data, picture yourself at the top of a pyramid. You get to be number 1. (You can start it with another ancestor for whom you want to create such a record, and assign the number 1 position to that person instead.) Each level of the pyramid represents a generation, so your parents begin on the next line. Your father gets number 2, and your mother is number 3. Here's how the first two levels look:

You (1)

Your Father (2) Your Mother (3)

Observe the mathematical formula: Your father's number (2) is twice yours (1), and your mother's number (3) is twice yours plus one.

Your paternal grandfather's number starts off the third level, with number 4. Your paternal grandmother's number is 5. Notice that this combination still follows the doubling rule—your grandfather's number is twice your father's, and your grandmother's number is your grandfather's number plus 1:

Your Father (2)

Your Grandfather (4) Your Grandmother (5)

The process repeats just like that. Your paternal grandfather is 4, and your paternal grandfather's father is 8. Your paternal grandfather's mother is 9:

Your Paternal Grandfather (4)

Your Grandfather's Father (8) Your Grandfather's Mother (9)

This works in the same way for your mother's side. Your mother's number is 3, so your maternal grandfather's number is 6. Your maternal grandmother's number is 7, and so on. You can see a graphical representation of the system at www.genealogytips.com, on the Chapter 4 page.

The nice thing about the ahnentafel system is that it provides a spot for each of your direct ancestors, giving you an easy way to refer to them. A drawback is that it doesn't leave room for aunts and uncles or brothers or sisters. To get around that, genealogists usually modify the system, incorporating other numbering systems to keep everything straight. (You'll learn about other numbering systems later in this chapter.)

Another problem that can arise in the ahnentafel system is when the same person comes into the genealogy twice. To better understand how somebody might be in a genealogy twice and end up with two numbers, consider this scenario: Say that in your distant past, there was a death in the family. Your father's great-grandmother, Sophie, is left a widow. At the funeral, she happens to meet Sid, from a neighboring town, and they hit it off. (You often see this type of occurrence in royal genealogies.) If Sid is your mother's great-grandfather, then he needs to have two numbers, meaning that you have to duplicate all his information in order for the system to work perfectly.

Some people find the ahnentafel system cumbersome because the numbers get quite large very quickly. However, you'd have to research 20 generations before you reached 1 million in your numbering system. The numbers really aren't that bad to work with when you understand the process.

Formal descendant numbering systems

In order to present a descendent report in a format that can be understood by other people, genealogists had to come up with ways to list an ancestor and all his or her descendants, using a common numbering system. A descendant report starts with a common ancestor and works forward in time, instead of working backward, like the ahnentafel method.

The Register and Record Systems are sometimes referred to as *formal systems*, because they're most often used to publish completed genealogies.

The Register System

The Register System is often seen in published works. You may have already come across it in your research. It is a formal numbering system because it requires what would be considered a complete genealogy—one that needs no more research—before you can even start numbering. Simply stated, it's a way of presenting information, used historically, that other people understand. It's not a system that works well with evolving genealogies.

The Register System starts with a common ancestor, and gives him or her the Arabic numeral 1. His or her children are also numbered, using lowercase Roman numerals, such as i, ii, iii, and iv. If any of those children had children of their own, they would have Arabic numerals. In the Register System, if a person has an Arabic number, it means that he or she had children.

Timesaver
If you're using a computer database for your family history, you shouldn't have to worry about the numbering system. Most programs look after that for you.

The following is an example of a descendant report in the Register System:

First Generation

1. Joseph Smith, born 29 January 1835 London; married c1855 Jane Wilde

    Children:

    2. i. Norman

Second Generation

2. Norman Smith (Joseph-1), born 2 November 1857 London; married c1876 Mary White

    Children:

    3. i. John

Third Generation

3. John Smith (Norman-2), born 1 August 1881 Leeds County, OH; married c1896 Margaret Chapel; died 1937 Leeds County, OH

    Children:

    i. David Smith, born 25 March 1905 Leeds County, OH; died 1921, farming accident

    4. ii. Henry

Fourth Generation

4. Henry Smith (John-3), born 7 December 1909 Leeds County, OH; married Sarah Bouvier 1 June 1931

    Children:

    i. Danielle, born 19 October 1933 Leeds County, OH

    5. ii. Andre

    iii. Philip, born 5 April 1938 Leeds County, OH

    6. iv. Bruce

Watch Out!
Dates in a genealogical report are recorded in a consistent format. U.S. genealogists use the format 4 September 1951, whereas Europeans would show the same date as 4.9.1951. In your own research, if you aren't consistent with your dates, you might think the second date is April 9, 1951, when in fact it's not.

Fifth Generation

5. Andre Smith (Henry-4), born 2 February 1937 Leeds County, OH; married Sarah Jones 15 July 1959

   Children:

   i. Andrew, born 11 May 1961 Leeds County, OH

   ii. Joanne, born 2 February 1962 Leeds County, OH

6. Bruce Smith (Henry-4), born 15 December 1940 Leeds County, OH; married Beatrice Ward 7 June 1962

   Children:

   i. Sarah, born 25 June 1963 Leeds County, OH

   7. ii. Eric

Sixth Generation

7. Eric Smith (Bruce-5), born 18 September 1965 Leeds County, OH; married Alice Levine 1992

   Children:

   i. Annette, born 2 June 1996

As you can see in this example, the Register System builds on the ancestor, showing his or her children. An Arabic number indicates that the line is continued and will be addressed in the next generation. This allows you to trace the lines back through the levels of generations.

The Record System

The Record System is very similar to the Register System, and is another formal descendant numbering system. It differs from the Register System in that it numbers everyone instead of just those with

Unofficially...
Web site and company information for the most popular geneaology programs are covered in Chapter 3. Links to those sites are available at www. genealogytips. com.

children. If a line is continued in a subsequent generation, the Arabic numeral assigned to the person is preceded with a plus sign. Because of this slight change, the Record System is often referred to as the Modified Register System.

Using the same family information used in the Register System example, a Record System report would look like this:

First Generation

1. Joseph Smith, born 29 January 1835 London; married c1855 Jane Wilde

   Children:

   +2. i. Norman

Second Generation

2. Norman Smith (Joseph-1), born 2 November 1857 London; married c1876 Mary White

   Children:

   +3. i. John

Third Generation

3. John Smith (Norman-2), born 1 August 1881 Leeds County, OH; married c1896 Margaret Chapel; died 1937 Leeds County, OH

   Children:

   4. i. David Smith, born 25 March 1905 Leeds County, OH; died 1921, farming accident

   +5. ii. Henry

Fourth Generation

5. Henry Smith (John-3), born 7 December 1909 Leeds County, OH; married Sarah Bouvier 1 June 1931

Children:

6. i. Danielle, born 19 October 1933 Leeds County, OH

+7. ii. Andre

8. iii. Philip, born 5 April 1938 Leeds County, OH

+9. iv. Bruce

Fifth Generation

7. Andre Smith (Henry-5), born 2 February 1937 Leeds County, OH; married Sarah Jones 15 July 1959

Children:

10. i. Andrew, born 11 May 1961 Leeds County, OH

11. ii. Joanne, born 2 February 1962 Leeds County, OH

9. Bruce Smith (Henry-5), born 15 December 1940 Leeds County, OH; married Beatrice Ward 7 June 1962

Children:

12. i. Sarah, born 25 June 1963 Leeds County, OH

+13. ii. Eric

Sixth Generation

13. Eric Smith (Bruce-9), born 18 September 1965 Leeds County, OH; married Alice Levine 1992

Children:

14. i. Annette, born 2 June 1996

This example looks very similar to the Register System example, but each person has his or her own number. This is a popular system, used even by the *National Genealogical Society Quarterly*, which is an

80-page publication of the National Genealogical Society, in print since 1912 and one of the oldest, most respected genealogy sources on new methodology, little-known resources, and other information useful for the genealogist.

The Register and Record Systems provide an organized format for published genealogies. The main drawback is that if one change is made, all subsequent numbering has to be redone. Therefore, these systems are used only when a genealogy is considered complete.

Modified descendant numbering systems

Because of the rigid and inflexible approach of the Register and Record Systems, other methods have been developed to simplify the process of numbering and renumbering descendants. Whereas the formal systems are most often seen in published genealogies, the modified systems described in the following sections are also widely used. Even if you don't plan to use the following methods, you should still be familiar with how they work.

The Henry System

The Henry System is convenient because each individual receives a number that tells the relationship of that person to the common ancestor at a glance. It is widely used, and some genealogists now consider the Henry System to be a formal system, like the Register and Record Systems.

The first digit of the Henry System number indicates the first-generation level. Starting with your common ancestor, you assign that person the number 1. His or her children are indicated, in sequence, by the second digit, so that the first child born would receive the number 11, and the next 12. For instance, the number 14 tells you that

Watch Out!
Remember that when you have to add anything to a genealogy, a formal system takes a lot of work to renumber. If you still have blank spots on your genealogy, choose one of the alternative descendant numbering systems instead. (Keep in mind that some software programs do the numbering for you automatically, depending on how you set the program preferences.)

the person is in the second-generation level in your list, and that he or she is the fourth child born to the common ancestor.

Because each number place means something, though, having more than nine children would knock the system out of whack. To get around that, an X is used for number 10; after that, the regular alphabet is used—A for 11, B for 12, and so on.

Here's how the examples used earlier would appear in the Henry System:

First Generation

1. Joseph Smith, born 29 January 1835 London; married c1855 Jane Wilde

    Children:

    11. Norman

Second Generation

    11. Norman Smith, born 2 November 1857 London; married c1876 Mary White

    Children:

    111. John

Third Generation

    111. John Smith, born 1 August 1881 Leeds County, OH; married c1896 Margaret Chapel; died 1937 Leeds County, OH

    Children:

    1111. David Smith, born 25 March 1905 Leeds County, OH; died 1921, farming accident

    1112. Henry

Fourth Generation

    1112. Henry Smith, born 7 December 1909 Leeds County, OH; married Sarah Bouvier 1 June 1931

Children:

11121. Danielle, born 19 October 1933 Leeds County, OH

11122. Andre

11123. Philip, born 5 April 1938 Leeds County, OH

11124. Bruce

Fifth Generation

11122. Andre Smith, born 2 February 1937 Leeds County, OH; married Sarah Jones 15 July 1959

Children:

111221. Andrew, born 11 May 1961 Leeds County, OH

111222. Joanne, born 2 February 1962 Leeds County, OH

11124. Bruce Smith, born 15 December 1940 Leeds County, OH; married Beatrice Ward 7 June 1962

Children:

111241. Sarah, born 25 June 1963 Leeds County, OH

111242. Eric

Sixth Generation

111242. Eric Smith, born 18 September 1965 Leeds County, OH; married Alice Levine 1992

Children:

1112421. Annette, born 2 June 1996

In this example, Andre Smith receives the number 11122. That tells us that he's the fifth generation, and the second child of the second child.

The nice thing about the Henry System is that it allows for expansion when new information is discovered. As mentioned earlier, the main problem with the Henry System arises when a family has more than 10 children. Adding letters to the numbering system is convenient, but it slows people down. It might take a bit of work to decipher something like 1DE27: You know that it's the fifth generation, but where do the D and E fit in? Well, if X is 10, and A is 11, D must be 14. If D is 14, E must be 15. So 1DE27 is the fifth generation, seventh child of the second child in the fourth generation, who was the 15th child of the third generation, and so forth.

The Modified Henry System

As you have learned, the Henry System can cause difficulty with very large generations. In order to address this, some people have modified the Henry System to make it a little simpler. Instead of using letters to indicate two-digit numbers, the two-digit numbers are used, but separated from the rest of the numbers by parentheses or other punctuation. It makes the Henry System much easier to follow. Suppose that Henry is actually the 13th child of John, instead of the second:

First Generation

1. Joseph Smith, born 29 January 1835 London; married c1855 Jane Wilde

    Children:

    11. Norman

Second Generation

11. Norman Smith, born 2 November 1857 London; married c1876 Mary White

Unofficially...
Keep your data in an easy-to-understand-and-interpret format. It is a good idea to use one of the most common numbering systems rather than to invent one that will not be familiar to others.

Children:

111. John

Third Generation

111. John Smith, born 1 August 1881 Leeds County, OH; married c1896 Margaret Chapel; died 1937 Leeds County, OH

Children:

1111. David Smith, born 25 March 1905 Leeds County, OH; died 1921, farming accident

(Note that rather than list another 11 names, this example jumps right to Henry.)

111(13). Henry

Fourth Generation

111(13). Henry Smith, born 7 December 1909 Leeds County, OH; married Sarah Bouvier 1 June 1931

Children:

111(13)1. Danielle, born 19 October 1933 Leeds County, OH

111(13)2. Andre

111(13)3. Philip, born 5 April 1938 Leeds County, OH

111(13)4. Bruce

Fifth Generation

111(13)2. Andre Smith, born 2 February 1937 Leeds County, OH; married Sarah Jones 15 July 1959

Children:

111(13)21. Andrew, born 11 May 1961 Leeds County, OH

111(13)22. Joanne, born 2 February 1962
Leeds County, OH

111(13)4. Bruce Smith, born 15 December
1940 Leeds County, OH; married Beatrice
Ward 7 June 1962

Children:

111(13)41. Sarah, born 25 June 1963 Leeds
County, OH

111(13)42. Eric

Sixth Generation

111(13)42. Eric Smith, born 18 September
1965 Leeds County, OH; married Alice Levine
1992

Children:

111(13)421. Annette, born 2 June 1996

As you can see from this example, with the Modified Henry System, you know at a glance that Andre is the fifth generation, and is the second son of the 13th son, and so on, right back to the common ancestor. If you want to look up Andre's father, you can go back to the previous generation and look for the 13th child.

As you can see, the numbering in this system is much easier to follow than that in the Henry System. The only drawback to the Modified Henry System is that the levels can be hard to count when you're dealing with a large number of records.

The d'Aboville System

The d'Aboville System is very similar to the Henry System, but it takes the logic one step further. Instead of indicating larger numbers in brackets, you separate the positions with a period, making the generations easier to see.

Watch Out!
Be consistent. It may seem liberating to list the wife's name first, but if you do so, you could cause confusion because you won't be in compliance with how others record information on their family group sheets.

Keeping Henry as the 13th child, look at the same example, this time using the d'Aboville System:

First Generation

1 Joseph Smith, born 29 January 1835 London; married c1855 Jane Wilde

   Children:

   1.1 Norman

Second Generation

   1.1 Norman Smith, born 2 November 1857 London; married c1876 Mary White

   Children:

   1.1.1 John

Third Generation

   John Smith, born 1 August 1881 Leeds County, OH; married c1896 Margaret Chapel; died 1937 Leeds County, OH

   Children:

   1.1.1.1 David Smith, born 25 March 1905 Leeds County, OH; died 1921, farming accident

   1.1.1.13 Henry

Fourth Generation

   1.1.1.13 Henry Smith, born 7 December 1909 Leeds County, OH; married Sarah Bouvier 1 June 1931

   Children:

   1.1.1.13.1 Danielle, born 19 October 1933 Leeds County, OH

   1.1.1.13.2 Andre

1.1.1.13.3 Philip, born 5 April 1938 Leeds County, OH

1.1.1.13.4 Bruce

Fifth Generation

1.1.1.13.2 Andre Smith, born 2 February 1937 Leeds County, OH; married Sarah Jones 15 July 1959

Children:

1.1.1.13.2.1 Andrew, born 11 May 1961 Leeds County, OH

1.1.1.13.2.2 Joanne, born 2 February 1962 Leeds County, OH

1.1.1.13.4 Bruce Smith, born 15 December 1940 Leeds County, OH; married Beatrice Ward 7 June 1962

Children:

1.1.1.13.4.1 Sarah, born 25 June 1963 Leeds County, OH

1.1.1.13.4.2 Eric

Sixth Generation

1.1.1.13.4.2 Eric Smith, born 18 September 1965 Leeds County, OH; married Alice Levine 1992

Children:

1.1.1.13.4.2.1 Annette, born 2 June 1996

The d'Aboville System uses the best points of the Henry System, but makes information much clearer and more understandable than the Henry or Modified Henry Systems do.

The de Villiers/Pama System

The systems covered so far tend to be widely used in North America. If your genealogical search takes

Unofficially...
There is not one most commonly used numbering system. If you plan to publish in a journal that has an established system, you must use that system. Be certain to ask any publication to which you plan to submit material for style guidelines to determine its preference.

you outside North America, you may encounter the de Villiers/Pama System.

The de Villiers/Pama System uses letters and numbers to indicate relationships. Letters are used to indicate the generation level, and numbers are added to the letters to indicate the rank of each child.

The common ancestor of a descendent report is given the letter a. That is the first-generation level. The second-generation level is indicated by the letter b; therefore, his or her firstborn child will receive the designation b1, with the next oldest receiving b2.

Grandchildren receive the letter c, and are ranked by number according to birth. Rather than list all the letters, the de Villiers/Pama system lets you use periods in place of the letters. The periods tell you what generation it is; you just look up the list to find the parentage.

Here's what the Smith family example would look like using the de Villiers/Pama System:

First Generation

a Joseph Smith, born 29 January 1835 London; married c1855 Jane Wilde

Children:

.b1 Norman

Second Generation

.b1 Norman Smith, born 2 November 1857 London; married c1876 Mary White

Children:

..c1 John

Third Generation

..c1 John Smith, born 1 August 1881 Leeds County, OH; married c1896 Margaret Chapel; died 1937 Leeds County, OH

Children:

...d1 David Smith, born 25 March 1905 Leeds County, OH; died 1921, farming accident

...d2 Henry

Fourth Generation

...d2 Henry Smith, born 7 December 1909 Leeds County, OH; married Sarah Bouvier 1 June 1931

Children:

....e1 Danielle, born 19 October 1933 Leeds County, OH

....e2 Andre

....e3 Philip, born 5 April 1938 Leeds County, OH

....e4 Bruce

Fifth Generation

....e2 Andre Smith, born 2 February 1937 Leeds County, OH; married Sarah Jones 15 July 1959

Children:

.....f1 Andrew, born 11 May 1961 Leeds County, OH

.....f2 Joanne, born 2 February 1962 Leeds County, OH

....e4 Bruce Smith, born 15 December 1940 Leeds County, OH; married Beatrice Ward 7 June 1962

Children:

.....f1 Sarah, born 25 June 1963 Leeds County, OH

.....f2 Eric

Sixth Generation

.....f2 Eric Smith, born 18 September 1965 Leeds County, OH; married Alice Levine 1992

Children:

......g1 Annette, born 2 June 1996

Here, because Andre is the second child of the second child of the first child of the only child of the common ancestor, he receives the designation b1.c1.d2.e2. Each person in the descendent list should receive a similar designation, showing the level and relationship to the other people in the report.

The de Villiers/Pama System can also be used in an expanded format, listing the children with the parents, as in the following example:

a Joseph Smith, born 29 January 1835 London; married c1855 Jane Wilde

.b1 Norman Smith, born 2 November 1857 London; married c1876 Mary White

..c1 John Smith, born 1 August 1881 Leeds County, OH; married c1896 Margaret Chapel; died 1937 Leeds County, OH

Children:

...d1 David Smith, born 25 March 1905 Leeds County, OH; died 1921, farming accident

...d2 Henry Smith, born 7 December 1909 Leeds County, OH; married Sarah Bouvier 1 June 1931

....e1 Danielle, born 19 October 1933 Leeds County, OH

....e2 Andre Smith, born 2 February 1937 Leeds County, OH; married Sarah Jones 15 July 1959

Watch Out!
According to Elizabeth Shown Mills, author of *Evidence: Citation & Analysis for the Family Historian*, any random sequential numbering system "for narrative text is impractical for data accumulated on group sheets and charts. Both of these items are 'working documents' on which data are added in a random pattern as new information is found."

.....f1 Andrew, born 11 May 1961 Leeds County, OH

.....f2 Joanne, born 2 February 1962 Leeds County, OH

....e3 Philip, born 5 April 1938 Leeds County, OH

....e4 Bruce Smith, born 15 December 1940 Leeds County, OH; married Beatrice Ward 7 June 1962

.....f1 Sarah, born 25 June 1963 Leeds County, OH

.....f2 Eric, born 18 September 1965 Leeds County, OH; married Alice Levine 1992

......g1 Annette, born 2 June 1996

When you use this expanded version of the de Villiers/Pama System, you spend less time tracking back and forth across the generations.

Combined numbering systems

In order to include information on other people in your family (such as aunts and uncles), a modified system is required. The ahnentafel system is invaluable for keeping track of direct ancestors. However, it leaves no room for collateral family members, such as brothers and sisters or aunts and uncles. The Register and Record Systems don't provide much help with this, either, because they can only be used for a finished product. Combining the ahnentafel system with one of the alternative descendant numbering systems can provide a better way for you to keep track of your data.

Some genealogists use the d'Aboville System, inserting the ahnentafel number at the beginning. For example, say that John Smith isn't one of your

Watch Out!
Remember that ancestor listings and descendant listings are two different things. One works upward, and one works downward. When combining systems, you have to remember the difference.

direct ancestors, but is in fact a great-great-uncle on your father's side, and you want to produce information about him to give to a distant cousin.

As your great-great-uncle, John was brother to your paternal great-great-grandfather, who would receive number 8 in your ahnentafel system. The father's number is going to be double that of the son's, which makes number 16 where you and your distant cousin connect.

Here's what a combined system would look like, using the same family as the earlier examples:

First Generation

> 16.1 John Smith, born 1 August 1881 Leeds County, OH; married c1896 Margaret Chapel; died 1937 Leeds County, OH

> Children:

> 16.1.1 David Smith, born 25 March 1905 Leeds County, OH; died 1921, farming accident

> 16.1.2 Henry

Second Generation

> 16.1.2 Henry Smith, born 7 December 1909 Leeds County, OH; married Sarah Bouvier 1 June 1931

> Children:

> 16.1.2.1 Danielle, born 19 October 1933 Leeds County, OH

> 16.1.2.2 Andre

> 16.1.2.3 Philip, born 5 April 1938 Leeds County, OH

> 16.1.2.4 Bruce

Third Generation

> 16.1.2.2 Andre Smith, born 2 February 1937
> Leeds County, OH; married Sarah Jones
> 15 July 1959

> Children:

> 16.1.2.2.3 Andrew, born 11 May 1961 Leeds
> County, OH

> 16.1.2.2.4 Joanne, born 2 February 1962 Leeds
> County, OH

> 16.1.2.4 Bruce Smith, born 15 December 1940
> Leeds County, OH; married Beatrice Ward
> 7 June 1962

> Children:

> 16.1.2.4.1 Sarah, born 25 June 1963 Leeds
> County, OH

> 16.1.2.4.2 Eric

Sixth Generation

> 16.1.2.4.2 Eric Smith, born 18 September 1965
> Leeds County, OH; married Alice Levine 1992

> Children:

16.1.2.4.2.1 Annette, born 2 June 1996

With this combined system, you can keep track of collateral relatives in your system and expand the information you are able to keep regarding your family.

Just the facts

- Forms help organize your research and are available at a number of Web sites.

- A numbering system is necessary to keep track of descendants; each numbering system has advantages and disadvantages, and regardless

Bright Idea
Feel free to devise your own system, but remember that it should be easy for others to use. Better yet, you can let a computer database do most of the work for you.

of the method you prefer to use, it's a good idea to become familiar with them all.

- Many software programs do numbering for you, and they handle renumbering when you make changes.

- Formal systems aren't conducive to research because they don't let you insert new information as it becomes available.

- You may encounter combinations of numbering systems in your research, and you can design your own numbering system to meet your needs.

Beginning Your Online Adventure

GET THE SCOOP ON...
How email works ▪ Common email features
▪ How to check your email on the Web
▪ Subscribing to newsgroups and mailing lists

PART III

Chapter 5

Expanding Your Online World

Over the past 10 years, email has become one of the most popular forms of communication. Forrester Research predicts that by 2002, the number of emails transmitted daily will exceed 1.5 billion. Email can instantaneously link people together, even if those people are in different countries, and it provides a low-cost alternative to telephone calls. You'll find email a vital part of your online genealogy research.

Someday in the near future, you may get an email in which the correspondent tells you that she saw your name on a surname list and wondered if you were related to those with that last name who reside in Illinois. I sent an email to a woman, and based on the list of "sounds like" possibilities she'd listed on her Web page, I gave her one more possible surname spelling for an ancestor she'd yet to find.

Later in this chapter, you'll learn about newsgroups and mailing lists; they also provide excellent research tools for genealogical researchers. Not only do they impart current information, but they give you access to other individuals interested in the same topics. You can use newsgroups and mailing lists to help establish a network of people to help with your search. You'll also learn about email programs (or *clients*, as they are commonly called) that retrieve your mail and let you read it.

Read on, and you'll learn why, when it comes to expediency, email beats licking a stamp any day!

How email works (incredibly simplified)

Email is a lot like regular postal mail, but it's sent to an address over the Internet rather than being hand delivered. Like postal mail, it's passed along until it reaches its final destination. Unlike regular "snail" mail, however, email is delivered almost instantly.

An email address consists of two parts. The beginning of the address—the part before the at sign (@)—shows the username. The part after @ shows the Internet service provider (ISP). Together, they form the address, identifying the destination server (the ISP) and the username (the account on that server).

Most email that you send reaches its destination almost instantaneously, but this is not always the case. If the destination server is down, the mail servers hang on to the message for a while and re-send it at periodic intervals. The server usually notifies you if it has been unable to deliver a message you've sent. Often, it tries to re-send the message every few hours, and gives up if it is not able to deliver the message within three days.

Email features

Some features are common to just about every email client available. Use of these components tends to

Timesaver
Some email clients (that is, programs) offer an option to place someone in your address book automatically when you reply to an email.

be a personal preference; deciding whether these features are important to you will help you determine which email client you should use.

Address books

Address books help you organize your contacts. Within an email client, it's nice to be able to store email addresses along with other information. Some email clients limit the amount of information you can save—for example, they let you save the address and telephone number, but little else. Other clients have extensive room for other information, and even have fields for birthdays, fax numbers, distinct home and business addresses, and other personal information. Figure out what kind of information you believe you'll need to store, and decide how important it is to have this information in your email client.

You'll also want to see how easy you find using an address book. If it's hard to create a message from the address book or to access the address book from within a new message, you may want to use a different email client.

Another consideration with address books is the ability to transfer information. Most email clients can import address books from other file formats, so if you already have an address book in one client, you may be able to import it into a new email client.

cc, bcc, and distribution lists

Email clients give you the option of specifying carbon copy (cc) addresses, so that each person you specify receives a copy of the email and each person sees who received it. Blind carbon copy (bcc) works just like cc, in that people receive copies of the message, but bcc doesn't include that email address in

Watch Out!
Although it's a nice idea, most people don't have time to maintain detailed address books. Be careful that you don't spend more time editing your address book than doing research.

Watch Out!
Email clients handle the distribution list feature in a variety of ways, so be careful. Some clients, for example, show the recipients the name you've assigned your list or convert the list name to individual addresses.

the main message. The bcc option is an easy, convenient way to protect another's privacy; when you send a message to a number of recipients using the bcc address option for each address on your list, each address is hidden from the others on the list.

Distribution lists allow you to send email messages to a number of people. If you think this might be something you want to do, you can consider doing it from your email client or using one of the free distribution list services listed at www.genealogytips.com, on the Chapter 5 page. I know several people who have established mailing lists to keep family members apprised of news.

Signatures

A *signature* consists of a few lines of text that are added to the end of a message. Signatures often include Web site addresses and additional email addresses. You can include a *signature line*—a line of text with a cute or witty saying.

Remember that some signature lines aren't appropriate for business use; so if you plan to use a cute message or quote in personal email messages, make sure you know how to turn it off when you're sending a formal business email. Many users create a few different signatures, and then choose the most appropriate one with each message. Most of the popular email clients make it very easy to choose a signature.

Many genealogy email lists that are archived discourage signature lines that include lists of surnames because they generate so many false hits on archives searches. Such signatures can, however, be a useful tool in one-on-one email and in introductory messages, when permitted. Some people try to get around the problem by using . or - between letters (for example, H.a.h.n.). That solves the search problem, but it doesn't look very pretty.

Email attachments

Attachments are an excellent way to exchange information using email. You can attach a file (such as a word processing document or a picture) to an email message and send it to another user. The other user is able to open the attachment as if it were transferred by disk.

An email attachment is usually sent as one message, which can result in some long downloads. You can use a file compression utility (also known as a *zip program*) to shrink the files and make the messages shorter. If your email client splits large messages into smaller chunks, make sure that the person receiving the file is going to be able to put them back together.

You'll find attachments useful, especially when exchanging research documents or GEDCOM family history data files. Check with the recipient to make sure that he or she can open a particular type of file, and never send an attachment unless it's invited. Most genealogy-related email lists frown on or prohibit attachments.

For specific help with attachments, look in your email client's online or program help section.

Some popular email clients

Email clients range from very simple to fairly complex. Different clients emphasize different features, so identifying the features that are most important to you is beneficial in choosing the right email client.

Ultimately, it becomes a matter of choice. If you're not happy with a client, don't be afraid to

Bright Idea
I have my email client set as no signature as the default preference; I physically select a signature when I want to include it in a message so that I don't accidentally send an inappropriate signature to someone.

Bright Idea
Before you install an email client, ask your ISP if it offers technical support for that program. If your ISP supports the client you choose, it'll be able to help you with any problems you encounter.

download another one. You may find that another client better meets your needs.

You will most likely find an email client that appeals to your personal tastes among the following software. If not, you can find more freeware and shareware email clients by conducting a Web search.

Outlook Express
www.microsoft.com/windows/oe

Microsoft's free Outlook Express incorporates an email client with a newsreader, and it supports hypertext markup language (HTML), which means it can display email and newsgroup messages as Web pages.

Outlook Express allows you to specify filing options, so that email messages can be automatically stored in the appropriate folder as they're downloaded. This can also be an effective tool against *spam* (that is, unsolicited advertising messages). You can have the program automatically delete messages that use certain words or come from certain email addresses.

If you have more than one email account, you can specify them and have Outlook Express check all the accounts when it goes to the server to retrieve new messages. You can also program different identities so that you and another person can use the same computer and still keep your personal email messages separate. If you have an email account at work, you could also access those messages by creating another identity.

Outlook Express has a Find People option, which allows you to select from the most popular search databases by using a pull-down menu. You can search for email addresses or other contact information. This information is also accessible via the Web, but if you think you might need to access it a lot, it can be nice to have quick access to it in your email program.

If you have a Microsoft Hotmail account, you can access it from within Outlook Express, and even exchange your address book information between the two accounts. This feature does not work with any other free Web-based email provider; however, if your free Web mail provider offers POP3 and SMTP access, you can add the account as an identity and access the information in much the same way. You'll have to check your free mail provider's Web site for information on importing address books.

Outlook Express also offers specialized electronic stationery—so that the people you send a message to can view your message with the graphical background you select.

Watch Out!
Only use email stationery or place pictures within a message itself in casual or informal messages. Most formal business usage still calls for email messages to be in plain text and for graphics and other extras to be sent as attachments.

Netscape Messenger
www.netscape.com

Netscape Messenger is free as part of Netscape Communicator, and it includes mail filtering and HTML support. Many people use it because it is simple and has an easy-to-use interface, which includes the following:

■ It is automatically activated when you click on a mailto: link on a Web page.

■ Like other email clients, it offers a confirmation of delivery option and a confirmation of reading option.

■ It allows you to attach a file to a message with the click of a button.

Netscape Messenger doesn't support more than one POP3 address, so unless your ISP supports IMAP, you might want to try another email program.

Bright Idea
Most email
clients will let
you request a
return receipt to
make sure that
your message
reaches its desti-
nation. Keep in
mind, however,
that some people
turn off the
option to reply
to message-read
requests.

Pegasus Mail
www.pegasus.usa.com

Pegasus Mail is a free email client that offers advanced filing and message-filtering options. Corporate users are encouraged to purchase manuals to support the development of the program; home users are permitted to use the software for free.

Pegasus Mail has a more basic interface than the other clients, but it offers good control over folders and message-filing options. Messages can be filtered (so that they go directly into designated folders rather than to the in box) as they are downloaded, or a filter can be applied when a folder is opened. A variety of options are available, including subject keywords and other filing tools. One particularly nice feature is the ability to select the folder in which to file a copy of an email message as you send it rather than having that copy placed in a generic sent-messages location.

Pegasus Mail allows you to specify other accounts that should be checked along with your main account. It also offers identities, so that you can move easily between a home and a work address, for example. Pegasus Mail also supports distribution lists, allowing you to send a message to a number of people. Because some servers limit the number of cc or bcc messages in an effort to reduce spam, distribution lists may be an attractive option if you plan to send messages to quite a few people at the same time.

Eudora
www.eudora.com

Eudora offers support for most of the major email functions, including multiple email accounts, spellcheck, filters, and HTML messages.

Whereas Eudora used to come in a free Lite version and a shareware Pro version, it now comes in a single program with different usage options. Users can choose to use the program in a restricted free mode, which limits access to some of the more advanced features. In the sponsored mode, the program displays advertisements, but all features are available. Users also have the option of purchasing the software, eliminating the advertising, and activating all features.

Checking email on the Web

Some sites allow you to access your home email account using your browser via the Web, which can be convenient when you're traveling or accessing the Internet from the library. Some ISPs provide Web-based access as a service, and other companies provide it as a commercial advertising enterprise. You can find links to a few of them at www. genealogytips.com, on the Chapter 5 page.

Choosing a Web-based email service

In addition to sites that offer free email access so you can check your email via your browser, there are also sites that offer Web-based email accounts. When you use a Web-based email account, you establish an email address that's different from the one assigned to you by your ISP. For example, a Web-based email account email address might look something like pam@excite.com or pam@yahoo. com. This is a convenient way for you to be able to receive email if you don't have Internet access on a home computer or if you need to access your email from a variety of locations; in such cases, one of these services might be the best option for you.

Watch Out!
If you want to check your email at work, check your employer's policy first. Some employers log computer activity, so find out if it's allowed.

Many people use a Web-based email account before they even have a computer. If you don't have a computer yet, you may want to consider a Web-based service, which provides all the email options a regular ISP offers, and can be accessed from any Web browser—whether it's in a library or a cyber-café. Even without a computer of your own, you can still participate in the online world.

When choosing a Web-based email service, you'll want to make sure that it offers all the features you'll need, and you'll want to make sure that you won't be inconvenienced by any of its limitations. The following sections cover a few areas you should consider. You can find links to free Web-based email at www. genealogytips.com, on the Chapter 5 page.

Size restrictions

You need to consider whether the service allows attachments, and whether it limits the file size of attachments. Some services don't allow any attachments, and some allow them only if they're under a particular size. If your mailbox gets full, you may miss important messages because the service may begin to reject them. Knowing the amount of email storage space in advance and limiting the number of messages you store on the server will help you avoid that problem. It can also help you avoid spending a long time downloading what results in only a partial file if that file exceeds the maximum size allowed. Size restrictions are an important consideration if you know you'll be receiving large attachments.

Speed

Another consideration is whether the service seems fast enough to you. Some Web-based services might be particularly busy at certain times of the day. You might want to try a few of them to see which will suit you best. Create some accounts you'd like to test, and then send email messages (with and without attachments) to each of them. This way you can base your decision on your firsthand experience regarding the service's performance. When you find one that best meets your needs, you can cancel the others you created during your test phase.

Technical support

You should also take into consideration whether the service offers technical support. If you think you'll need technical assistance in using the service, you should find out if the service offers prompt technical support via email or another means, such as online help pages.

Compatibility

Another consideration is whether the service will work with any browser. Make sure that you're not going to be stuck trying to access a Netscape-only service using Internet Explorer at the library. If you need to access your email from a variety of locations, compatibility may be a deciding factor. If a site requires a special plug-in, you may not be able to access it from the library or other locations that don't permit you to customize the browser.

Filing systems

You should find out whether the service allows you to store messages on the server. Most services store messages with a size limitation. If you subscribe to a lot of mailing lists, you might find your account becoming full in a short period of time.

Most services also allow you to establish storage folders, so that you can organize your stored email messages.

66
I subscribe to some genealogy lists, but I only get to read them about once a week. I use a free Web-based email service for those lists. I delete the messages I don't need, and I forward the important ones to my home account.
—Don, father and Web-based email service user
99

Timesaver
If you don't have time to sit and type a message in a Web form, you can use a word processor to type your message. Then, when you're online, highlight the text in the word processing program, copy it, and paste it into the Web form.

Filters

Some services let you specify instructions, or filters, for certain types of messages. Filters can be an effective tool in reducing spam or filing large numbers of mailing list messages. If you have a large volume of email from a variety of sources, filters may be important to you.

Signatures

Some services allow you to specify more than one email signature. If you want to use different signatures for business contacts and personal contacts, or for close friends and acquaintances, this may be an important consideration for you.

Composition

Remember that when you're using a Web-based email service, you have to be online. You lose the convenience that an email client provides by allowing you to work offline, storing your messages until they can be sent when you're connected to the Internet.

Advertisements

Many Web sites that offer free email accounts place advertising on those pages. If they're not displayed on the Web page you're viewing, the ads are usually attached to the end of your message. If you are bothered by ads, you can search for a service that doesn't display them.

Longevity

If you plan on using a Web-based email account as your main email address, you will want to make sure that the service will be around for a while. With the constant mergers of Internet companies, this can seem like a difficult goal to achieve; however, recognizing that the company could disappear is an unfortunate but necessary reality.

Keep a backup copy of your address book in case your Web-based email ever goes down. If you have to get another email address with another server, you can use your address book to notify all your friends about your required email address change.

Privacy

Anything advertised as free often comes with a hidden price. Free Web-based email services tend to ask for demographic information when you sign up for the service. They may even offer to add you to particular mailing lists that may be of interest. The information you provide is often used to determine the type of advertising that most suits you.

Nothing can be unconditional: consequently nothing can be free.
—Bernard Shaw

Read the information carefully when you're signing up for a free service. You'll probably want to find one that doesn't sell information to third-party companies that in turn use it for mass mail delivered by post or for spam sent by email.

You should also think about what kind of information you are going to make available on the Web. Some providers ask for your home address and then offer to include you in a white pages directory of users. You may not want information such as your home city available for view in a Web search.

Newsgroups

Newsgroups, put simply, are group discussion lists. Newsgroup messages can be read by anyone who downloads them. Newsgroups can be on any subject; people interested in the subject can post articles, which are then relayed to other computers throughout the world. Because of the way newsgroups exchange information, these postings can sometimes take one or two days to reach all the servers.

You post to newsgroups using your email address. Other people can respond to you privately by email or openly through the newsgroup.

In order to access newsgroups, you need a news server and a newsreader. A news server stores articles submitted to newsgroups and makes them available to other users. Newsreaders are discussed later in this chapter.

Check your ISP's policy: Some offer a family-oriented selection that filters out adult sites. If you allow your children to have access to newsgroups, you might want to subscribe through an ISP that offers safe content.

Newsreader software

Newsreader software lets you download a list of all the available newsgroups on a server so that you can select the ones you'd like to read. Most let you sub-scribe to your choice of newsgroups.

After you've selected newsgroups, the newsreader downloads the message headers, which include information about the subject of a message, the size, when it was sent, the sender's address, and any attachments the message may have. The newsreader then displays a list of available messages, which you can sort by date, subject, or sender. You click on a message to open it, which downloads the text mes-sage and any files that are attached to it.

The newsreaders described in the following sections are the ones most frequently used. Links to these and others, as well as links to genealogy news-groups, are provided at www.genealogytips.com, on the Chapter 5 page.

Timesaver
Your ISP can help you access newsgroups. Because the information is traveling from your ISP's home network, your ISP's newsgroup server will probably be faster than free services. However, if it tends to be busy when you use it, try another free or commercial news server.

Outlook Express
www.microsoft.com/windows/oe

Microsoft Outlook Express combines email and newsgroups in one program. You can access newsgroups from Outlook Express by clicking on the Read News icon on the main page. If your newsgroup information is not already stored in Outlook Express, the client will prompt you for your account information and news server. Outlook Express allows you to specify more than one news server in the Accounts section. If you have more than one ISP or news server, you can access them from within Outlook Express.

After Outlook Express downloads the list of available newsgroups, it displays a dialog box that lets you display newsgroup titles that include certain text. For example, you can type *genealogy* into the dialog box to narrow the list to only newsgroups that have *genealogy* somewhere in the address. You can also use filters to identify keywords to ignore and thereby restrict the types of newsgroups displayed.

Netscape News
www.netscape.com

Netscape News is integrated with Netscape Communicator, and it is easily accessible from the Netscape Navigator or Netscape Messenger screens.

Although Netscape doesn't support multiple email addresses, it does support multiple news servers. You can add additional servers by adding them to the Newsgroup Servers category under Preferences.

Netscape downloads the list of available newsgroups. When it has finished, it displays the list, allowing you to select the newsgroups to which you'd like to subscribe. It then downloads the message headers for you to review. Netscape displays the newsgroup list in a hierarchical filing system, which means that it uses folders to hold similar categories. For example, rather than display an entire list of alt.adoption.* sites, it displays a file folder. You can click on the folder to open it and get access to alt.adoption.issues, alt.adoption.searching, and other alt.adoption sites. This feature can save time when searching for newsgroups, as it allows you to hide the newsgroups you feel aren't relevant to your search.

Free Agent
www.forteinc.com/agent/freagent.htm
Free Agent is a free newsreader that is also available in a shareware version that has additional features. Free Agent, like most other readers, includes an offline reading option that allows you to review messages when you're not connected to the Internet.

With Free Agent, you can specify a list of messages you'd like to read, and then have the program download them all at once. If you are downloading large attachments that have been split into smaller posts, Free Agent will put the pieces back together for you.

NewsFilter
www.easybyte.com
If you like to customize your software applications, you might want to try NewsFilter, a freeware newsreader that lets you create display templates. You can even configure the program to generate content for a Web site that contains that news and displays it in the style you want.

Tifny

www.tifny2.com

Tifny is a free newsreader designed to accentuate multimedia in newsgroups, with the emphasis on displaying image and sound files. It includes an MP3 music player and a video slideshow presentation for pictures you download. Tifny lets you filter out such things as redundant messages and unwanted file sizes or formats. You can even eliminate messages written by certain authors, which could be one way to avoid messages written by known flamers. (You'll find information on flamers later in this chapter.)

Mailing lists

Mailing lists rely on email to convey posts. Users can subscribe to the list and choose to receive posts on a message-by-message basis or have messages saved into a digest format and sent at periodic intervals.

You can use mailing lists with an email client or a Web-based email address. Mailing lists can be found in two formats:

- *Discussion lists*   With a discussion list, subscribers can post messages that are distributed to all the other subscribers. Discussion lists may be moderated, which means the list manager first screens a message and decides whether to authorize it before sending it to the other members of the list. If the list is not moderated, all posts are forwarded automatically.

- *Announcement lists*   Announcement lists work like moderated lists: Only people with the proper authorization can post messages. These types of lists are often used by associations to announce events or by software companies to provide information about program updates.

Mailing lists are run on one of three software packages—ListServ, MajorDomo, and ListProc—each with slightly different ways of handling information:

- *ListServ (www.lsoft.com)*   Submission requests for ListServ mailing lists are sent to ListServ@*siteaddress*.com. To subscribe, put "subscribe *listname yourfirstname yourlastname*" in the body of the email message, and send it to the appropriate ListServ address.

- *Majordomo (www.greatcircle.com/majordomo)* Majordomo submission requests are handled by majordomo@*siteaddress*.com. Send your submission request to that address, with "subscribe *listname*" in the body of the message.

- *ListProc (www.listproc.net)*   To subscribe to a ListProc mailing list, send a message to ListProc@*siteaddress*.com, with "subscribe *listname firstname lastname*" in the body of the email message.

Newsgroup commands are usually handled by a special email address. Trying to send a subscribe or an unsubscribe message to the list's general address will result in your request being forwarded to all the subscribers. List administrators usually send out periodic reminders about how to access the mailing list's commands.

Free mailing list hosts

A number of Web sites offer free mailing lists, allowing users to set up new lists easily. You can subscribe either by emailing the mailing list software or subscribing using Web forms.

Unofficially...
Remember that each mailing list usually has two different email addresses. One is the address from which the list itself is generated; that's the email address you use to reply to the entire list. The other email address is for commands, such as subscribe and unsubscribe.

A mailing list can be a great option for bringing together family and friends. If you want to start one of your own, you may want to investigate one of the free hosts listed at www.genealogytips.com, on the Chapter 5 page. Remember that these services are provided at no cost to the user, so advertisements are usually inserted at the end of each post.

General mailing list instructions

You can subscribe to many mailing lists using Web forms. If a site offers to add you to a mailing list, you can give your email address and follow the instructions.

Generally, you will receive a confirmation email. You have to respond to this message in order to complete the subscription process. Keep the message you get from a mailing list server. This message probably includes instructions on how to unsubscribe, so you can consult it if you have any difficulties.

Remember that when you send commands to mailing list software, you are dealing with a computer program. Don't put extra questions or information in the email, as the program won't know how to handle them; it will simply delete what it views as any unnecessary information in your replies. Extraneous information, such as signature lines, may result in your request being ignored. But if you follow the instructions carefully, you should have a painless mailing list experience.

Netiquette

Netiquette refers to the manners people use when corresponding over the Internet. Certain behavior is unacceptable. Understanding the rules will keep you from being removed from a mailing list and may ensure that you never upset other users.

Timesaver
It's a good idea to filter the email you receive from mailing lists into folders created for each list. You can still delete messages after you've read them; however, those you want to keep will already be stored in the appropriate place.

Flamed is the term used by Internet users to describe receiving attacking messages. Many people get flamed on lists for making inappropriate posts, or even for making silly mistakes. (Some *flamers* seem to thrive on causing or creating problems by complaining about posts made by others.)

To make sure you don't upset other users or get flamed, you should observe the following basic Netiquette:

- *Study the material before you jump in*   Read the messages for a few days to get a general feel for the type of things usually discussed on the list. This is entirely acceptable on the Internet, and is referred to as *lurking*. Sending a message asking "What's this group about?" to a newsgroup named alt.soc.genealogy.methods won't only make you look stupid, it may also get you a lot of email messages saying you are.

- *Read the frequently asked questions (FAQ) list*   The FAQ for a mailing list or newsgroup is usually posted at regular intervals. Alternatively, it may be available on the Web. A FAQ provides answers to basic questions you are likely to have.

- *Listen to the list owner*   The Internet is not always a democracy. You must abide by the rules of the list's owner or moderator. If there is no owner or moderator, as with some newsgroups, you must defer to the Netiquette defined by the other subscribers.

- *Keep on topic*   Don't get off topic in a discussion. When users reply to threads, it can be easy for a discussion to wander. Make sure that your subject line reflects the actual content of the message and doesn't refer to a discussion

Unofficially...
When you reply to a mailing list post, be sure to preface the subject line with RE: (for *reference*). Most, but not all, email clients automatically do this for you.

that has evolved into something completely different.

■ *Don't send inappropriate posts*   Don't go off on a tangent. In other words, don't post something to the newsgroup or mailing list if your discussion has nothing to do with the list's subject matter. Either move to a more relevant list or keep your discussion private.

■ *Edit your posts*   Don't forward an entire email message with a note at the beginning that says only, "Me, too," "I agree," or another short response that doesn't contribute to the discussion. This wastes bandwidth and aggravates users. Delete the information that isn't directly relevant to your message. When forwarding messages, delete nested headers—long lists of email addresses that also received the forward.

■ *Respond in private when appropriate*   If you're sending a reply that is applicable to only one person, send it to that person directly, rather than through the list or newsgroup. This reduces volume and makes more space available for other messages. However, if you have a response that would be beneficial to other users, feel free to post it.

■ *Don't cross-post*   *Cross-posting* means sending a message to more than one list or newsgroup. If the content of the message is directly relevant to the list, cross-posting is acceptable; indiscriminate usage of cross-posting will result in complaints to your ISP.

■ *Don't flame*   If someone makes a silly mistake, don't send email messages complaining about it. The person has probably already realized

Bright Idea
Some of the
large mailing
lists have thou-
sands of list
members.
Subscribing to
the digest for
that list prevents
your email
program's in
box from being
filled with
several hundred
individual mes-
sages everyday.

his or her mistake, and your message will only
rub it in. Plenty of users will have already sent
rude messages. You don't have to be one of
them.

■ *Request personal email replies*   Encouraging
people to email you directly with comments
reduces the server load and allows more bandwidth for other messages. If someone sends
you a particularly good idea, follow it up with a
note suggesting that he or she forward it to the
newsgroup or mailing list so that others may
benefit from it.

■ *Don't plagiarize*   Newsgroups and mailing lists
are forms of publication, and copyright laws
apply to them. Don't use information that isn't
yours without giving proper credit. If you need
permission to post something, get the permission or don't post it. The law is constantly
evolving with regard to the Internet, and you
don't want to get caught up in any legal battles
stemming from inappropriate use of someone
else's material.

■ *Ignore off-subject posts*   Once again, responding
to messages that don't relate to the list's subject matter will only aggravate the problem.
Ignore off-subject posts, and they'll go away.

■ *Verify your addresses*   Mailing lists can sometimes appear tricky; although a message might
look as though it's coming from a particular
individual, the mailing list processing software
has probably modified the message to give the
mailing list address as the reply-to address.
Verify the address before you send it to avoid

sending a personal message to all the subscribers of a list.

- *Verify information*   Remember that you don't know the people who post the information received from newsgroups and mailing lists. You may want to do additional research to confirm the information, or you may want to use the information to confirm your own prior research. Regardless of your approach, be wary of relying completely on information received from newsgroups and mailing lists. The more you use these services, the more you will become familiar with the people whose information you can trust.

- *Don't spam*   No matter how good a money-making scheme seems to you, the readers of a newsgroup or mailing list won't appreciate hearing about it. Sending spam to a list is an excellent way to have your ISP suspended for breaching its acceptable use policy.

- *Don't repost right away*   If you don't receive any replies to your query, wait a week or two, and then send it again. Examine your question, and ask yourself if you would have received more replies if it were less specific or more specific. Sending the same message many times over the span of a few days infuriates users and makes them less likely to respond in a positive fashion.

- *Don't give out personal information*   Don't volunteer personal information about yourself, and be cautious in giving it when you're asked about it. Your personal safety could be at stake, so be cautious in trusting people with information.

Just the facts

- Email provides you with an almost-instantaneous means to communicate with others who have similar interests.

- Email attachments allow you to send pictures of family members, GEDCOMs, and other files across the Internet.

- If you're traveling, you can check your email on the Web.

- You can use newsgroups and mailing lists to find other people who are researching the same topic.

- It's important to follow the rules of Netiquette when sending email and submitting posts to newsgroups.

Genealogy Web Sites

Chapter 6

Web sites fall under two main categories. The first type requires some sort of commercial transaction in order to fully participate on the site, such as buying a membership or buying and registering a product (as in the case of shareware).

Keep in mind that while commercial sites charge a membership fee to access certain information, almost all of them also provide free content; this applies to genealogy sites as well as to others. For example, most of the commercial genealogy sites mentioned in this chapter provide time-limited free access to certain areas of the site (such as databases and archives) to nonregistered users. Almost all of them also have tutorials and tips sections you can access for free. Another example of this would be a newspaper archive site that lets you search its data; oftentimes you can read a synopsis of each article that matches your search criteria, but you are required to pay a fee to retrieve the entire article.

The second category of Web sites is free sites, offered by people who want to share the information they have gathered in order to make your search easier. This doesn't mean that such a site won't have any sort of commercial affiliation; it just means that the Web site is provided as a service without charge. Government Web sites fall into this category; even though you may be required to pay a processing fee for materials you order through the agencies represented on those pages, you don't pay a fee to access the pages themselves.

Sometimes even free sites fall within what could be described as a hybrid area—they don't require a membership fee, but they might strongly encourage that you do something like make a donation. Some might consider the companion Web site for this book, www.genealogytips.com, such a hybrid. Anyone can use the companion site as a free source of online bookmarks or favorites for Web pages described in this book, but I sure love it when those who visit the Web site own a copy of the book—and I'll make it easy for them to do so by providing links to where they can purchase it.

In this chapter you'll learn about a sampling of genealogy Web sites. First, I'll cover commercial Web sites and then free Web sites. Government sites are broken out separately so that it's easier for you to find them. You'll also learn about genealogical societies that maintain Web sites. It's impossible to rate any one site better than another because each of those mentioned here fulfills a need or needs for genealogy research.

This chapter ends with some tips that should make your computer work a little easier, especially if you're a beginner. You'll learn how to use copy and paste to make your online life easier, how to read Web pages offline, and how to perform some other handy computer tricks.

Timesaver
As you read this chapter, keep in mind that you don't have to type in the URLs mentioned here. You can find them at www.genealogytips.com, on the Chapter 6 page.

Evaluating the information you see

As you read about the sites presented in this chapter, you'll discover that some of them duplicate information maintained at other sites. That doesn't necessarily make such sites redundant. Eventually you'll discover which sites are updated most frequently and are maintained well. When you learn your way around them, you'll also develop preferences based on how you are able to navigate your way around a site, as well as other factors that match your personality or your research needs.

Your needs and wishes for Web sites may evolve as you broaden the scope of your research. You might start out wanting to read tutorials, find state archives addresses, and learn more about how others conduct their research. Later, you might want to consult census or military records. Your favorite site today may be different from the one that you choose tomorrow. The sites in the chapter are not a comprehensive list of all that you can find on the Internet, but are key locations where you can begin your genealogical journey online.

In Chapter 1, I told you about how I chose the Web sites mentioned in this book. Now that you're ready to start looking at Web pages, there are several questions you can answer to help determine your needs and find the sites that will be most helpful for you:

- *Do you like going on a treasure hunt?* If you answer yes to this question, you will probably prefer to go in search of information yourself, utilizing the techniques you'll learn about in Chapter 7 to use online search engines and directories.

Bright Idea
Many genealogy sites maintain message boards where you can post questions. The more information you include with the query, the better your chances of finding the data you need.

- *Do you have more money than time?*   If you answer yes to this question, you may prefer to subscribe to a commercial genealogy Web site. Some are organized in such a way that they reduce the amount of time you need to spend looking for information.

- *Do you have more time than money?*   If you answer yes to this question, you may want to concentrate on the free sites and cull what you can from them first. Later, you can try some of the trial memberships to the commercial sites. That should give you sufficient background to make a decision about whether it would be worth it for you to invest in a full membership.

- *Is it convenient for you to spend large amounts of time online?*   If being online means that you tie up your only phone line, it may be more practical for you to do your preliminary research online and then order data CDs or visit a Family History Center to gather the information you need.

Bright Idea
In Chapter 7 you'll learn that a true *search engine* is a database of indexed material. A *directory* is also a database, but usually that index is categorized and manually produced. A site that combines both a search engine and a directory of Web pages arranged by individual categories is known as a *hybrid*.

You can also ask yourself some questions while viewing a Web site to determine whether the site will meet your needs. Those who rate Web sites refer to the ones people return to time and again as "sticky sites." To choose whether a site will be sticky enough for you to want to add it to your bookmarks or favorites file and return to it, ask yourself these questions:

- *Is the site easy to navigate?*   If you don't like how the information is arranged on the site or it takes too long for pages to load, this might not be a site you like.

- *Is there anything that annoys you about the site?*
  My personal pet peeve is a Web page that automatically plays music and doesn't give me the
  option to turn it off. Sure, I could turn down
  my computer volume, but that would mean I'd
  miss my email notification sound. If a site
  doesn't give me the option of whether I want
  music playing in the background, I don't
  return to the page if I can avoid it.

- *Are there a lot of errors on the site?*   A large number of incorrectly spelled words and grammar
  errors can mean that the person maintaining
  the site doesn't pay much attention to detail.
  The reliability of the data you'll need depends
  on accuracy, so details are important.

Commercial Web sites

Most of the sites in this section require a membership fee or other payment before you can access all
their features.

Ancestry.com
www.ancestry.com

Ancestry.com has more than 500 million names in
2,000 databases, including census indexes, early
U.S. marriage records, Civil War records, and other
information.

Some areas of the site are available for free, but
most require that you sign up for a paid membership. Ancestry.com does, however, offer a free 30-day
money-back guarantee plus a quarterly dues-paying
option.

This site offers some features that don't require
a membership, such as access to the Social Security
Death Index, a daily or weekly genealogy tips email
newsletter, and daily genealogy news summaries.

Timesaver
Some of the sites
in this chapter
have areas where
you can submit
questions
(queries) by
using a form on
the site or by
email; others
discourage sub-
mitting queries.
Be sure to follow
the appropriate
instructions and
guidelines before
you submit a
query.

Ancestry.com also maintains the Ancestry World Tree database of visitor-submitted, nonverified family tree data. This search area is free; you can use this area to find clues and valuable secondary source material.

Genealogy.com
www.genealogy.com

Maintained by the creators of Family Tree Maker software, this site doesn't require a membership fee or the purchase of software. Genealogy.com provides numerous articles on genealogy and other online assets. This site mirrors much of the information available on the official Family Tree Maker software Web site (www.familytreemaker.com).

If you are new to genealogy, you can find help at the site's New? Start Here link (www.genealogy.com/newstart.html). Other points of interest include a virtual cemetery tour (www.genealogy.com/vcem_welcome.html), which is part of the Virtual Cemetery Project collection of tombstone photos and searchable transcriptions archive.

Everton's Genealogical Helper Magazine
www.everton.com

Like Ancestry.com, the Everton's site is maintained by the publisher of a genealogy magazine and other reference materials. Everton's also offers a free daily genealogy email newsletter.

Nonmembers can access several charts and forms on the site, including pedigree charts, relationship charts, and family group sheets. Other preprinted charts and forms are available through the Everton's online genealogy supply store.

The Everton's Ancestor Research Tool is available as a shareware program at the site's download area. With registration, you receive a printed manual and unlimited technical support.

GenealogyLibrary.com
www.familytreemaker.com/glc_deny.html

GenealogyLibrary.com offers monthly and annual memberships, which allow you to access 2,346 online databases and primary resources and other special sections of the site. Membership also allows you to receive assistance on ordering vital records and performing other research that once required a visit to the library.

Kindred Konnections Family History Research Center
www.kindredkonnections.com

I'm a believer in keeping site navigation as easy as possible. Evidently the creators of this Web site believe the same thing. Here you'll find links to free services, member services, subscription services, and how to obtain a free hour or month of the site's services.

Kindred Konnections has more than 374 million names (and is still growing), as well as a Demo Room link to an area where you can learn how to use the site's research center.

National Genealogical Society
www.ngsgenealogy.org

The National Genealogical Society (NGS) site offers some general information, but much of what's on the site requires an NGS membership. You can find information on the types of memberships available at www.ngsgenealogy.org/member/content/type.html. This information is also available by calling NGS's toll-free number: 800-473-0060, extension 114.

Watch Out!
Navigation isn't always easy at commercial genealogy sites. It is sometimes difficult to tell whether you can't get the material you want because you're trying to access a members-only area or if a Web page is inaccessible due to server problems or other occasional Internet difficulties.

Free Web sites

Free Web sites are great because they don't charge for the information they provide. Some may utilize advertisements to offset the costs of running the site, but the overall objective is to provide the information, not to generate revenue.

A caution with any site, of course, is that you should not rely completely on the information it provides. For example, information taken from published materials, even when it's known to have some errors, can still have research value, despite those known problems. That isn't to imply that what you'll find on the free sites—or, for that matter, the commercial sites—is all necessarily error prone. (The verification and proofreading of transcribed materials done by volunteer efforts is commendable!) It means the basic rule of thumb is that you should verify everything you find.

American Local History Network
www.alhn.org

The American Local History Network is a site with links to individual state information, as well as a Migrations section for U.S. territories. A chosen volunteer Web page editor maintains the information associated with each link on this site. This site is hosted by the United States Genealogy Network (www.usgennet.org), which provides safe-site services on the Internet for not-for-profit historical and genealogical organizations.

Ancestors
www.kbyu.org/ancestors

Ancestors is a Web site maintained by KBYU-TV (www.kbyu.org) in association with PBS Online (www.pbs.org) for the family history and genealogy television series called *Ancestors*.

In addition to a new activities sheet about using forms, the site provides a number of forms in readable or printable .pdf and .gif formats, including pedigree charts, family group records, time line pages, research logs, and source checklists.

Family-Reunion.com
www.family-reunion.com

This site provides lots of information, including a newsletter and software, to help you plan a successful family reunion. The site includes suggestions on setting a theme for a reunion, feeding the crowd, choosing activities, picking a location, deciding what time of year to hold the reunion, and handling the invitations.

The Genealogy Home Page
www.genhomepage.com/full.html

In existence since 1994, The Genealogy Home Page (maintained on one long page) is sponsored by Family Tree Maker Online (www.familytreemaker. com) and has links to numerous help files, guides, and resources. It also has links to maps and deeds online; archives by state, country, and ethnic and religious groups; and family and personal Web sites.

GenForum
genforum.genealogy.com

GenForum is a surname message board and forum site that categorizes surnames in alphabetical order. The site also has areas for general and specific genealogy topics and computer hardware and software questions. There's a search engine on the site that you can use to search for specific topics.

Watch Out!
Many of the forms available on the Internet require Adobe Acrobat Reader, a program that doesn't work with WebTV. You can review the information on forms by taking another look at Chapter 4.

Gensource.com
www.gensource.com

Gensource.com provides links to historical records sites, databases, and resources intended to help genealogists find others who are researching the same names.

GENTECH
www.gentech.org

GENTECH is a nonprofit, all-volunteer organization. GENTECH's mission is to facilitate communication and knowledge among those interested in genealogy and technology by presenting national conferences, sponsoring programs with other societies, and publishing white papers based on analyses of problems of common interest to genealogists and technologists.

Helm's Genealogy Toolbox
www.genealogytoolbox.com

Helm's Genealogy Toolbox is the site maintained by the authors of *Genealogy Online For Dummies* (IDG Books, 1999). There you will find links to genealogy services, including news, search engines, Web magazines, and software reviews.

Heritage Quest
www.heritagequest.com

Heritage Quest provides information on how to get a free trial issue of *Heritage Quest* magazine. The site also has a genealogy tutorial, plus a bookstore, a software store, a magazine stand, searchable directories, an email newsletter, an events calendar, a query center you can use to link up with others with whom you can exchange information, access to professional genealogists who for a fee will help you with your research, and more.

Journal of Online Genealogy
www.onlinegenealogy.com

The *Journal of Online Genealogy* site provides an online magazine promoting the use of computers and the Internet in genealogy research. This site is maintained by Matthew L. Helm, coauthor of *Genealogy Online for Dummies* (IDG Books, 1999).

Lineages
www.lineages.com

Lineages promotes itself as "a major genealogy reference library and resource center built and maintained by professional genealogists who understand the needs of beginning researchers and experienced family historians." The First Steps beginner's area of the site (www.lineages.com/FirstSteps) offers forms and checklists for beginners that can be downloaded for free.

RootsWeb Genealogical Data Cooperative
www.rootsweb.com

The RootsWeb Genealogical Data Cooperative started out as a volunteer organization; it is now sponsored by Ancestry.com. It provides newsletters and articles; more than 806,000 surname entries in the RootsWeb Surname List; the means to do queries and searches; millions of pages of free genealogical data—with millions of individuals on file in the WorldConnect Project; and a comprehensive listing of genealogical topic mailing lists, including the site's own list, ROOTS-L.

RootsWeb publishes two of the world's largest online genealogy magazines (often called *zines*): *RootsWeb Review* and *Missing Links*. You'll find individual links to many of the services available at RootsWeb at www.genealogytips.com, on the Chapter 6 page.

Rory's Stories
users.erols.com/emcrcc/Tools.htm

Tutorials on this site include information on genealogy numbering systems and doing online searches. Rory's Stories also includes charts in hypertext markup language (HTML) format, printable to an $8\frac{1}{2} \times 11$-inch page. If you can't use the .pdf files available at other sites, you may want to check out this site.

Treasure Maps
www.firstct.com/fv/tmaps.html

The Treasure Maps site bills itself as the "How-to Genealogy WWW Site." In addition to a free email newsletter, it offers links ranging from the Research Room U.S. Federal Census and other tutorials to Old & Treasured Recipes.

Yourfamily.com
www.yourfamily.com

Yourfamily.com maintains a database of family home pages (and includes information on how you can add yours), a genealogy bulletin board to help you locate long-lost relatives, and information on how to create your own family home page, taped oral history, and heirloom photo albums.

General genealogy directories

General genealogy directories can range from sites that simply provide links pages with the listed Web site page titles and a brief synopsis of the opening lines on the site to those maintained on About.com and Suite101.com that feature a guide or an editor who personally updates the information and provides frequently updated material and articles. The major sites in this category include the following:

- *About.com* www.genealogy.about.com/ hobbies/genealogy

- *Excite!* www.excite.com/family/genealogy

- *Suite.101* www.suite101.com/welcome.cfm/ genealogy

- *Yahoo!* dir.yahoo.com/Arts/Humanities/ History/Genealogy

Newspaper columns online

Newspaper columnists often provide specific information, such as seminars and classes, geared for the local newspaper audience. However, newspaper columns can also be a wealth of tips and tricks to help you with your research. You can find links to newspaper columns online at www.genealogytips.com, on the Chapter 6 page.

Other genealogy search engines and databases

Genealogy search engines allow for a focused search because they don't index anything that isn't related to genealogy. At this time, there are three true genealogy search engines:

- *GenealogyPortal* (www.genealogyportal.com) A part of the Helm's Genealogy Toolbox, described earlier in this chapter

- *Internet FamilyFinder* (www.genealogy.com/ genealogy/ifftop.html) A part of Family Tree Maker/Genealogy.com

- *GenPageFinder* (www.ancestry.com/search/ rectype/directories/gpf/main.htm) A part of Ancestry.com/FamilyHistory.com

These three sites contain searchable databases of information contributed by site users. None of

Unofficially...
When you need to find information that was published in a recent newspaper, you can go to Newspapers Online (www. newspapers.com), which provides a search engine that lets you search newspapers within the United States, by country, and for business, industry, the arts, state press, religious, college, and specialty publications.

these sites automatically checks the Internet for new content.

You can find links to site-specific and other genealogy search engines at www.genealogytips.com, on the Chapter 6 page.

GeneaNet Genealogical Database Network
www.geneanet.com
GeneaNet is a searchable, worldwide list of user-registered, genealogy-related Web sites.

I Found It!
www.gensource.com/ifoundit
I Found It! is a free service offered by GenSource. It is a searchable database composed of pages submitted by users. Results are based on keyword hits, which are matched against the keywords supplied by the site owner.

Internet FamilyFinder
www.genealogy.com/genealogy/ifftop.html
Internet FamilyFinder allows you to perform a search in some or all of the available categories, including message boards, family home pages, commercial genealogy CDs, GenealogyLibrary.com, Civil War databases, and the Internet. There's also a link on this site to submit your Web site's URL.

Government archive sites
Government-maintained archive sites can be a source of valuable information. Even though you won't be charged to access the information on these pages, government departments may have fees if you request more specific information from them.

Library of Congress
www.loc.gov
The Library of Congress site has links to the Library of Congress American Memory collection of writings, music, and pictures related to U.S. history. The Library of Congress maintains millions of books, manuscripts, maps, music selections, and photographs. The site has information on how to use the research tools available, such as the searchable Library of Congress catalogs; country studies and area handbooks; military personnel death, missing in action, and prisoner of war records; and the copyright office records from 1978 to the present.

U.S. National Archives: The Genealogy Page
www.nara.gov/genealogy/genindex.html
This National Archives and Records Administration (NARA) page contains government archives links to pages specifically of interest to genealogists. NARA maintains regional research facilities; however, NARA recommends that you search its online microfilmlocator (www.nara.gov/nara/searchmicro.html) to verify that the regional office will have the document you need. The Web pages for the regional offices and for archives outside the United States are listed at www.genealogytips.com, on the Chapter 6 page.

Genealogical society sites

Genealogical and historical societies not only exist on the national and international levels, but on the local level as well. (You can find more information on historical societies in Chapter 12.) Most maintain Web pages, so there are thousands of such sites. You can do a search engine or directory search to find societies for your area (see Chapter 7). Other resources are the Genealogy SiteFinder (www. genealogy.com/links/index.html) and the other genealogy search engines mentioned in this chapter.

Federation of Genealogical Societies Society Hall
www.familyhistory.com/societyhall

Federation of Genealogical Societies (FGS) is a non-profit organization of genealogical and historical societies, family associations, and libraries. The site provides areas where you can search for information about societies (for example, if you want to locate one in your area; searches can be done by society name, keyword, city, state/province, or zip code) or submit a society to the FGS directory.

American Historical Association
www.theaha.org

The American Historical Association (AHA) provides research articles and grant availability information for history students. The site provides links to two noted publications in that field—*American Historical Review* and *Journal of American History.*

American Association for State and Local History
www.aaslh.org

Headquartered in Nashville, Tennessee, the American Association for State and Local History (AASLH) was founded in 1904 as a department within the AHA. It provides leadership and support assistance to more than 5,000 institutions and individuals who work in the fields of state and local history.

America's First Families
www.linkline.com/personal/xymox

The America's First Families—An Online Genealogy Society for 1600s Ancestors site includes an ancestor roll of honor of biographies and the 1600s ancestor database that includes thousands of proven 1600s colonial ancestors.

Association of Professional Genealogists
www.apgen.org

The Association of Professional Genealogists (APG) supports genealogists in all phases of their work—amateurs and experienced professionals alike. It provides a forum for those seeking to exchange ideas with colleagues, and it protects the interests of those engaging the services of a professional genealogist.

Genealogical Speaker's Guild
www.genspeakguild.org

The Genealogical Speaker's Guild (GSG) has a listing of speakers plus the means to search for speakers by topic or subject. It also provides information on how to go about hiring a speaker.

National Genealogical Society
www.ngsgenealogy.org

The National Genealogical Society is an educational service for the genealogical community. Its services include an online course, scheduled trips, and a library for its 17,000 members, which include individual genealogists, families, genealogical societies, family associations, libraries, and other related institutions.

National Institute on Genealogical Research
www.rootsweb.com/~natgenin

Founded in 1950 under the sponsorship of The American University, The American Society of Genealogists, NARA, and the Maryland Hall of Records, the National Institute of Genealogical Research (NIGR) is a leader in genealogical education. It is geared toward experienced genealogists.

Computer hints and shortcuts

The general tips described in the following sections will make your life online and your work on the computer a lot easier.

Be honest about your abilities

If you're not a good typist, consider recruiting someone else to enter your data. Also get help proofreading your work. Unfortunately, incorrect information travels as fast as correct information. One typo may seem insignificant when you consider the vast number of facts you're putting on your computer. But if that typo makes it into one of your GEDCOM files, which you put online, and which others later duplicate on their sites, that one lone typo can create big problems.

Use copy and paste

It isn't always necessary to retype information. Many times you can manage data by clicking, dragging to highlight, copying, and pasting. Place the cursor at the beginning of the text you want to copy, and then click and continue to hold down the left mouse button as you drag the cursor across the words you want to copy. When you lift your finger off the left mouse button, the chosen information will be highlighted.

To copy that information, press the Control and C keys (Control + C) at the same time, or from the Edit menu, choose Copy.

To paste the information, place the cursor where you want the information to go. This can be in the same document or in an entirely different window or program. When you have the cursor in position, press Control + V, or from the Edit menu, choose Paste. The duplicate information now resides at its new location.

Read Web pages offline

To spend less time online, select File | Save As to read a Web page offline. Newer browsers save a Web page, complete with any graphics, if you use the Save As option from the File menu. After you click Save As, follow the prompts to set the file path (that is, select the folder where you want to store the page). If you need to do so, you can even create a new folder into which you can save the page. You can later open the page in the browser; some newer word processing programs also let you view the page in Web page view.

Watch Out!
Don't forget that when you read a page while you're offline, none of the links will work.

Work around URL errors

URL errors are frustrating, but often they can easily be resolved. Webmasters sometimes move a page without creating a refresh page to take you to the new location. You can often get to the Web site by starting at the right end of the URL and deleting some of the letters.

For example, imagine you have a link to www. ricehahn.com/illustration_purposes/exampleonly. html. You paste or type that URL into the Address line in your browser and press Enter or Go, but the page won't load. First try deleting exampleonly.html. If the Webmaster has an index page—that is, a page for which the filename is invisible to the viewer but is recognized by the browser, even though the browser doesn't display it as part of the URL—for the illustration_purposes area of the site, using the URL that now reads www.ricehahn.com/ illustration_purposes will call up that page. If that still doesn't work, drop back and punt again: Delete illustration_purposes so that you're left with just the domain address: www.ricehahn.com. With any luck, the domain is still in existence and you'll be able to find a site map that tells you where you can now find the information you need.

Copy a URL

Say you're at a fantastic Web site and you want to send the URL to a friend in an email. You don't have to type in the information. You can copy it and then paste it into the body of an email message. Click on the Address line in your browser. That highlights the entire URL. Now follow the usual steps for copying: Use Control + C (or Apple + C, on a Mac) to copy the URL, and then place the cursor where you want to paste that information, and use Control + V to do so.

Find it fast

Imagine that you created a file containing some important notes, but now there's a problem: You can't remember the filename or the name of the folder in which you saved it. From the Start menu, choose Find | Files or Folders. If you remember any part of the filename, you can enter the part of it that you remember and use wildcards for the rest of the filename. For example, you use an asterisk * to replace the unknown portion of the filename in a search on *notes*.*. Check the Look In window to make sure the correct drive is selected for your search. If it isn't, you can use the drop-down menu or click the Browse button. Also make sure there's a checkmark in the Includes subfolders box. Now click Find. Any filenames that match the search criteria (*notes*.*) show up in the lower pane.

If you remember some keywords in your notes, you can also use Find, even if you no longer have a clue about any part of the filename. Leave the Named area blank and type the keywords in the Containing text window.

Just the facts

- A number of online directories and search engines are devoted to genealogy.

- Carefully preview the services offered by a Web site before you submit a query to make sure the site can answer the kinds of questions you're asking.

- Although a Web site might appear reliable, don't take chances: Verify everything.

- Some sites require a membership fee, and others offer free information.

- Government Web sites provide a wealth of information.

GET THE SCOOP ON...
Streamlining your research by using
online tools ▪ Using search engines, directories,
and hybrids ▪ Saving and printing Web pages
▪ Online timesavers

Strategic Online Research Tips

A few short years ago, in the dark ages before the Internet, if you wanted to do research, you made a trip to the local library. Once there, you'd ask the librarian for something like "everything you have about genealogy," and unless she asked you to narrow your search, you would have spent days sifting through the books, journals, pamphlets, local histories, personal histories, magazine articles, public records, and documentary films she placed in front of you. Then, for good measure and perhaps smiling while she did so, she'd probably come by later with another stack of materials, which she'd just remembered.

Seriously, most librarians are far more helpful than that. They're a lot more user friendly than most search engines and directories seem. Chapter 6 lists Web sites to use to start your research until you feel more comfortable doing your own searches. And that shouldn't be too long from now, with the tricks I'll show you in this chapter. Humans have

Chapter 7

Unofficially...
Genealogy won't be the topic of all your searches. Sometimes you'll need to do such things as confirm historical events, look up terms or words found in journals that are unique to the time a diary was written, or find an article in a periodicals archive.

their place in research, but computers are generally quicker.

Doing it digitally

Although the digital age demands some changes in the manner in which research is done, the research itself hasn't changed much. You still need to have a good idea of what you're trying to find. For example, I recently did a search on *genealogy* at a popular search engine, and I got 5,186,470 hits! I don't know about you, but that's more than I can read in an hour. Heaven only knows how long it would take to load that many Web pages.

It might be a good idea to learn how to narrow that search. Doing so is a craft, an art, a science. I promise that if you learn to do it well, it will solve quite a few of your online woes. By the time you finish this chapter, you'll know some of the tricks you'll need to master that skill.

The search

A search, basically, is a request for information. You type a few words and click the Search button; the site then checks its database of pages to see which of your search words appear there, and it gives you a list of the ones that match.

Whether you realize it or not, much like The Top 10 Countdown on the music charts and *The New York Times* Bestseller List, you are—if not consciously, at least subliminally—influenced by the rankings of the returns on your search. The closer a page appears to that number-one position on the list, the better the odds that you will be drawn to that page. So if you think of the results of your searches as a hit list, and if you're like the typical Web surfer, you'll only venture about 10 deep into the search list that's returned before you give up on that list.

Knowing where and how to search

I've talked to a lot of people who think searching the Web is nearly impossible. They think that they need to learn strings of complicated codes and search commands (called *syntax*) if they want to gain control over their search results.

If you're one of those people, I have good news and better news. The good news is that the commands aren't that hard, and I'll show you how to use them later. The better news is that a lot of times you don't need any syntax at all. Syntax is helpful when you want to reduce the overall number of hits; however, I believe that there's a lot more to searching than getting fewer hits. What you really want to do is get the good results to appear at the top of the list. This is getting easier as search engines grow smarter and more powerful—almost by the day.

First, you need to use the right search for the job. Sure, you could try using a wrench to put a nail through a board, and eventually you might even get it to work. But you wouldn't be using the easiest method possible. Likewise, different searches call for different tools. But before you can select a tool, you need to know something about the options.

Understanding search engines, directories, and hybrids

Hundreds of millions of Web pages offering a seemingly endless supply of information exist on the World Wide Web, and more arrive literally each minute. As you attempt to wade through this information, you can make sense of it if you know how the major search engines, directories, and hybrids gather and present that data. Then, with any luck, you'll be able to move past wading and get down to some serious surfing of your own.

Watch Out!
You'll see the term *search engine* used generically throughout this chapter to refer to any search-capable Web site. A true search engine, such as AltaVista (www.altavista. com), is a database of indexed material. A directory is also a database, but usually that index is categorized and manually produced.

Search engines

Search engines consist of three major elements:

- A spider (also known as the crawler, robot, or bot) constantly scans the Web to retrieve the information it needs by visiting a Web page, reading the content, and then following the links to other pages on that site. Because a spider is blind to image and audio or video clip information, the system isn't perfect. But a lot can still be categorized from the textual content on a page.

- The index or catalog is an archive of indexed pages.

- The search engine software determines which pages in the index are relevant to a given search.

Watch Out!
According to Search Engine Watch (www. searchenginewatch.com/ facts/size.html) no search engine indexes *everything* on the Web. Search engines miss pages because of problems with frames (a style of Web page design), lack of image maps (site indexes), and the inability to index dynamically created Web pages (another Web page design style).

AltaVista (www.altavista.com) is the granddaddy of the search engines. Its archives are huge, with recent statistics from Search Engine Watch (www.searchenginewatch.com/reports/sizes.html) placing its numbers at more than 350 million pages. AltaVista isn't the only search engine out there, though.

Directories

Unlike a search engine that goes out looking for content, a directory usually only selects its listings from the Web pages submitted to it for consideration. In most cases, a directory search only looks for hits on the words included in the Web page description submitted with the other page information (such as the URL, or uniform resource locator, which is the address to the Web site, such as www. genealogytips.com).

Yahoo! (www.yahoo.com) is the leader in the directory category. For general topic searches, this is probably the best place to start. Current statistics credit Yahoo! with 1.2 million pages in its catalog. One advantage to Yahoo! is that if what you need doesn't show up in your initial search on that site, Yahoo! provides the means to forward your search to a number of other search engines.

Now that many search engines are adding subcategory directories to their sites, which they combine with their search engines, the distinction between search engines and directories is quickly becoming blurred.

Another directory, The Study Web (www.studyweb. com), places its directories on links pages, organized by topics, with more than 120,000 URLs categorized on those pages. It doesn't allow for searches within those categories; however, even without that searchable capability, such directories can often save time until you better understand how to narrow a keyword search. The Study Web also has a feature for students, called the Study Buddy—a separate window of links to an encyclopedia, measurement and money converters, dictionaries, CIA World Fact Book (which does include a keyword search option at the bottom of its CIA Publications page), and other helpful sites.

Some directories, including the following, use spiders to search for sites outside the directory:

- *Excite (www.excite.com)* Excite offers special features, such as letting you customize your start page. You can select the features that you want to appear on that page. Your choices include stock quotes, shopping sites, news

Bright Idea
Pages on sites that use frames can't be bookmarked directly. To escape the frames, right-click on the link and either select the Open in a New Window option or the Copy Shortcut option and paste the copied URL into your browser's Address window.

tracking, personal horoscope, local weather, and comic strips.

- *Snap (www.snap.com)* Snap provides category directories, plus links to e-cards (greeting cards sent by email), chat communities, and other features.

- *About.com (www.about.com)* Like Yahoo!, About.com (formerly known as the Mining Company) has handpicked links. On these sites, an expert who publishes articles and commentary on the subject edits each category. (You can find a list of genealogy subcategories at www.genealogytips.com, on the Chapter 7 page.)

Hybrids

Hybrid sites include a search engine and also maintain an associated directory of pages grouped by category. These sites allow you to do a search of the sites included in the subdirectory. Subdirectory searches include such options as searching by zip code, a keyword option limited to searches within that category, and a general search area. You can find links to hybrid search engines and see the listing of genealogy subdirectories at www.genealogytips. com, on the Chapter 7 page.

Multiple-search-engine sites

A multiple-search-engine site, often called a *meta-search engine* or an *all-in-one search engine,* searches several search engines and directories simultaneously. In many cases, these sites allow you to choose between searching all the engines included on the site or searching a selection of sites based on such criteria as fastest three or best three. ProFusion (www.profusion.com) even lets you decide whether you want it to verify all or some of the resulting links, which can help you avoid the dreaded 404 File Not Found page error. You can get links to ProFusion and other multiple-search-engine sites at www. genealogytips.com, on the Chapter 7 page.

Natural-language searching

A natural language search is one where, instead of searching on a number of key words, you use common, everyday language as your search criteria. Some people swear by Ask Jeeves! (www.askjeeves. com), which lets you use natural language to ask a question. Instead of using keywords and searches, you simply type a question like "Where can I find census records?" The results are shown as a series of boxes with drop-down menus.

Ask Jeeves! is a hybrid site; it also contacts other search engines and provides the results in drop-down menus. If you find what you're looking for on one of those menus, you select it from the list and then click the Ask button beside the menu to jump to that site.

For times when you're having trouble deciding exactly how to phrase a question, Ask Jeeves! even provides an area on its home page that shows you what other people are asking.

Giving a Web search a whirl

Now that you understand what goes into a searchable online database, it's time to learn how to refine your searches and use some specific search sites. The trick to using any search engine is knowing what to ask. The more specific you are, the better your results at the top of the stack will be. With a little bit of practice, you'll quickly develop a knack for conducting searches.

Timesaver
After you type in your search information, you don't have to move your fingers off the keyboard and grab your mouse to click the Search button. Pressing the Enter key at most search engines will accomplish the same thing.

Some search engines require *Boolean operators*, which are characters used to connect search terms. Other search engines are simpler. For example, Google (www.google.com), developed after more than three years of research at Stanford University, doesn't require any Boolean operators or special characters before or between words. To try a simple search, go to www.google.com and follow these steps:

1. In the box under Search the Web using Google, enter *genealogy*, *new*, and *jersey*, making sure you have a space after each word.

2. Click on the I'm Feeling Lucky button on the right.

3. Google sends you to what it thinks is the best page to start on. With the search words entered in this example, Google took me to the Genealogy SiteFinder, at www.genealogy.com/links/c/c-libraries-and-archives.html.

If you don't like the results you get from the I'm Feeling Lucky search, you can click the browser's Back button and do a plain old Google search by clicking on the Google Search button or pressing the Enter key.

One of my few complaints about Google is that the home page doesn't offer a search results drop-down menu option box for increasing the number of hits displayed. Unfortunately, you have to conduct a search first to get to those other pages. For example, if I do a search from a search results page, I can increase the number of hits from 10 all the way up to 100. This isn't necessarily contrary to the point I made earlier about refining your search so that pages that are more apt to match your criteria land

Bright Idea
If you're having trouble with a word's meaning, try Google. Enter a word into the search box, click I'm Feeling Lucky, and the resulting page will often give you an idea of what the word means. This is great for proper names and words that aren't defined in dictionaries.

at the top of your results list. There are times when it's convenient to skim through an assortment of the hits to get a better feel for the pages that are out there; being able to do so on one long page is nice because it means you don't have to switch between the results pages, but instead can easily skim the list and return to anyplace on that list to choose the site you want to click on. It does, however, mean that in a roundabout way, one of the first rules of a successful Web search is perseverance: There are times you just can't be tricked into believing that those at the top of a results list are necessarily the best sites, and you may need to dig a little deeper.

Again, you'll develop a knack for how best to conduct a search that meets your needs. At some point, you'll probably realize that you prefer one search site over another. Searching is an art, and as a budding search artist, you need to experiment until you feel comfortable.

Zen and the art of searching

Sometimes a search engine isn't enough. That doesn't mean that if at first you don't get the results you want, you jump from search engine to search engine until you do. Searching is easiest if you use a little logic and intuition. Let me give you an example.

While researching information for parts of this book, I needed to find the Web site for the U.S. Colored Troops database. Normally, typing in those words will bring back results for each individual word: *U.S.* and *colored* and *troops* and *database.* However, putting quotation marks around the keywords limits the search to the specific phrase, in this instance, *U.S. Colored Troops database.*

For this search, I used Google, and clicked on the I'm Feeling Lucky button. I was taken to

Genealogy.com's Genealogy SiteFinder for History: United States:American Civil War (www.genealogy. com/links/c/c-history,united-states,american-civil-war.html).

You might think that the last thing I'd want is a links page. However, I've learned that Control + F (which opens the Find dialog box in the browser) is my friend. As I said earlier, sometimes a search engine can only do so much. I decided to see if I could find one of the primary words in my search phrase on that page. In this case, *colored* seemed the best choice.

Using the find feature landed me on a descriptive information page—the Web page for the 54th Massachusetts Infantry (1863)—with history, service records, letters/book excerpts, a database of more than 230,000 names of U.S. Colored Troops, re-enactment information, and some links. At the page I found a link to the 54th Massachusetts Infantry page (extlab1.entnem.ufl.edu/olustee/54th_MS_inf. html).

On first glance, that page didn't look like it was going to be of much help. It appeared to be nothing more than a narration on the history of the 54th Massachusetts Infantry. Once again, I decided to see what I could find on *colored*. A Control + F search took me all the way to the bottom of that page, to two links, one of which was the one I needed. The Web site for the U.S. Colored Troops database is at www.itd.nps.gov/cwss/usct.html, a page that informed me that there are now 235,000 names in that database.

Out of curiosity, I also did a Google search on the original phrase; the site didn't appear directly in any of the 20-plus results.

Searching directories

As discussed earlier, a directory is a handpicked listing of Web sites, divided into categories. It's important to remember that searching a directory is not the same as searching the Web. If the directory's editor hasn't selected a site, that site won't come up in your search. However, many times when a site has been included, your search can really pay off. Most often, if a site is listed in a directory, it means it's passed some sort of criteria to make it there.

As mentioned earlier, not every search engine or directory lists every site on the Web. Eventually you'll learn which ones give you the best results to meet your needs. The only mistake you can make is to stick to using only one; you'll miss finding some valuable resources if you do that.

The biggest advantage of a directory is its structure. You can start out with a very broad search, and then narrow it down by using categories. If you enter a broad term such as *genealogy* into Yahoo!, the first link is to Yahoo's Arts:Humanities:Genealogy category, which is divided into a number of subcategories. From there, you can choose from one of those subcategories or narrow the search by entering one or more keywords and clicking the button for the search within that site.

If you wanted to go in another direction, on Yahoo!'s home page, you could broaden your search by clicking one of the categories under the Yahoo! logo. Clicking History and then By Region lets you look up information about a specific state. Or you might want to click on a country name to research, for example, Sicilian origins.

> **❝**
> Judging whether sites in a directory are just listed or have passed a review is something like assessing the relative value of a comprehensive bare-bones bibliography versus an annotated selected list of reading. They each have value, but the appropriate selection depends on your previous knowledge and your research goals and needs.
> —John Scroggins
> **❞**

Timesaver
It's a good idea to jot down notes on pages from your first few searches. That will help you come up with good keywords for later searches.

Looking in unexpected places

Help isn't always at the places run by the big boys. There are times when you can find what you need on smaller, sometimes amateur, sites as well. For example, if you're doing a medical history genealogy, you might be interested in a site I maintain that I modestly call The Ultimate Chronic Illness Resource Directory, at www.ricehahn.com/resource. The site provides links about specific illnesses, links to medical reference guides, health news sites, and other resources of medical interest.

It often seems that the people who maintain such amateur sites are driven by real excitement and interest in the subject about which they write. Yahoo! started out as an amateur site, too. Some of these sites may become the big boys of tomorrow. Who can tell?

Expect some personal bias when you visit these sites. One person's fluff may be another person's treasure. Different sites offer different ways to filter or sort the information. The filter determines which sites appear at the top of the list, but no filter is perfect. But at least with sites maintained as a labor of love and without the benefit of venture capitalist funding, you know up front that you're getting information that has been of benefit to somebody. You can find links to some of these smaller sites at www.genealogytips.com, on the Chapter 7 page.

Syntax

There are times when it's best to use a powerful search engine like AltaVista (www.altavista.com), the 200-million-page-strong Fast Search (www.alltheweb. com), or HotBot (www.hotbot.com). These are the closest you can get to literally searching the entire Web. Their databases index every word on each page. These search engines give you a very broad range of results, so this is when you'll need to narrow your searches the most by learning to be as specific as possible. Syntax can help a lot in these searches.

To practice such a search, first add to the search. Now that you've been through a few directories, you know what types of things you can look for that apply to the genealogy category. Many of the genealogy directory sites list pages for diaries and journals. Rather than peruse all those offerings, suppose you want to search for diaries or journals that pertain only to war.

On AltaVista, your entry would look like this:

+war +diar +journal* +genealogy*

The * acts as a wildcard. Using wildcards in the manner shown here tells AltaVista to include both *diary* and *diaries* and *journal* and *journals* in the search. The + lets AltaVista know that you want each word to show in the results—you don't want separate results on each word. When I tried a search using the + before each word, I got 4,116 hits; without them about 11,338,554 pages were found. A big difference! Four thousand pages is still a lot, but at least they're all related to a specific topic. You can do better.

You can also use minus signs to force AltaVista to exclude words from the search. Now try a search on this:

+war –"world war" +diar +journal* +genealogy*

That results in 3,498 pages found. It shaves off a few hundred hits, but perhaps it's better to include the war you want, rather than exclude all wars you don't want:

+war +"civil war" +diar +journal* +genealogy*

Watch Out!
When you use the + sign as part of a search on AltaVista, the spaces between the words are important. When I tried a search on *+war+diar*+ journal*+ genealogy*, the result was "no pages found."

Bright Idea
The syntax discussed in this section can be used in almost any search. The quotation marks are especially useful at Google and AltaVista.

You see even more improvement—this time 2,910 pages are found.

Maybe it's an even better idea to make your search as specific as a certain battle:

+war +civil +gettysburg +diar* +journal* +genealogy

Only 148 pages found!

Now your search depends on what exactly you need to ascertain from those Battle of Gettysburg journals. If you're looking for any written by your ancestors, you could add a surname to your search. A search on this yields 6 pages:

+war +civil +gettysburg +diar* +journal* +genealogy +hahn

Out of curiosity (to see if there are any non-genealogy-related sites matching the criteria), try doing one more search, dropping *+genealogy* from the previous one. A search on this gets 53 hits:

+war +civil +gettysburg +diar* +journal* +hahn

Changing the word order doesn't affect the hit number in this instance. Those results are still within reason.

Sometimes adding, deleting, or substituting a word in a search query can get you better results. You'll get the hang of this and other tricks after a while. Depending on the amount of time you have to devote to a particular search, you may or may not want to search on all the possible keywords you can think of and then drop them one by one to broaden the search. You might want to begin a search on a single keyword and hope you can find the information you need on one of the top hits.

Advanced search options

There are times when you want to require certain words and allow others to "float" to the top of a search. Most sites have instructions about how to conduct even more advanced searches than what's discussed in the previous section. Many also have help pages.

Most search sites display such information prominently at the top of their pages; however, if you don't see it there, scroll down; the bottom of the page is another good place to look for links specific to a site.

Other sites worth mentioning

Search sites, just like people, come in all shapes, sizes, and personalities. Finding the one that meets your needs is almost like looking for a spouse. A lot depends on whether you like the appearance. Can you trust what you're told? And, like all people, chances are it will have some nasty habits that'll drive you up the wall at times, so you just need to decide which ones you can live with.

Just like when you're dating, you may have to see a few sites before you find "the one." This section is a little black book of sites for you to try; this is a sample of what's available, so don't let your quest end here. Be on the lookout for new sites and use the ones that appeal to you.

WorldPages.com
www.worldpages.com/whitepages

Not all your searches will be for information on deceased individuals. There will be times when you want to track down long-lost relatives or people from your past. One place to start is on the WorldPages People Finder site. Here you can search Canada and the United States by last name only. The site also provides boxes for first name, city, and state/province, but those are optional fields.

555-1212.com
www.555-1212.com

555-1212.com is a site sponsored by AT&T, InfoSpace.com, LocalEyes, and NameSecure that provides free online telephone and Web directory services. Specific information includes area codes, white pages, yellow pages, reverse lookup (that is, entering a phone number to learn who that number is registered to rather than searching for a phone number by a person's name), international calling codes, international directories, and email addresses.

HotBot
www.hotbot.com

The exact phrase option at HotBot is one I use frequently. If you use that option, you get the same result as using quotation marks around the phrase, but without needing to use the quotation marks.

I've used HotBot to find the origins of an obscure quote—such as determining the speaker and the date and time of the speech when all I had to go on was a line mentioned in a journal, song lyrics and the associated copyright information, the author of a poem my grandmother had clipped from a newspaper, and so on. Plus, HotBot lets you increase the number of hits displayed on a page to up to 100.

> 66
> The Internet is like a giant jellyfish. You can't step on it. You can't go around it. You've got to get through it.
> —John Evans, www.quoteland.com/quotes/author/147.html
> 99

deja.com
www.deja.com

Formerly known as DejaNews, deja.com is best known for searching for information that's been posted on Usenet newsgroups. That area can be found in the Discussions section at www.deja.com/usenet. (See Chapter 5 for more information on newsgroups.) One nice touch is that deja.com provides a link on the left of the home page for a tour that will walk you through how to use the site.

Practice makes perfect

Remember that there are a large number of search engines and directories out there. Search Engine Watch (www.searchenginewatch.com) has listings and information on all of them. Search engines are like friends. I've introduced you to the ones I know well. It's important to get acquainted with as many as you can so you can determine which ones you like the most.

Searching can become an addiction for a trivia buff. But what better way to relax and educate yourself at the same time than to put on some music and practice searching for random things? It's a surprisingly good pastime, and you'll learn a lot in the process.

As with anything else in life, the more you practice, the more naturally searching will come. Eventually, your initial searches will be close to perfect. Soon you'll know just what type of search to use and how to select keywords to get the results you want.

Saving time online

You need to know some basics when it comes to browsing. The following tips will save you hours of time. I learned them the hard way; but there's no reason you should have to, too.

Saving a Web page

Anyone who has spent any time at all on the Internet knows that Web pages come and go. Therefore, it's in your best interest when you find a page that contains the information you need to save

Watch Out!
Unless you're doing a specifically case-sensitive search, don't use capital letters or punctuation marks (aside from the quotation marks used around a phrase) in a search. The search engine will either throw them away (making them a waste of keystrokes) or use them as syntax (which can really mess up your results).

it in some format. Say you don't have time to copy and paste all the data you need on a page, and you want to be able to work with that information when you're offline or at least ensure that the information is close by *when* you need it. If you have plenty of hard drive space, the quickest way to save the information is to save the Web page. Both Microsoft Internet Explorer and Netscape Navigator provide this option. To save a page, you follow these steps:

1. From the File menu, choose Save As.

2. Choose the folder in which you want to save the page.

3. Confirm that the filename is descriptive enough and change it if necessary; the page will save as an .html file. Newer browsers save any accompanying graphics in a folder bearing the same filename as the file when you save the file.

4. Click Save.

Later, when you're ready to view the page, you need to open it. To open the file in your browser, you follow these steps:

1. From the File menu, choose Open.

2. In the Open dialog, either type in the file path and filename (for example, C:\My Documents\ genealogy\tutorials\lesson1.html) or click on the Browse button to locate the file you want to open, and then click Open.

3. Click OK.

Printing a Web page
To print a hard copy of a Web page to keep with your files, follow these steps:

1. Open the page in a browser. If you are online, enter the URL or click on one of your bookmarks or favorites, and wait for the page to load. If you want to print one of the pages you've saved, follow the earlier instructions to open the page in the browser.

2. In the browser, click on the Printer icon, or from the File menu, choose Print.

3. Choose your options in the Print dialog box, and click OK.

Consider the number of pages that will be in the printout before you decide to print an entire Web page. You may be able to save a lot of paper by copying and pasting the information you need into a separate word processing file. If you choose this option, be sure to cite the source of the information so you remember where you got it.

Grabbing pictures from a Web page

You might find a graphic on a Web site that you want to preserve as an image file rather than in only printed format because you may want to do one of the following:

- Send the image to others via email or on disk

- Save it as a file in order to incorporate it into your own Web site (But if you don't first receive permission from the copyright holder or owner of the graphic, don't do it.)

- Examine details using another program (such as PhotoShop, Paint Shop Pro, or a shareware program) that lets you zoom, adjust the contrast, or use other viewing options

- Preserve the image with your other family history data by putting it in a digital scrapbook

Moneysaver
If you can't choose Print Preview in your browser, choose the Print dialog box option Print Range Pages from 1 to 1. Print the first page; the total number of pages will appear in the footer. You can then decide whether you want to print the remaining pages.

Unofficially...
Some Web pages
disable the
copy/paste
function, but
there's a little
trick you can
use to override
it. Just copy
the URL into
Netscape
Composer or
FrontPage
Express. You'll
have the page
open in a
document you
can edit.

Isolating and saving a graphic from a Web page is easy:

1. Place the cursor over the image you want to save.

2. Choose Save Image As (in Netscape) or Save Picture As (in Internet Explorer).

3. In the resulting Save dialog box, choose the location to which you want to save the file, and alter the filename if you want to make it more descriptive.

4. Click Save.

Just the facts

- No one search engine can fill all your needs; try searches using several different search engines, directories, and hybrids to find what works best for you.

- Directories are arranged so that you can conduct your searches within specific categories.

- There are a number of ways to narrow or broaden a search.

- You can sometimes find the information you need by taking the road less traveled—using an amateur search site.

Starting Your Personal Discovery

PART IV

GET THE SCOOP ON...
Why you should do research on yourself first
■ Finding the documentation you need ■ Writing
your personal biography ■ Getting the kids
involved

Chapter 8

Starting with Yourself and Involving Others

Whether you plan to keep all your records on a computer or keep a series of notebooks, you've got to start your research somewhere. It's best to start with yourself, and in this chapter you'll learn why.

Just because you start with yourself doesn't mean that you have to do all the work yourself. When you involve your friends and family, you do everybody a favor. At the end of this chapter, you'll learn how to get others involved, ways to make it work, and why it's a good idea.

Before you reach that point, however, you first need to make a commitment to be honest with yourself. Some of the tasks of recording and preserving your personal history may be unpleasant (for example, dredging up details about an ex-spouse). Just remember that even if you hate those times—whether it's while gathering your personal documents and filling out your forms or while writing an autobiography—your grandchildren and their grandchildren will thank you later for your efforts.

Bright Idea
During your
study of gene-
alogy, you may
hear a pedigree
chart called by
other names,
such as an
ancestry,
a *family tree,* or
a *lineage chart.*

Gathering information for your story

As you begin to gather the documents that prove that you are you (your birth certificate and other documents that you'll read about in this chapter), it's important to remember that your goal is to learn how to organize your research efforts. Gathering the information that's easiest for you to access—the stuff about yourself—will help you develop good habits at the beginning.

First, you'll start with a pedigree chart, which you learned about in Chapter 4. Begin by writing down all that you know about yourself. Start with your date of birth and place (city, state, and county) of birth. Label this Chart no. 1. Whether you fill in as much as you know of the other information on the pedigree chart at this point is up to you. If you're a "handle each piece of paper once" type and it'll bug you to save the rest of your pedigree chart for later, by all means fill it out now. However, this is one of the forms that you'll be finding yourself returning to work on again and again.

Next, you need to prepare a family group record (sometimes referred to as a family group sheet) for yourself. You're not quite ready to start gathering the documentation (that is, proof or primary records that support what you write); you're simply recording your personal data. So, again, fill in as many blanks as you can on the form. You'll need to record the following:

- Your name (if you're a married female, your husband's name goes at the top of the form and yours in the next section down, under "wife")

- Birthday (day, month, year) and birthplace (town, county, state or province, and country)

- Christening date and place (adapt for other ceremonies)

- Father's name

- Mother's name

- Indication of whether you have had other marriages

You'll need to leave room for date and location of your death, as well as date and location of burial, which, obviously, someone else will have to add later.

If you're married, you can include the date and place of your wedding and your spouse's name, birthday, and birthplace; you can do this now or get back to it later. The same applies to your children. Your primary purpose at this point, however, is to keep this a self-involved endeavor. This chapter is about you, you, and then for good measure, some more about you!

One of the reasons for focusing on yourself is that in the beginning it's much easier to start disciplining yourself to organize your data (and to figure out how you want to do so) if you don't have lots of papers for lots of different people. You are also not just doing this research for yourself. Someday all the family history information you gather will be valuable to others, too, and they will want to know about you.

Even though you're only recording information about yourself, write down and document all the information that you find and where you find it. Later on you'll keep a similar report sheet on each person you research. This helps you keep everything straight as you uncover more and more information. Without proper recording techniques, it'll be impossible to keep everything straight. At this

Unofficially...
It may not seem like the politically correct thing to do, but you should always put the husband's name first on a family group sheet. If you don't comply with this standardization, your records may be difficult for others to follow.

Watch Out!
Remember that you should complete a separate family group sheet for each marriage. If you've been married twice, you should have two family group sheets—one for each marriage. (Some sheets allow space for other marriages. If no children resulted from the marriage, you won't need much data on that spouse.)

point, you will find that you still have a lot of blank spaces, even in your own chart. When you get into the heavy research (and detective work), you'll be glad you laid your groundwork so carefully.

Remain focused as you do your work. Your mission is to start with yourself and work your way backward. You want to avoid going off on tangents— jumping around or skipping generations "to learn the good stuff." Avoid the temptation to go off in search of stories about a relative's brushes with the law during Prohibition. You'll get to that eventually. And, when you do, it'll prove interesting, no matter what tales you uncover or myths you debunk. However, unless you've laid the proper groundwork, you may overlook vital facts when you're exploring that past generation of kinfolk simply because you didn't have a full understanding of what you needed to complete the job.

Treasure hunts

Now that you've filled out your personal pedigree chart and preliminary family group sheets, it's time to work your way through your home. You'll be looking for records that prove who you are. Later, you'll do the same thing for your spouse, children, grandchildren, and others, working backward in time. But for now, focus on cleaning out drawers, organizing closets, and dusting off papers in the attic, tool shed, or wherever it is that you've stuck (er, efficiently stored) important papers in the past.

You have a wealth of documentation around the house, or in some cases, in a safety deposit box. You'll want to check these sources for the following information on yourself:

- *Birth* Documents such as a baby book, a birth certificate, or an adoption record

- *Religious affiliation* Documents such as a record of blessing, baptismal record, dated bulletins, christening record, or confirmation record or other record of coming-of-age ritual

- *Citizenship* Documents such as a naturalization record, an alien registration, deportment papers, a passport, and a visa

- *Civil and legal activity* Documents such as a bond, a contract, guardian papers, subpoenas, and summonses

- *Death* Documents such as a death certificate, a funeral book, an obituary, a memorial card, and a will; you can complete this information at this time, if you want, for a deceased spouse or child, and for obvious reasons, you leave this area about yourself blank

- *Employment* Documents such as achievement awards, apprenticeship records, citations, disability papers, income tax records, membership records, union papers, severance records, retirement records, and a Social Security card

- *Family records* Documents such as a family Bible, bulletins, a coat of arms, genealogies, histories, lineages, and newsletters

- *Health* Documents such as hospital records, medical records, immunization records, insurance papers, and vaccination records

- *Heirlooms* Items such as dishes, engraved items, needlework, quilts, silverware, stitched samplers, tapestries, travel souvenirs, and trophies

- *Licenses* Documents about pursuits such as business (including occupational and professional licenses), driving, possessing firearms, fishing, and hunting

Unofficially...
The confidentiality of medical records varies from state to state and agency to agency. *Your* records are one thing; getting them for somebody else may prove difficult. If you have access to them, they're another important form of documentation. Otherwise, you may have trouble getting such records released to you.

- *Marriage*   Documents such as a wedding announcement, a marriage license, a wedding album, an anniversary announcement, and divorce papers

- *Military service*   Documents and artifacts such as citations, disability papers, discharge papers or records, insignias, national guard service records, pension records, ribbons, selective service records, service medals, service-related weapons, and uniforms

- *Personal information*   Documents such as autograph albums, calendars, journals, letters, newspaper clippings, photos and photo albums, publication clippings, and scrapbooks

- *Proof of residence*   Documents such as lease records, rent receipts, utility bills, and property tax records

- *Property ownership*   Documents such as abstracts of title, deeds, estate records, land grants, mortgages, other financial records, and water rights

- *School*   Documents and artifacts such as awards, grade transcripts, graduation diplomas, honor roll listings, report cards, and yearbooks

- *Miscellaneous information*   Documents such as published works (not necessarily directly family history related) and sales receipts

You can find a link to a printable home document form that lists the items in this chapter as a checklist, at www.genealogytips.com, on the Chapter 8 page.

You know better than anyone else where you keep the records you need to gather in order to check off each item listed on your checklist. If you need to get copies of some of the records, find the appropriate sections of the book, where I give information on how to do that. If you find that you don't have some of the important documents on hand and need to obtain copies, now is the time to indicate that on your to-do list.

As you are gathering the documents that help you add validity to your family tree records, decide where you will store them. By now you've probably established the area in your home where you'll be doing your genealogy work. Even if at this point it's only a portable cardboard file box and some hanging folders, put each thing in its correct place as you find it.

Even though you're concentrating on yourself at this point, don't ignore documents that you find for other family members, or you'll wind up backtracking and duplicating your efforts. The same holds true if your preliminary document gathering takes you to the homes of family members. Establish a file for the other records you retrieve so you'll know their location when you are ready for them. Eventually you'll have copies of birth certificates for every person in your family, as well as other pertinent papers.

Citing

It is important to differentiate between actual documentation for an event or a relationship described and other source information. You'll encounter primary versus secondary information, and primary versus secondary documents during the course of your research. You'll also be accessing various kinds and qualities of reproductions, transcripts, indexes, and other records. Some sources will prove more reliable than others, so keep in mind that in and of

Unofficially...
You don't need to have original copies of all the certificates you're gathering; photocopies will suffice. Cite on each copy that it is a photocopy of a certified copy and mention where the original is stored.

themselves, they do not necessarily establish the validity of the "fact" they reference. At the time you locate a document, you need to cite several important factors about that document; if the document is later somehow discredited, you indicate that by adding additional citation remarks. Your citation is there to do the following:

- Remind yourself where you acquired the information

- Provide an indication of the relative accuracy of the information

- Act as a pointer to where additional information might be found

- Advise of discrepancies, such as "this date differs from that reported as transcribed from earlier-cited church record"

- Allow the placement of additional notes and reminders to yourself; it's important to write these down as they occur and in the context in which they occur

The importance of documenting your work cannot be overstressed. In the beginning, it might help if you ask other family members to read over your citations to see if they are able to fully grasp your explanations. Citation formality isn't as important as clarity. However, by their very natures, formal citation styles do lend clarity. See Chapter 1 for additional information on how to cite information and documentation.

Remember that your citations will help you keep yourself on track. They're your memory on paper. Citations will also help anyone else with whom you share your records or anyone who might come across your documentation in the future. So even

Watch Out!
Be consistent in how you prepare your document citations: It will help others as well as you, if at some future time someone wants to check the sources.

though you know when you were born, add a citation to your own birth certificate. As you now know, documentation (in this case, the document and your citation) is considered a more reliable "proof" of the stated information. In other words, a document with a citation is considered more trustworthy than the document alone. The citation is a means of showing that somebody verified the information.

When there isn't conflicting information, documentation generally satisfies the requirement that what is stated is factual and substantiates any inference you made. For example, your citation to a will can be used to document other statements that you record regarding information discovered in that document.

The best documentation always comes from a primary record. Later, when there are questions concerning other members of your family for which primary records aren't available, there will be times when you have to play a logic game of putting together pieces of the puzzle in a sort of well-documented answer key.

In the beginning, you may fool yourself into thinking that you can remember it all. Later, after you've moved beyond yourself and are gathering facts and documentation about others, you'll thank yourself for establishing the citation habit from the beginning. Nothing will be left to chance. You'll have your own written proof of how and where you acquired each piece of data in your records.

Recording the story of you

Now that you've gathered the documents proving who you are, it's time to begin thinking about using your own words to tell the world who you are. Don't worry about the length and format at this point.

66
If you can't write a story about yourself, you cannot write about someone else. Do the research on yourself, before you go on to the rest of the family.
—Loretta Sheldon, Ancestors Web site Tips & Tricks, www.kbyu.org/ancestors
99

Begin by asking yourself some questions:

- How do you want people to remember you?

- What are your favorite memories of childhood?

- What are the milestones thus far in your life?

- What early projections did you make for your life that you've yet to obtain?

- What are your goals for the future?

- What obstacles have you overcome?

- What are the current challenges you face?

- What are your worst fears?

Now that you've answered some questions, you've done what is sometimes referred to as "going to the well." You dip your bucket and hope it doesn't come up dry. "Priming the pump" with those questions helps ensure that it doesn't.

Next, you need to decide what style of biography (or autobiography—this *is* about *you*, after all) you want to write. You can choose from several formats, each of which allows you to use the first-person, *I,* style of writing:

- *Narrative*   This is the least intimidating format because you can just imagine you're writing a letter to a friend. In this case, it's like you're writing to a friend who will read your autobiography in the future. Just like a letter, you write a narrative bio in a casual, conversational style.

- *Chronological*   Similar to narrative, in this format your "letter to your friend" begins with your writing about your earliest memories and then progresses through your life, year by year.

- *Personal essay*   In this format, you select a specific event about which you want to write, including conclusions about how the experience

Bright Idea
Regardless of how you tell your personal story, don't get distracted early on, trying to choose just the right words. It's called a *first draft* for a reason. You can always make changes later. The most important thing at first is to get the story down on paper.

affected you and the significance it held in your life.

- *Humorous* Everybody enjoys a good laugh. Think of these stories as *Reader's Digest*-style anecdotes. Preserve the memories of when something said or done made for a funny situation.

- *Photo essay* Think of this format as a documentary of your life. One way to write this style of personal biography is to pick up one of your family photo albums and simply begin writing out your recollections about what was taking place at the time specific photographs were taken. It's okay to also write down what other things were going on in your life at the time. It helps if you develop some sort of system for keying your writings to the photographs.

- *Memoir* Similar to the personal essay, in this format you combine the stories of several events in your life.

- *Journal* Even if you've never kept a diary before in your life, if you choose to use this format to record your bio, it doesn't mean that you have to ignore everything that's happened to you before the date of your first journal entry. Allow for flashbacks. On days when nothing out of the ordinary occurs, begin your entry by writing a "something today made me think of this" story.

- *Biographical sketch* When you use this format, you write down an introduction to yourself that is similar in style to what a master of ceremonies would use to introduce a speaker. Include facts about the significant events and honors in your life, but be brief.

Whichever way you choose to tell your life's story, strive to make it interesting. Allow for some flexibility. If what you're doing evolves into the great American novel, that's wonderful, but it doesn't have to be your primary purpose. Even if you're writing about events in chronological order, you can skip around. Record things as you remember them. Don't feel you have to stick to just one style. Use whatever you feel works best for the event you're describing. Think of your personal essays as chapters in a book. Whether you ever put those chapters into book order is up to you. The important thing is that you're getting your story down on paper.

Date each entry you make in your bio. If you later revise what you've written, put the revision date after the date the story was first written. You might also want to keep a running citations list of others mentioned in the writings. It's a good idea to have a master sheet that tells who the people in your writings are; that way, casual, first-name-basis references to others will become a valuable additional resource for your heirs.

Getting others involved

Most people welcome the chance to be helpful. In fact, requesting assistance in your research will offer other people some unique benefits.

Genealogy can, for example, make history come alive for kids. (Even if you don't have children of your own, you can probably get your nieces, nephews, or adult relatives involved.) Chances are kids know their way around the computer better than you do anyhow. Why not take advantage of that and have them help with the research? First, send them to some of the tutorial sites geared specifically for their age group; you'll find a list of such sites at

Bright Idea
Get family members involved in genealogical research by asking them to make a time capsule together. Ask everyone to write a brief biography and include some mementos from the year. Seal it together, and choose a year for it to be opened.

www.genealogytips.com, on the Chapter 8 page. Later you can give the kids specific research questions to work on.

Drop hints that get your family members and friends involved. Have children look over the Genealogy Book List for Kids and the Genealogy Word Search on GenExchange's Kids Corner section, at www.genexchange.org/kidscorner.cfm. Involving them will help your children develop a sense of pride in their heritage and a respect for their ancestors. As a bonus, you'll be helping them develop their investigative, organizational, and reasoning skills.

Put one of the kids in charge of making photocopies. Another can use the three-hole punch to make printouts ready for the three-ring binder. A preschooler can put return address labels and stamps on envelopes. Set aside one night a week as family tree night, and put everybody to work.

When you've got the hang of getting the children involved, delegate some more. Let your children write some of the letters to relatives, asking for information. Consider having them conduct some of the oral interviews, even if it just means you start out letting them interview you. (See additional interview suggestions later in the chapter.)

Scope out the terrain together by reading a book or watching a video about the history of an area before you go there on a visit. Plan part of a family vacation around your genealogical research. Visit some of the historic sites in the area you're visiting. Places like Colonial Williamsburg and Deerfield Village help give everyone a sense of what life was like in the past. Make history, and therefore your heritage, come alive.

Another benefit to this approach is that it can help everyone develop certain other skills, too. Consider some of the possibilities described in the following sections.

Interview and research skills

You can use role playing to teach interviewing techniques. Begin by having your child pretend to be a historical character—one from a video you recently watched together or somebody you know your child will be comfortable portraying. Ask your child's character a series of questions (for example, "How did it feel to first see land after spending so much time at sea aboard the Mayflower?" "Were those boxes of tea heavy? Did you have to have somebody else help you throw them overboard?"). Later, reverse the roles and let your child interview you.

You'll find opportunities for developing yet another skill when the person being interviewed isn't sure of the answer: research skills. Coming up with interview questions to ask you will spark your child's imagination and uncover things about which he or she is naturally curious. Depending on the age of your child, you can either assist or turn the child loose on the Internet and let him or her go in search of the answers. (If you plan ahead, you can already have some sites saved in your bookmarks or favorites that you know will provide some of the answers.)

Organizational skills and logical thinking

Something as simple as helping you put papers into a notebook helps reinforce a child's organizational skills. Then, when you're ready to file that notebook, get your child's opinion. ("We'll probably be putting papers into this notebook once a week. Where do you think it'd be most practical to keep it—here at my desk or on one of the bookshelves?")

Genealogy and the visual arts

You might want to plan a monthly photo album night. Have all your supplies at the kitchen table and turn the kids loose, letting them create their own pages for the album. If you'd rather not mess around with paste, glitter, and stickers, you can use one of the numerous graphics programs that let you use the computer to design onscreen frames to go around snapshots.

Here are some other ideas:

- Older kids can scan photos into the computer. Chances are that an adolescent would welcome the chance to create a digital slideshow.

- You don't have to limit children's involvement to snapshots. Let them develop graphic arts skills by creating digital images for your family Web site (which you'll learn more about in Chapter 14).

- When a child is old enough to respect the equipment and learn how to operate it, put him or her in charge of setting up the tripod and using a camcorder.

The possibilities are endless. Everybody—friends and family alike—will think they're just having fun. You can remind them occasionally that they're creating their own history.

Just the facts

- Regardless of whether you keep most of your research data on the computer, you'll still have

Bright Idea
Afraid you don't have the time to do your family tree research and figure out ways to get others involved? Then take a shortcut. Contact a home-schooler. He or she will probably already know numerous other techniques to help history come alive for kids.

paper records to organize, too.

- Starting by gathering records and preparing other documentation about yourself helps you become familiar with the genealogy research process, learn how to complete some of the paperwork, and make some decisions about the best ways to organize your research based on that experience.

- Your personal biography can be in any form you believe is best.

- Family history research is a wonderful way to share time with others; children can learn their history as well as many new skills.

GET THE SCOOP ON...
How to complete a pedigree chart ▪ Finding
your famous (or infamous) relations ▪ Web sites
that help you search ▪ Filling out family
group sheets

Your Immediate Family and Beyond

Chapter 9

A few years ago, my friend came across an obituary when she was cleaning out her mother's house. The obituary was for my friend's grandfather, and it referred to a son named Lawrence; until then, my friend didn't know Lawrence existed.

Lawrence posed a great mystery. There were no living relatives left to ask about him, and my friend had very little documentation from her mother's side of the family. The obituary was the only reference to Lawrence that seemed to exist. She checked at the courthouse, but didn't find any mention of Lawrence. A search of the parish records yielded no results—no marriages, baptisms, or death certificates. The trail was cold.

Several months later, that friend was doing some research on the Internet on her great-aunt, and she found a site that listed her great-aunt's husband's lineage. She was surprised to find a Lawrence listed as her great-aunt's nephew, whom she had raised as a son. After a little more digging—which involved correspondence with the person who had posted that information to the Internet—she managed to find out that her grandfather's marriage to her grandmother was a second one. She visited some old family friends and discovered that her grandfather's first wife had died giving birth to Lawrence, and her grandfather had left Lawrence in his sister's care while he went off to war. When he returned, Lawrence had bonded well with his aunt, and even though no formal adoption ever took place, her grandfather agreed to leave Lawrence with his sister. Her grandfather then found employment in another state, where he met and married her grandmother.

Had my friend not come across the obituary, she might never have learned this part of her family's history. Had she not dug further, she might never have come into contact with Lawrence's descendants. The experience taught us both a valuable lesson: Never give up completely, and use every tool at your disposal. The answer will likely come eventually, probably from an unexpected source. Keep this in mind as you begin your research on the rest of your family.

The rest of the family

Bright Idea
Always record the maiden names for your female relatives. Also write out everyone's middle names—not just the initials.

Now it's time to return to your pedigree charts and family group sheets to add the rest of your family. If you haven't done so already, fill in the information on your spouse and your children. If any of your children are married, complete forms to reflect those marriages and any children they may have (your grandchildren), too.

Now you're ready to go back a generation. Fill in as many of these charts and as much of each as possible for as far back in your lineage as you can.

Primarily, this chapter focuses on your immediate family; however, if you have information on hand on your ancestors, there's no reason to delay recording that information. Don't worry about blank spaces for now. Also remember that you'll be confirming your memory later when you check the dates on the primary records you amass against what you've filled in on the forms.

Pedigree charts

A pedigree chart serves as a comprehensive outline of a bloodline. In this case, you're starting with yourself and working your way backward, creating an ascendant chart.

Keep in mind the following as you complete a pedigree chart:

- Write surnames in ALL CAPS.

- Use a pen to complete information; pencil tends to smudge.

- Draw a line through any incorrect information and initial and date the change.

- For geographic locations, show city or town, township, county, state, and country, in that order.

- Add blank parentheses—that is, ( )—when a maiden or a middle name is unknown.

- Put a nickname in quotation marks or list it as an aka (that is, also known as).

- Show dates in a consistent format, such as day/month/year format (that is, dd/mm/yyyy); other date styles are discussed later in this chapter.

Each pedigree chart is a visual guide to your research. It's in your best interest to keep them all

Timesaver
You can order blank genealogy wall charts online from Misbach.org, at misbach.org/ charts. Genealogy forms are also available from the National Genealogical Society, at www. ngsgenealogy. org/education/ content/ gen_forms.html.

up to date. Pedigree charts are only the efficient research tools they're meant to be if you update them as you gather new information and correct any mistakes on them as soon as you uncover any errors.

Also keep in mind that because a pedigree chart does not allow for proper source citations, you should not share it with other people unless you also include an attached source citation document or a properly cited family group sheet.

You can find hints and suggestions on completing a pedigree chart or alternative forms at www. genealogytips.com, on the Chapter 9 page.

Family group sheets

Now you're ready to generate (no pun intended) even more paperwork: family group sheets. Each family group sheet is the information on an entire family. Each person on your pedigree chart will have at least two family group sheets—one as a child (with parents and siblings) and another as an adult (complete with information on his or her spouse and children, if appropriate).

Keep in mind the following as you complete a family group sheet:

- Write surnames in ALL CAPS.

- Use a separate family group sheet for each marriage or union.

- Link each fact to a full source citation.

- List all sources for a given fact (such as date of death found on a death certificate, obituary, and tombstone or cemetery record).

- Use the back of the form to record source data, if necessary.

- List children eldest to youngest, using an additional sheet if necessary.

You can find links to information on filling out family group sheets and other forms at www. genealogytips.com, on the Chapter 9 page.

Paper versus computer records

The point at which you use your genealogy software is up to you. Some prefer to enter all their data into a program and let it generate the charts. However, the downside to doing this is that each time you record new information, you need to print out another series of reports in order for your notebooks to be accurate and up to date.

Some people print charts only after significant changes and make small pencil notes on the existing printed charts until new ones are produced. (Remember that I prefer to always use ink because it's less likely to smudge; I then write in any changes and date that change, crossing out the inappropriate information, if necessary.)

Other people avoid paper charts entirely and keep everything on the computer. I can't tell you what will work for you, but it's a good idea to find a method you like and stick to it.

Putting your tools to use

As you've already learned, you use pedigree charts as a broad outline and tracking form to determine which of the following answers you've been able to uncover about each ancestor:

- Date of birth
- Place of birth
- Date of marriage
- Place of marriage
- Date of death

> 66
> What I did was wait to do my program print-outs until a goal number of people had been reached. For me, it was 200.
> —Keith Giddeon, author and Web page designer, www.giddeon. com
> 99

- Place of death
- Place of burial

You've probably been able to uncover most of those details on your immediate family. To prepare for some of the work you'll be doing in subsequent chapters, pick one of your ancestors from the pedigree chart and identify the questions you need to answer about that person. To find those answers, you'll be looking through two basic types of genealogical records:

- *Compiled records*   These biographies, family histories, or genealogies are found on microfilm or microfiche, in books, or online and are the records that have already been researched by others.

- *Primary records*   These are the original records that were created at or near the time of an event, copies of which you'll want for your documentation. They consist of birth, marriage, death, and other selected records.

Looking for compiled records first can save you a lot of time—they are available on some Web sites, at Family History Centers, and on data CDs—but it doesn't eliminate your need to find primary records, too.

When the going gets tough

You don't want to allow yourself to get bogged down and discouraged by what can seem at times to be insurmountable odds. Allowing for variety and flexibility in your routine will help you avoid genealogy burnout. When you don't know where to turn next, try using this problem-solving questionnaire:

Moneysaver
Unless you are unable to visit a Family History Center (FHC), don't invest a lot of money in data CDs. In her tour of an FHC site (www.firstct.com/fv/fhctour.html), Edie Mixon, director of the Jacksonville, Florida, FHC says, "You can usually do 90% of your Family Research from an FHC."

GENEALOGY PROBLEM-SOLVING QUESTIONNAIRE

Surname: _____

First name: _____

Middle name: _____

Address: _____

Telephone: _____

Date: _____

Email address: _____

My primary search components: _____

Surname: _____

Given names: _____

Location(s): _____

Time frame: _____

My goals and what I'm hoping to find: _____

Libraries and other archives visited for this search:_____

_____

_____

Family sources used: _____

Other sources consulted:

    Courthouses: _____

    Cemeteries: _____

    Churches: _____

    Organizations: _____

Resources already checked:

    Census: _____

    Land: _____

    Probate: _____

    Other: _____

Famous genealogies

Probably the first curiosity search beginning geneal-ogists do is to try to discover any relationship to somebody who is famous, or in some cases, infa-mous. If you insist on checking out some of the famous lineages posted online, check out the

> **❝**
> Misinformation in genealogy did not start with online research. The savvy genealogist believes nothing without a primary source citation which they personally, painstakingly, verify. Anything else is just a clue and maybe an incorrect clue at that.
> —Sherry Schaller Marshall, genforum. genealogy.com/ success/ messages/ 333.html
> **❞**

following Web sites (remember that you'll need to verify any association your family may have with one of them):

- *A Shakespeare Genealogy*   daphne.palomar.edu/ shakespeare/timeline/genealogy.htm

- *Appleseed Alley: Johnny Appleseed*   www.geocities. com/Heartland/Fields/9587

- *Biographical Dictionary of more than 28,000 Notable Men and Women*   www.s9.com/biography

- *(Daniel) Boone Ancestors and Descendants* booneinfo.com

- *Boone-Lincoln Genealogical Connection*   www. everton.com/usa/GENEALOG/GENEALOG. BOONLINC

- *Brigitte's The Royalty Pages (includes The White House Connection)*   www.worldroots.com/ brigitte/royal/royal11.htm

- *Celebrity Family Trees: I Dream of Genealogy (includes Lizzie Borden, Amelia Earhart, Diana Spencer, and Titanic survivor Margaret Tobin, aka Molly Brown)*   www.idreamof.com/ famous.html

- *Celine Dion's Family Tree*   members.spree.com/ sip/bons_achats/cdiongen-a.htm

- *Donner Party Descendants*   members.aol.com/ danmrosen/donner/index.htm

- *Elvis Presley (includes a family portrait)* www.rootsweb.com/~rwguide/notable/ elvis.htm

- *Elvis Presley: I Dream of Genealogy Family History Research*   www.idreamof.com/tree_elvis.html

- *HMS Bounty Genealogies*   www.lareau.org/bounty6.html

- *Laura Ingalls Wilder*   members.tripod.com/~PennyN/LIWgen.html

- *Lewis & Clark Corps Of Discovery Descendant Project*   home.pacifier.com/~karenl/lewis&.htm

- *The General Society of Mayflower Descendants*   www.mayflower.org

- *Pocahontas: Descendants of Powhatan (Father of Pocahontas)*   www.rootscomputing.com/howto/pocahn/pocahn.htm

- *Presidential Genealogies on the Web*   homepages.rootsweb.com/~godwin/reference/prez.html

- *Relatives, Friends and Associates of Isaac Newton*   www.newton.org.uk/glossary/Gpeople.html

- *Robert Burns Family History*   fox.nstn.ca/~jburness/burns.html

- *RootsWeb.com's Notable Kin*   www.rootsweb.com/~rwguide/notable

- *RootsWeb.com's Notable Women Ancestors*   www.rootsweb.com/~nwa

- *RootsWeb.com presents Royal and Noble Lineages*   www.rootsweb.com/~rwguide/royal

- *RootsWeb.com's U. S. Presidential Ancestor Tables/Pedigrees*   www.rootsweb.com/~rwguide/presidents

Thirty thoughtful research tips

Now that you're moving beyond yourself and researching others in your immediate and extended family, remember these tips:

Bright Idea
If you want to read more about the lineages of wealthy and famous people, consider *Roots of the Rich and Famous* by Robert R. Davenport (Taylor Publishing, 1988).

Unofficially...
Never make fun of a pack rat again. Family members who hoard old papers and memorabilia are a genealogist's best friends. Read *Hector, the Collector* by Shel Silverstein. This will give you a better appreciation for those who treasure their "stuff."

- *Write down every nit-picky detail*   Never leave a library, courthouse, or other research site without consistent, complete citations for each piece of information you've found. You should also record the citations and general content for books in which you didn't find anything. Keep a list of these titles so you don't repeat your efforts later. Your list might also come in handy later, when you need sources for newly discovered ancestors.

- *Always list who told you what*   If Aunt Gertie told you that family rumor has always had it that Bessie Mae was a dance hall girl in the California Gold Rush, record that information, as well as information on where you can find other known data (such as full name, date of birth, and other information) on both Aunt Gertie and Bessie Mae. Casual comments may not seem important now, but they may prove valuable in the future.

- *Keep a correspondence log*   Similar in format to a research log, a correspondence log is where you record the date and the action of each letter or email message you send. Cross-reference this log to the names of those with whom you correspond.

- *Be grateful for relatives from small towns*   Not everybody who lives in a small town keeps up with what everybody else is doing, but if your great-granny is one who does, you'll uncover all sorts of interesting tidbits and family lore.

- *Take advantage of your local library's interlibrary loan system*   You can use this service to retrieve needed books from other libraries and request free microfilm from other states such as that for a newspaper by range of dates.

- *Reread your notes from time to time*   You'll be surprised by what you've forgotten. You'll also uncover new information. Even though it was there all the time, it may not have made sense to you until you filled in some other pieces of the puzzle.

- *Don't accept other people's data as fact*   Verify all that you find. Something may not even be known to be an error until you explore matters further. For example, my grandparents' mailing address was in one town, but they actually lived in another; that town was small enough to be considered a rural route of the neighboring town. Similar discrepancies can make a difference when you try to find plat maps and other important records.

- *Find alternative ways to look for relatives*   If you run into a roadblock trying to find data on a woman, try searching for records on her brothers.

- *Don't forget to check church records*   Church records are often more reliable than early courthouse records because immigrants went to a church where they could speak their native language. English-speaking people recorded most courthouse records, which especially caused problems when they recorded information gathered from immigrants for whom English was not the native language; it wasn't uncommon for such people to learn to speak English without acquiring the skill to read or write it, which made them functionally

"
I've learned more about my ancestry from second cousins in small-town Illinois than from the folks I grew up with in big-city Minnesota.
—John M. Scroggins, www/ancestry. com
"

illiterate. This also accounts for the variety of surname spellings. Knowing how to pronounce a surname in its native language can give you clues as to the variety of spellings for which you should look. Even various branches of the same family often ended up with different surname spellings because of this.

- *Be thoughtful* Enclose a self-addressed, stamped envelope when you write to somebody if you expect a reply.

- *Don't expect others to do your work for you* If you discover information on a book that you believe may contain information you can use, check with a local librarian to see if the book is available through interlibrary loan before you post notices online asking for somebody to look up the reference for you.

- *Join a surname-specific mailing list* If you are having difficulty finding information on a specific surname, even if he or she can't help you directly, someone on the list will probably be able to guide you to data sources that will help you in your search.

- *Know when to ask for help and give it* Despite my earlier warnings about asking others for help at the wrong time, don't think that you can always go it alone. Sometimes it's necessary to stop and ask for directions. The important thing to remember is that you should not just be a taker; provide information for others, too.

- *Advertise* You don't have to take out an ad in the paper, but do let all relatives with whom you come in contact and your circle of friends know about your genealogy research. Be sure to list the names you're researching online, such as on the RootsWeb Surname List, at rsl.rootsweb.com/cgi-bin/rslsql.cgi. Also submit them to any genealogical directories and surname lists published by genealogical societies to which you belong. This can help you avoid duplicating work that has already been done.

▪ *Don't get frustrated by delays or what can seem to be insurmountable odds*   Everyone encounters roadblocks. In most cases, you'll find the answers you need eventually—and often in unexpected ways.

▪ *Use the valuable online resources, but don't discount or overlook local sources of information*   Family Bibles and other records held by your immediate relatives are usually more reliable than what you'll find online. Local historical societies are another source of information you shouldn't overlook.

▪ *Invest in a microcassette recorder*   Dictating notes often takes less time than writing them down, and transcribing dictated notes can be quicker than rewriting notes you've handwritten, especially if your handwriting is hampered by carpal tunnel syndrome or other problems.

▪ *Your cameras aren't just for family photographs*   You can use a 35mm, digital, or digital video camera to photograph important documents and tombstones. Be sure to experiment with your camera's settings before you need to use it. Especially with important papers, you want to be sure your photographs show all the details. In this case, you want photocopy-quality images. It's important that the photograph you take clearly shows the data on the page.

- *Stay on top of your research*   Maintain a central location to keep documents until you can get them filed or stored in your three-ring binders. In an ideal world, you should file each page of notes, photocopy, or other document as you acquire it. That isn't always possible. Having a "to be filed" spot at least saves you the time of searching all over the place should you need to find a document you haven't yet filed; you'll only have to look in one place.

- *Double-check all dates*   It isn't unknown for somebody to "improve" a marriage date recorded in a family Bible to camouflage a "premature" birth. Other times incorrect date information occurs because somebody trans-posed numbers. You don't want to perpetuate such an error. Watch for red flags that should trigger your suspicions, such as a birthdate that would mean a woman became a mother at age 10.

- *Make a concerted effort to get complete name infor-mation*   As mentioned previously, you should make sure you record all parts of a person's name, including nicknames under which the person may have been known; nicknames are sometimes used in newspaper stories, for exam-ple. Chances are, however, that any request for a legal record will be rejected if the request is for a nickname rather than the person's full name.

- *Don't just rely on a book index*   Indexes to local history books usually don't include the names of all persons mentioned in the book. Take the time to skim the book's contents if you know that one of your ancestors lived in the geographic area covered by the book. You might stumble across an obscure reference that carries you to a new line of investigation.

- *Remember that boundaries and place names often change*   Verify geographic data in historical atlases or genealogical texts pertaining to the area to make sure you're directing your research to the proper location.

- *Look for clues even where you don't expect them*   Sometimes something that doesn't appear to be quite right can be just what you need. Don't overlook address names that are a bit different from the ones you're researching.

- *Stick with one common date format*   Start using the day/month/year format (for example, 5 September 1951) or dd/mm/yyyy (for example, 05/09/1951) format. To an English person 09/05/51 means May 9, 1951. Forty-eight years from now, it'll have a different meaning even for Americans. 5 September 1951 leaves no room for misinterpretation; if you use the 05/09/2000 format, be sure to indicate this in your citation. Using a four-digit year means that you'll always define the century.

- *Be grateful*   Send thank-you notes to those who assist you.

- *Consider yourself always on duty*   Carry a notebook and a microcassette recorder with you at all times. This way you'll be ready to record information anytime.

- *Take advantage of waiting time*   Don't let a long line at the supermarket get you frustrated; interview the elderly person behind you in line

Unofficially...
Take a trivia break and read Mark Howells's article about how back in the 1950s COMTRAM developer Bob Bemer, because of his genealogy background and appreciation for the importance of using a four-digit year, helped divert the Y2K problem. See www.oz.net/~markhow/writing/bemer.htm.

about changes he or she has witnessed in the community. (Then step aside and let him or her go ahead of you in line as a way of saying thanks.) Don't get stressed in rush-hour traffic. Instead, keep your microcassette recorder close by and dictate some of the letters you've been putting off writing.

Bright Idea
EMAZING's Genealogy Tip of the Day Archive is located at www.emazing. com/archives/ genealogy.

- *Make wise use of bookmarks or favorites*   When you're at a site where you've found valuable information, bookmark it or add it to your favorites or bookmarks. When you're done with that research session, take the time to organize your links so that you can easily find them later. Make sure you title links that aren't prenamed or that have hard-to-decipher names so you'll remember what they're for.

- *Remember to keep things fun*   Be flexible. Sometimes your research plans may change because of new information you uncover. Allow for some flexibility. Be spontaneous, and embrace the serendipitous moments when they occur.

Just the facts

- Keep your pedigree charts up to date, being sure to include complete names (surname, first name, and middle name—not just the middle initial) and maiden names.

- Complete one family group sheet for each family.

- When the going gets tough, review your research options and try a new approach.

- You can satisfy your curiosity online by checking to see if you are related to anyone famous—or infamous—at a number of sites.

GET THE SCOOP ON...
The value of a relationship chart
▪ Understanding different relationship terms
▪ Naming schemes ▪ Finding your relatives
online

The Rest of the Family Story

Now that you've gathered all the information and primary records on yourself and those in your immediate family, you're ready to move on to your ancestors.

Without having a plan to manage paperwork in place before you start this phase of your research, you could easily become overwhelmed by it all. Think about it.... Assuming no additional marriages in the mix, you have 2 parents, 4 grandparents, 8 great-grandparents, 16 great-great-grandparents, and so on. If you include your parents' and grandparents' siblings and try to learn about all your cousins, too, you're faced with a daunting task unless you keep everything organized as you go. As you move backward in time, you really begin to appreciate the concept that no man is an island.

With this in mind, you can also appreciate why it's much easier to make a concerted effort to do your research in a linear fashion than to skip around. Otherwise, it'd be like going to the store for

Timesaver
Certified
Genealogy
Records
Specialist Beverly
Whitaker recom-
mends that as
you gather bits
and pieces of
family lore,
dates, names,
and places, you
keep track of it
all by recording
the information
on standard
8½ × 11 paper
instead of
assorted scraps.
—GenTutor
Approach to
Genealogy page,
members.aol.
com/GenTutor/
tutor.html

the chocolate chips after you've preheated the oven and started mixing up the cookie dough. Any work is more fun if you make it as painless as possible.

Relationship charts and terms

Although your goal is to do your research in a manner that's as linear as possible, that may not always be practical. While you're conducting oral interviews with your relatives (covered in Chapter 11), for example, they may mention other ancestors. As granddaddy used to say, "Strike while the iron is hot." Don't walk away from information offered to you by another simply because you haven't reached that point in your research. File information you're not ready for until you're ready for it. Devise a way to remind yourself that you have that information. For some, a "papers on file" log keyed to a relation-ship chart helps.

A relationship chart lets you see at a glance exactly what your relationship is to another as you work your way through previous generations. It lets you see how far removed (that is, the generations away) from a common ancestor two people are. Because these charts have many variations, you should find the one that is easiest for you to understand.

You can find one example of a relationship chart as part of the Rory's Stories Web site, at users.erols. com/emcrcc/Rel_chart.htm. Another, adapted from *From Generation to Generation: How to Trace Your Jewish Genealogy and Family History* by Arthur Kurzweil (Jason Aronson, 1994), is at www.jewishgen.org/ infofiles/related.txt.

An example of a relationship chart and links to other charts are at www.genealogytips.com, on the Chapter 10 page.

You'll encounter some of the following terms as you work with relationship charts:

Timesaver
Many genea-
logical software
programs
calculate
relationships
on-the-fly as
you add people
to your file.

- *Half*   Shares only one parent, such as a half-brother and a half-sister who share the same mother but have different fathers

- *In-law*   People related by marriage rather than being blood kin

- *Kith and kin*   Friends and relatives; *kith* are friends and acquaintances and *kin* are blood relatives or in-laws

- *Step*   A close legal relationship formed due to the remarriage of a parent, such as step-mother, step-daughter, or step-sister

Dozens of cousins

Keeping all the cousins in a family straight can be a chore. Then, when you add all the names for cousins and other matters, it can get downright daunting. Here are some definitions of cousins that should help:

- *First cousins*   Blood kin in your family who share two of the same grandparents as you; the children of your aunts and uncles

- *Double first cousins*   A father's sibling marrying a mother's sibling results in double first cousins because the children of those unions are first cousins twice—once on their father's side and once on their mother's side

- *Second cousins*   Blood kin who have the same great-grandparents as you but not the same grandparents

- *Third, fourth, and other cousins*   Third cousins share the same great-great-grandparents, fourth cousins have the same great-great-great-grandparents, and so on

Bright Idea
If your browser can handle JavaScript, then you can use the Cousin Calculator that's available at www. prenticenet. com/roots/ tools/cusncalc/ cusncalc.htm. You can download DOS and Windows versions of this program, too.

Cousins removed

Removal occurs when cousins are separated (removed) by being generations apart. *Once removed* means one generation apart. Your father's first cousin is previous one generation to your grandparents, and you are two generations previous to the same grandparents; this one-generation difference equals once removed. That relationship is generally stated as "first cousins, once removed." But it doesn't always remain that simple. *First cousin, once removed* could also describe either the child of your first cousin (in the descendancy) or the child of your great-aunt (in the ascendancy).

Twice removed refers to a two-generation difference. You are two generations from your grandmother's first cousin; therefore, you and your grandmother's first cousin are first cousins, twice removed.

Relationship charts indicate the way these cousin relationships are numbered. Many use a *G* to indicate grandparents, so that the number of Gs you share with another cousin is equal to your relationship to that cousin; for example, 3 Gs equals third cousins.

Kissing cousins

In genealogy, the term *kissing cousins* usually refers to marriages between cousins. You'll also find instances of the term loosely applied to refer to neighborhood sweethearts or "allied families"—families linked by some means other than by blood.

Current conventions dictate that no intermarriage should take place between first and second cousins. Kissing cousins are third and fourth cousins for whom marriage is permitted; this is sometimes referred to as *strengthening the line.* Marriage is sometimes encouraged between distant cousins—fifth cousins or those further removed—and called *reconverging the line.*

In the past, marriage was only discouraged between first cousins. In the 19th century, second cousins were allowed to marry; that's where the term *kissing cousins* originated. At that time, distant cousins were considered those who were third cousins or greater.

Generations past

Your family's origins determine which records you'll need to use. If your family *did* come over on the Mayflower in 1620, most of your earlier searches will involve such records as church and civil, Mayflower Society, and later (1790 and beyond) U.S. records such as the census data described in Chapter 13. No two families' origins are the same. In addition to finding family history work already done by others, you can trace yours by searching for records pertaining to known country or origin, for example.

Tracing immigrant origins

As you research your immigrant ancestors, keep the following points in mind:

- An *immigrant* is someone who moves to one country from another.

- *Naturalization* is the legal procedure by which an alien becomes a citizen of a country to which he or she emigrates.

- Before the Revolutionary War, there was no United States; for example, at that time, immigrants to the "new world" of British North America would have been naturalized as British subjects.

- The first naturalization law in the United States was passed in March 1790.

Unofficially... According to Hartford Public Library Reference Librarian W. Robert Chapman, blanket statements such as "My family came over on the Mayflower" just aren't possible because the "Mayflower wasn't big enough" (*Noah's Ark Encounters the Mayflower,* www.main. nc.us/OBCGS/ descended.html).

- Naturalization certificates themselves do not convey much information; however, it is helpful to find the accompanying application materials because those document family names, relatives, and previous residence.

- According to the National Archives and Records Administration (NARA), "The only rule one can apply to all U.S. naturalization records—certainly all those prior to September 1906—is that there was no rule."

Unofficially...
A Summer 1998 *NARA Quarterly* article (www. nara.gov/ publications/ prologue/ natural1.html) explains that women are usually not represented in early naturalization records because although "immigrant women have always had the right to become U.S. citizens, not every court honored that right."

Immigration records and searches

There will be times when you don't know from where and how your ancestors arrived in a country. At these points your search becomes more difficult, but not impossible.

The U.S. Immigration and Naturalization Service (INS) site, at www.ins.usdoj.gov/graphics/ index.htm, offers helpful data on INS history and other topics. Refer to the Chapter 10 page at www. genealogytips.com for more information.

What's in a name?

Naming schemes originated from the Catholic practice of giving two names to a child: a spiritual name and a secular name. The spiritual name was usually the same for all children of the same sex; all boys got a male spiritual name and the girls a female one. The spiritual name was often chosen based on a favored saint. These names appeared first on the baptismal records. This practice eventually evolved to include Protestants.

The second name is the child's given (or secular) name. Most legal and other records are identified by the secular name; if you are researching a name and seem to hit a dead end, you should determine whether you're using a spiritual or secular name. If you're not searching on the secular one, there's a possibility that you might be researching someone else.

Titles attached to the end of names can cause similar confusion, such as the use in some cases of *senior* and *junior*. Nowadays, these titles indicate a father–son relationship, but in the past, they inferred no direct relationship. If two men of the same name lived in the same area, the older was referred to as *senior* and the younger as *junior*, even if they weren't actually related.

Being familiar with and remembering these naming schemes can help you avoid problems as you conduct your research.

Finding your relatives online

If you're looking for a living relative, the procedures you'll follow are a bit different from those you follow to track down deceased ancestors. To find a living relative, starting with his or her last-known address, you could check with directory assistance for a phone number. If an address is unknown, you can use a search engine, directory, or phone number and email directory to search for the person by name. Such searches may find Web sites that will take you to stories about that person in addition to potential phone number or email address info. You might even luck out and discover that your relative has a Web site online. Other times, it can be a fishing expedition. Keep in mind that unless you already have definitive proof that the person you've found is actually your relative, you should be brief and cautious in any of your correspondence. A number of sites let you do searches online. You can find a listing of the national and international sites for such

66
Finding an immigrant ancestor's place of origin is the key to finding earlier generations of the family. It provides access to many family history resources in that home area."
—*The Family History SourceGuide: How-to Guides Version of Data*, March 1998, www. familysearch. org/sq/ Guideto Research.html
99

searches at www.genealogytips.com, on the Chapter 10 page.

Finding your ancestors

The term *ancestor* usually refers to a person who lived in the generations before your grandparents. Finding your ancestors can present many challenges. There are a number of routes you can take to do so. One is to check to see if anyone from your family has entered information at a site such as RootsWeb (www.rootsweb.com), where you can do the following:

1. Type in the name you're looking for in the Search by Surname form.

2. Click the WorldConnect Project button. Don't be surprised if you find many people listed with the same name. With millions of persons in the United States, it's inevitable.

Other online sources for finding people are Ancestry.com and FamilyTreeMaker.com. However, some of the searches at these sites may cost a subscription fee, or simply lead you to an area where you will need to buy CDs that contain the information. Some people don't mind spending a few dollars for such information; just be sure that the purchase will give you the information you need. The site lists the type of data that's available on the CD; if it doesn't make a reference to what you need, you might want to email the publisher before you make a purchase.

Finding information between 1880 and 1920 will be the hardest in your searches, especially if you don't know where a person resided during that time. Census indexes are difficult to come by during that period. (For more information on census records, see Chapter 13.)

A good resource for finding data on deceased relatives in the mid-to-late 20th century is the Social Security Death Index (SSDI). You can use this to find a birth month or year, or a death month or year. You can also use the SSDI to find a Social Security number. To conduct a search of SSDI records, the person you're looking for must have been alive after 1936.

One way to access the SSDI is through RootsWeb:

1. Go to www.rootsweb.com, and type a person's name in the Search by surname form.

2. Click the Social Security Death Index button.

3. If the name is a common one, like Smith, click the Advanced Search button at the bottom of the first page of search results. Type in another search parameter, such as the two-letter state abbreviation in the Last Residence State box if you know where the person resided when he or she died.

For persons who lived prior to the 20th century, your online search efforts may be a bit easier. One place to conduct a search is at the USGenWeb Archives Project Web site:

1. At www.rootsweb.com/~usgenweb, click on the table of contents for the state you want to search.

2. After the state page loads, click the link to the appropriate county. The county page will show all files that have been placed online at the USGenWeb site that relate to this county. These can include

   ▪ Cemetery transcriptions

   ▪ Census records

Watch Out!
Don't make assumptions when it comes to relationship terms. Modern meanings used to describe relationships can differ from those in another century, or sometimes in another locale. *Cousin*, for example, once referred to almost any relative except for your sibling or your child.

- Land records

- Military records

- Wills and estate records

- Birth, death, and marriage records

- Miscellaneous records such as newspaper stories

It's a good idea to go back and visit these pages on a regular basis. New information is added daily.

Another great resource is census transcriptions. (You'll learn more about census records in Chapter 13.)

You can also search sites such as RootsWeb or Ancestry.com to see if the ancestor you're looking for appears in someone else's family history. If that doesn't work, try checking to see if he or she is listed in any books, at www.genealogylibrary.com.

For more searching help, refer to the other genealogy Web sites mentioned in Chapter 6. Experiment with your searches. Over time, you'll discover which genealogy sites you prefer and which are likely to give you the kind of information you're trying to find. Although it still isn't possible to conduct all your genealogy research online, you can find a great deal of valuable information. (As always, don't simply accept everything you find from any resource; verify all information.)

Timesaver
You can find DearMYRTLE. com's start-to-finish instructions on how she conducted an online search for someone at members. aol.com/ dearmyrtle/ 99/0120.htm.

Handling special circumstances in genealogy

Your research may require that you delve into specialized areas of information. Such circumstances can include, but are not limited to, categories such as adoption and Native American or Jewish heritage. There are Web sites or portals for almost any specialty you may encounter. The following are a sampling of the Web sites available for this type of research. More categories and Web pages are listed at www.genealogytips.com, on the Chapter 10 page.

Adoption Search
www.adoptionsearch.com
While not limited to genealogy-related research, the Adoption Search search engine can help you check birth mother resources and do birth relative searches.

African Americans and U.S. Federal Census Records
www.18004genealogy.com/tutorials/afamgen/afam1.htm
The African Americans and U.S. Federal Census Records site catalogs the evolving ways that African Americans have been included in the U.S. Census.

American Indian Heritage Foundation
www.indians.org./Resource/FedTribes99/fedtribes99.html
The American Indian Heritage Foundation page has an image map of the United States. You click on the geographic area in which the tribe you're researching was or is located, and the site directs you to a page of address and telephone number resources for that region.

Jewish Genealogy Cross-Index
feefhs.org/indexjew.html
The Jewish Genealogy Cross-Index site is one example of a specialized Jewish genealogy site. This one is maintained by the Federation of East European Family History Societies.

The Orphan Train Collection
pda.republic.net/othsa
From 1853 until 1930, orphans in the eastern states were often put on trains and shipped to families in the west. Dubbed the "Riders," these children were

sometimes bound to the families who accepted them by indenture papers rather than ever officially being adopted. On the Orphan Train Collection site, the Orphan Train Heritage Society of America provides links to information about this shameful, and sometimes denied, chapter of U.S. history.

Informal family members

Although they are not blood relatives, some people are or were so much a part of a family that they need to be included among the family history records. For example, throughout grade school and high school, I went on numerous vacations and short excursions with my best friend. A childless widower who usually traveled with us and who upon his death left an inheritance to my friend would be somebody who warrants mention among her family's history.

The definition of *family* is evolving as people place a greater value on the community of others. Blood relatives define where people come from, but the significant others in people's lives shape who they are. Don't feel you can't include them simply because they're not genetically related. These people won't be mentioned on any of your lineage charts, but you will want to include them in your family history stories and refer to them in your reference notes.

Just the facts

- Computer programs can calculate relationship charts for you.
- Understanding some terms commonly used in genealogy will help you avoid confusion in your research.

- An immigrant is someone who moves to one country from another; naturalization is the process of becoming a citizen of the new country.

- Most of the naming schemes you'll encounter in your research originated through Roman Catholic tradition and were continued by Protestant baptismal naming customs.

- There are times when people who are not related by blood are so much a part of your life that they warrant being included in your family history.

Broadening Your Research

GET THE SCOOP ON...
Conducting effective oral interviews ▪ The
research value of old newspapers ▪ How to
obtain old family photographs ▪ Making a
scrapbook, online or offline

PART V

Beyond Statistics: Portraits of Time

Chapter 11

As you work your way through this and the next few chapters, you'll learn about all kinds of documents and other items of proof you'll begin gathering about your ancestors. Your decisions regarding the most efficient ways to proceed with that work will be determined by a number of factors, such as the time you have to devote to your genealogy project and geographical considerations.

In addition to tangible items of proof, you should not overlook something that is unique to you and your family: your family stories. Ever since the time of tales of the woolly mammoth hunt, oral history has been an important part of family lore. Back then, clan members would wait for lightning to strike just so they could gather around a crackling fire and reminisce. Things were not much different then than they are now—except that now we have matches, marshmallows, and municipal burning ordinances. Then, like now, there was probably

221

Unofficially...
In addition to photographs, you should also obtain signatures of your ancestors. Signatures on original wills and other documents provide a lasting personal effect from someone's life.

somebody who would hog the conversation. You want to find that person in your family now, the one who is ready with story after story after story.

Seriously, the more willing a family member is to share his or her stories with you, the better it will be for your research and for preserving aspects of your family heritage. The adage "do it now" is very important when it comes to getting these stories. People of all ages die. Start gathering your family's stories today. In this chapter, I'll tell you how. I'll also show you how to preserve your family's pictures and paper mementos, such as newspaper clippings.

Oral interviews

Your work as a genealogist will focus on gathering facts, but the stories of your ancestors will make those facts come alive. Becoming your family's historian and conducting oral interviews will allow you to do the following:

- Better understand how historical and other events affected your family
- Fill in the gaps caused by missing or unavailable records
- Learn more about your family
- Preserve a record of your family's values and traditions for your descendants

Start by interviewing the storyteller in your family. (He or she is usually the person who also clips obituaries from the newspaper and saves them, along with other family memorabilia.) This person normally doesn't need prompting to move into a dialog about the things you need and want to know.

Others in the family may require some drawing out. Some may be shy, and others may not feel comfortable talking about the past. Keep focused on

your objective, but be prepared to use all the nego-
tiating skills you have. If your requests are viewed as
a sincere desire for the other person's assistance
and not as an intrusion into his or her privacy, most
people will be more than happy to help.

Preparing for an oral interview

You can increase your chances of conducting a
productive fact-finding interview by preparing for
each of your interviews in the following ways:

- *Do your homework*   Read over any material you
  already have about the interviewee. This preliminary work will help trigger questions that
  you should ask. In addition, the interviewee
  will find it flattering when you come to the
  interview prepared because it shows that you
  respect his or her time.

- *Confirm the appointment*   Write a brief note to
  thank the person in advance for agreeing to
  the interview. Include the date and time the
  interview is to take place so the person has
  one more opportunity to make note of that
  information.

- *Include a sample questionnaire*   If you know in
  advance that you have specific questions for
  which you need answers, let the interviewee
  know about them by preparing and sending a
  list. It's also a good idea to send along a copy
  of any relevant family group sheets and pedigree charts. That way, the interviewee can read
  over the charts and see what information
  you're missing. The sheets may also trigger
  interesting stories the interviewee had forgotten; seeing Aunt Millie's name might remind
  the interviewee about the story Aunt Millie

used to tell about Great Uncle Cedric during the Gold Rush.

- *Customize the questionnaire*   Take into consideration the educational level of your interviewee, which you may have to surmise from previous conversations and correspondence. Use a font size large enough for the person to read. Allow enough space between questions for the person to jot notes to himself or herself.

- *Don't bombard the interviewee with questions*   If you know that you have a large number of questions for which you need answers, plan on conducting more than one interview. Initially send only those questions that you can realistically cover in the first interview.

- *Consider the length of the interview*   The length of time you can reasonably spend with the interviewee will determine the number of questions you can cover. Some people tire sooner than others, and other people, including retirees, have busy schedules.

- *List any papers you'll need*   When you mail the questionnaire, send along a separate sheet listing any documents, photographs, or other papers you'd like an opportunity to look at while you're there. Be as specific as possible. Giving your interviewee the chance to gather these things before your arrival will cut down on disruptions or delays in your interview.

- *Call ahead*   You want to be certain the person you need to talk with will be there when you arrive, especially if you have to travel a great distance to conduct the interview. An elderly relative or someone with chronic health

Unofficially...
A simple "Hi, I'm just verifying that this is still a convenient time for you before I head over to your place" shows that you are understanding of the other person's needs without drawing undue attention to any specific problems.

problems may be unable to predict very far in advance when he or she will feel up to receiving a visitor. Call or send an email to confirm.

▪ *Save sensitive questions for last*   You don't want the interviewee ending the interview before it's begun because he or she doesn't like the tone of a question. Begin the interview with safe questions. Near the end of the interview, use your judgment, based on the amount of trust you've been able to build with the other person and on how forthcoming that person has been thus far, to determine whether you should introduce any questions that might pertain to sensitive subjects.

Conducting an oral interview

You should use a form for each interview that includes the following information:

▪ Interview number (which you can cross-reference on a research log)

▪ Date of interview

▪ Place of interview

▪ Your full name (or the name of the person conducting the interview)

▪ Interviewee surname

▪ Interviewee first name

▪ Interviewee middle name

▪ Interviewee address

▪ Interviewee date of birth

▪ Interviewee occupation (if occupation is relevant)

Below that information, provide spaces for each of the questions you plan to ask. These will be the

Timesaver
If you're making video or audio recordings, put a cross-reference number on the tape and on your form. You'll easily be able to match them later. If you're only using hand-written notes, record that on the form so you don't look for a cassette to go along with it.

questions that you sent to the interviewee earlier. Be sure to allow enough space to write notes after each question.

Also indicate on this form whether you recorded the interview and, if so, what equipment you used to do so. Any videotapes and audiotapes should show the interview number, the interviewee's name, and the date of the interview. In addition, write down information about any documents you looked at or copied while you were there.

The manner in which you phrase your questions can make the difference between a productive and a nonproductive interview. You can conduct an effective interview by incorporating the following tips:

- *Ask open-ended questions*   Do not limit yourself to questions that only require simple yes-or-no answers.

- *Don't shotgun the interviewee*   Ask only one question at a time.

- *Don't interrupt*   Allow time for the interviewee to fully answer one question before moving on to the next.

- *Listen to the answers*   The answers will provide you with clues to any additional questions you need to ask.

- *Allow yourself time to compose your follow-up questions*   If you aren't sure how to best phrase a question that wasn't in your script, don't be afraid to say so.

- *Record notes about the interviewee's body language and mannerisms*   Body language and mannerisms can indicate discomfort or confidence and provide depth to your transcript of the interview.

- *Use a recording device, but don't rely on it*   You'll need notes in case of a mechanical error.

- *Clarify responses*   If you're uncertain of an answer, repeat it to the interviewee in the form of a question. Ask for any needed clarifications on spellings, too.

- *Mix 'em up*   Insert some questions asking for specific information in addition to the open-ended ones.

Like any good reporter, you want to find out the who, what, where, when, why, and how information. An effective interview gives you a better understanding of the interviewee's feelings and opinions, as well as information about the interviewee's experiences.

Don't be discouraged if you don't learn everything you need to know during the first visit. Memories are often triggered by conversation or activity. Ask the interviewee to jot down anything else he or she remembers after you leave. If a follow-up interview would require a distance too far to travel in the near future, agree to a time to conduct another interview over the phone. Otherwise, try to set up a time to return for another interview before you leave. This helps ensure that you remain on task and complete the project.

Special considerations for oral interviews

When you conduct an oral interview, you are asking the interviewee to share family stories that the person may consider private. Not everybody likes being in the news. Respect for your interviewee's privacy regarding any use of the interview transcript in the near or immediate future requires that you do the following:

- *Be forthright*   Provide the interviewee with information on what you intend to do with your records, especially if you plan to publish the stories on a Web site or in a family history or give copies to a library or historical society. Give your interviewee the chance to advise you of which stories are off the record for sharing with people outside the immediate family.

- *Get permission to publish*   Get permission in writing from the interviewee if you plan to publish the results of the interview in any medium.

- *Get permission to record*   Get permission in writing from the interviewee if you want to record the interview on audiotape or video-tape and plan to make any portion of those tapes available to others. It's a good idea to wait until you arrive for the interview to handle arrangements and permissions regarding any recording that you want to do. It's easy for an interviewee to say no over the phone or in a letter beforehand. If you record the interview for the purpose of making sure you get every-thing documented, you can always obtain any additional permission you need later. Don't give the interviewee the right to approve the final transcript; this opens your material to selective editing.

- *Be observant*   Be a good listener. If something your interviewee says triggers a memory of your own about a similar instance, jot yourself a short reminder in your notes. Don't inter-rupt the interviewee to tell your own stories. You can listen to yourself anytime. If you need clarification about something being said, don't interrupt to get it. Again, jot a note to yourself and ask for the needed information later, when the interviewee is done talking.

You can find tutorials to help prepare for interviews as well as examples of completed interviews through the links listed at www.genealogytips.com, on the Chapter 11 page.

Putting your oral history records to use

As you transcribe your oral interviews, you need to decide how best to organize the facts you gather. You can do this by putting them in the following categories:

- *Autobiographical* Reminisces about how another person's life history directly affects or affected your own

- *Biographical* Compiled histories about individual members of your family

- *Chronological* A time line of events about your family

- *Folklore* A record of your family's favorite games, pastimes, poems, songs, and stories, plus information on any family legends

- *Genealogical* A record of what the interviewee told you about your ancestors

- *Historical* Facts on your family's immigration, significant contributions to local or national history, and other information of historical value

- *Health issues* Facts about diseases and causes of death in your family's past

- *Skills or occupations* Known information about family members' past jobs that may or may not

> 66
> A quilt can be a genealogical chart through which fabric remnants and stitches introduce us to our ancestors, and celebrate family history. A quilt can be a family's softbound encyclopedia filled with stories passed down from generation to generation. Such a quilt is a fabric "Griot" in the African-American tradition.
> —Raymond G. Dobard, coauthor of *Hidden in Plain View: A Secret Story of Quilts and the Underground Railroad*
> 99

Bright Idea
Family Tree
Maker's
Genealogy Help
section offers
suggestions for
oral history
topics, at www.
familytreemaker.
com/
00000030.html.

necessarily be employable skills today

- *Social history*   A record of such things as your family's gender roles, ethnic culture, and religious practices

- *Special significance*   Stories about things that are a part of the family, such as a family farm, homestead, or vacation cottage

- *Special event*   The stories surrounding an event, such as an award, a christening, or a wedding

- *Topical*   Any recorded information that focuses on a particular event not directly related to the family but in which the family took part, such as a world's fair

Resurrecting family traditions

Every family has traditions. Some are more elaborate and well celebrated than others. When I was a child, every Thanksgiving, the entire family would gather at my grandparents' house. While all the women in the family were busy cooking dinner, all the men and children in the family would retire to the backyard for the annual Thanksgiving skeet-shoot. The children would help put the clay pigeons in the launcher, and when one was plucked out of the sky, the child who put it in the launcher would get a treat. Even though it might not seem like such a big deal, it was greatly enjoyed by everyone in the family (at least those outside). It also taught us youngsters some valuable rules about gun safety and following instructions.

Regardless of where your traditions fall, you'll want to make note of them, even if it's only for reminiscing at family gatherings. Wouldn't it be fun if subsequent generations revived old family traditions? You can find links to pages about family traditions at www.genealogytips.com, on the Chapter 11 page.

Creating a family history book

After you've conducted some oral interviews and completed other research, you might decide you want to write a book about your family's history. Even if your intention is only to share it with your immediate family, you will be making an important contribution to your family's history. By documenting and publishing it or printing a few copies, you'll help to ensure that your family's stories aren't lost.

You could use a word processing program to create a document, which you could then print and distribute to relatives. A friend of mine printed a copy of the family history he created, including stories from his family, which he then took to a local copy store for printing and coil binding. To make 10 copies cost him less than $50, and his aunts and uncles were thrilled to get them as Christmas presents. He also kept a copy for himself, which now sits on his coffee table, where visitors can flip through it.

You could also choose to have such a book printed and bound professionally. You can find links for amateur, professional, and print-on-demand publishing at www.genealogytips.com, on the Chapter 11 page.

The value of newspapers and other ephemera

In the course of interviews and other research efforts, you'll come across documents such as newspaper clippings and other ephemera that will lend support and add color to your family's history. Newspapers can be of value to you because they include such information as

- Announcements

Moneysaver
Print-on-demand is fast becoming a popular choice among those who self-publish family histories. *Print-on-demand* means that the publisher prints a copy only when one is ordered.

- Birth notices

- Death notices

- Land transfer announcements

- Legal notices

- Marriage announcements

Studying newspapers published in the time and place your ancestors lived can provide an overall record of the times. It can be a time-consuming process, but you can often discover information that wouldn't have been available to you otherwise—especially in areas where court or other records have been destroyed by fire.

From your family group sheets, determine the names, dates, places, relationships, and any other information about your family for which you've yet to find the information you need. Many newspaper collections are on microfilm and available at archives and libraries.

Bright Idea
Not all family archives are paper ones. The Kirk Collection has Quilt Care and Conservation information, at www. kirkcollection. com/conserve_ acidfree.asp.

Newspapers are a record of a community's day-to-day news and events. In addition to providing information, such as marriage notices, obituaries (and sometimes the biographical data they can contain), and birth announcements, they can also give you a feel for the history of the area at the time. Many newspaper archives, usually on microfilm, require a page-by-page search. Therefore, you need to know the approximate date of the event you want to research, as well as the name of the community in which the event took place.

Many newspapers have recently started putting their archives online; some are free, and some papers charge a fee to retrieve more than a summary. Before you sign up for a fee-based service, make sure that the paper lists the information you'll need. If an archive only goes back 10 years, it probably won't have the obituaries, marriage announcements, and birth notices you need.

The Library of Congress (www.loc.gov) has a large collection of early American newspapers. And The United States Newspaper Program is a cooperative national effort among the states and the federal government to locate, catalog, and microfilm U.S. newspapers published from the 18th century to the present. Information on the program can be found at www.neh.gov/preservation/usnp.html. You can find other newspaper information at www.genealogytips.com, on the Chapter 11 page.

If an ancestor you are researching was an active member of a church or another organization, newsletters and other periodicals published by these groups can prove valuable as well; however, expect these materials to be fairly difficult to find.

You might also be in search of other information that's of little value to somebody but invaluable to you. *Ephemera* is anything short-lived or with a short-term usefulness; in addition to newspapers, this non-book printed material includes the following:

- Advertising cards
- Almanacs
- Annual reports of towns and businesses
- Bookplates
- Business brochures
- Calendars
- Community cookbooks
- Deeds and other legal documents
- Greeting cards
- Investment prospectuses

Timesaver
Whether you're looking for old newspapers or other paper documents (old annual reports, for example), try the Antiqibles.com site, at www.antiqibles.com/antique_collectible/ephemera.htm.

- Invitations
- Labels
- Letters (correspondence)
- Magazines
- Maps
- Matchbooks
- Museum exhibition catalogs
- Pamphlets
- Posters
- Promotional material
- Sheet music
- Stock certificates
- Theater and other event programs
- Tickets
- Trade catalogs
- Transportation timetables

Watch Out!
Be sure to archive documents responsibly. Some tapes and other adhesives can yellow documents. Rubber bands get brittle over time and can stain documents. Likewise, you should use acid-free paper, and be sure that the ink you use in your printer won't fade over time.

Care of newspaper clippings and other ephemera

Documents don't last forever. Paper is treated with chemicals when it's made, and these chemicals can wreak havoc later. In addition, oil on your hands may damage certain documents. Because they used paper with cloth content, earlier newspapers didn't become as brittle as those do today. But even the type of rag content can make a difference in how well the paper will endure. Keep in mind that newspapers always have been somewhat fragile because newsprint paper serves as a cheap way to spread the news; it wasn't and isn't made to endure. You can take steps now to ensure that any documents in your hands last as long as possible, by using the following:

- *100% cotton gloves*   Used to keep finger oils

and acids off documents and photographs

■ *An acid-free ink pen*   Used to mark the backs of photographs without depositing acid on the paper

■ *Self-adhesive linen cloth tape*   Used for acid-free book repair, and mounting and framing of artwork

■ *Transparent mending tissue*   Non-yellowing, acid-free, pressure-sensitive, archival-mending adhesive used to restore documents

You can find links for more information about preserving documents at www.genealogytips.com, on the Chapter 11 page.

Before you try to repair any document, check with a professional. Preservation is an art; museums have entire departments dedicated to this and specialists trained for years in conservation. Make sure that you are able to perform restorative work before you begin, or you could risk destroying the very thing you are trying to save.

Finding old newspapers

Although it might be difficult, you *can* track down copies of old newspapers. Dealers who specialize in selling old and historic newspapers often issue mail-order catalogs listing papers dating back as early as the 1600s, some of which sell for as little as $10 each. Content can vary from typical to key event issues such as Civil War battles, the Lincoln assassination, the Lindbergh flight or kidnapping, and the San Francisco earthquake of 1906. If you can only find old newspapers on microfilm, but you'd prefer to purchase photocopied or original documents, check out the dealers listed at www.genealogytips.

Watch Out!
You should never laminate old newspapers or other documents. Collectors consider it akin to painting your own preferred color changes on a Rembrandt. Plus, the plastics in laminates can get sticky and discolored if the items are stored where the documents get too hot, or they can get brittle if your storage area is too cold.

com, on the Chapter 11 page.

Online newspaper resources

The New York State Newspaper Project (www.nysl.
nysed.gov/nysnp/index.html) identifies, describes,
preserves, and makes available to researchers the significant newspapers in all communities in New York
State since the first publication in 1725. The site
includes information on how to borrow, donate, or
purchase microfilm.

Family photos

As discussed throughout this book, sometimes the
backdoor approach is the quickest way to narrow
your quest for information. In the case of verifying
the identification of those in the photos you found
in your grandmother's attic, it often helps to determine the type of photo print. The print type date
range can help you narrow your options.

For example, let's say that while looking through
a box labeled "Bobby," you find a collodion print of
a young boy. At first you think you've found an early
picture of Uncle Bobby. However, if you know that
your Uncle Bobby wasn't born until 1931 and that
collodion prints went out of vogue around 1910,
you've just narrowed your search by eliminating
your Uncle Bobby as the subject in the photograph.
Perhaps the handmade birthday card or other trin-
kets in the box can help you determine that, in this
case, Bobby was a family member's school or neighborhood friend. You use your powers of observation
and logic to draw that conclusion. You then verify
the information, applying the research tips you've
gathered throughout this book.

If you have old photographs and you're not sure
when they're from, you might be able to date them
to a particular period if you can figure out what

Bright Idea
You can educate
yourself on
the details
about older
photographs
at the site
Photohistory:
19th Century
Photography for
Genealogists, at
www.genealogy.
org/~ajmorris/
photo/photo.
htm.

process was used to make them. You can begin your search with the descriptions of photographic types at www.genealogytips.com, on the Chapter 11 page. You might also want to consult with a commercial photographer or an expert on old photographs.

Commercial photo preservation

Like newspapers and other old documents and items, photographs require special care and attention. Thankfully, plenty of resources online can help you learn how to handle these precious visual records of your family's history.

If you have photos in need of repair, you can visit the Web sites listed at www.genealogytips.com, on the Chapter 11 page, to get an idea of whether you want to hire a professional to do restoration work. Photo restoration is a more involved process than just sending film to a generic photo lab like the one available at a local supermarket. Remember that you're taking a risk when you send old, irreplaceable photos through the mail. If you don't have anyone locally who can do the restoration work for you, consider using an insured courier service to send the photos to the professional you choose to work with.

An additional option for preserving older photographs is to have the pictures photographed by a professional photographer. The strong light from a scanner can damage some delicate prints. You should check with a professional before even attempting to take a digital or other photograph in natural light or daylight conditions. Some photos are more prone to light damage than are others. A professional will know best how to tackle the job. Consider having both prints and transparencies

Watch Out!
It may be fun to
experiment with
digital imaging
and your new
fancy software;
however, if you
manipulate
photographs
(such as placing
a picture of
yourself shaking
hands with the
president), be
sure to identify
the image as one
that is not an
original.

made.

Photos and other memorabilia online

A number of Web sites maintain information on lost and found family treasures. Visit them, and you might just find a long-lost photograph of one of your ancestors. The fees vary for the photos and other documents, but if you find an item that solves one more piece of the puzzle, you might think of it as priceless. You can find a listing of such sites at www.genealogytips.com, on the Chapter 11 page.

The following are some of the image formats you'll encounter online:

- *BMP (bitmap)*   An image saved in pixilated format wherein each pixel determines the color to display; the collection of tiny dots or squares (pixels) are then arranged on the screen to form the pattern. *Bitmap* can mean the image file itself or the data file for the image.

- *GIF (Graphics Interchange Format)*   A file format used to compress digital images.

- *JPEG or JPG (Joint Photographic Experts Group)*   A group that defined a means for encoding photographs and other graphics containing a large number of colors into a format that uses fewer bytes than the pixel-by-pixel approaches used by GIF and PNG, with little visible degradation in quality. The format JFIF is now commonly referred to as JPEG. The World Wide Web Consortium (W3C) has JPEG pointers at www.w3.org/Graphics/JPEG.

- *PNG (Portable Network Graphics)*   A file format for compressing digital images. W3C recommendations regarding this format can be found at www.w3.org/Graphics/PNG.

Keep in mind that because of their smaller file size, GIF and JPG are better suited for Web pages or for sending as email attachments. Although a BMP file doesn't degrade (that is, lose image integrity) during repeated resaves during edits like those you'd perform in PhotoShop or Paint Shop Pro—such as resizing the image or cropping it—the file size is too large to be practical to use as a transportable file. I recently received a family photo saved in BMP format, and it was more than 3.5MB! That same digital photo, while still too large for use on a Web page, was only a little more than 300KB when it was saved in JPG format.

Scrapbooks: Standard and digital

My grandmother used to keep a separate photo album for each member of the family. She documented everything she could with a camera—baptisms, birthdays, school plays, graduations, weddings, awards ceremonies, anything that she wanted to remember. After she had the film developed, she'd sort the photographs and add them to the appropriate books. When we became adults, our entire lives had been documented for us.

You can do the same thing for your family, but technology now provides a variety of options. In addition to the standard photo album or scrapbook, you can also archive your photographs and burn them on CD scrapbooks. Or you can use one of the many online scrapbooks that are available.

If you're going to take the time to maintain family documents and photographs in a scrapbook, you want to do so in a manner that preserves and

Bright Idea
Consider investing in voice recognition software (instead of a transcription machine) so you can read your notes and interviews out loud, instead of typing them. You can get answers to many of your questions about voice recognition software on the Voice-Users Mailing List, at voicerecognition. com/voice-users.

protects the items you're archiving. You can read suggestions on how best to do that at the sites mentioned at www.genealogytips.com, on the Chapter 11 page.

A number of sites offer free Web space for digital scrapbooks. You can put your family's scrapbook online, but before you post any photos on one of these sites, ensure that you maintain your rights to any photos you post. Also make sure you have permission from living family members before you include any of their photos online. Photographs taken by professional photographers are often covered by copyright and can't be used online without permission of the owner.

Some scrapbook sites allow you to include video clips. Some let you send digital postcards that you create using family photos. Others are for specialized uses, such as a new baby announcement. One thing is certain: Even if you don't want to maintain a Web site elsewhere, there are plenty of free sites online that will let you create an online scrapbook, and they'll hold your hand by providing easy instructions while you do so. Look over your choices before you decide. I've put links to some public scrapbook sites at www.genealogytips.com, on the Chapter 11 page.

Just the facts

- Oral interviews are a great way to discover important facts about your family, especially when you know how to ask the right questions.

- Respect your interviewee's wishes; regardless of whether your work is to benefit the entire family, an interviewee is entitled to privacy.

- Ephemera is any non-book paper record or artifact that was considered at the time it was produced to be short-lived or with a short-term usefulness.

- Old newspapers, photographs, and other items require special care.

- You can create a digital scrapbook and give people access to it via the Web.

GET THE SCOOP ON...
Discovering your local library's resources
▪ Using interlibrary loan ▪ How to find libraries
online ▪ Expanding searches by using Telnet
▪ Locating distant resources

Chapter 12

Libraries and Historical Societies

I do a lot of research, and before the Internet came along, I went to the library often. I used to enjoy the weekly trips, taking with me a notebook filled with all the things I needed to uncover. As romantic as I used to find it, I don't really miss poring over small index cards, trying to find relevant books on obscure topics.

Now I rarely have to leave home to go to the library. My local library has its card catalog online, and I can access it to find out what books are available. If my library doesn't have what I need, I can request it from another library through the interlibrary loan service. You can take advantage of these kinds of resources, too.

Libraries provide excellent resources. If a particular library doesn't provide actual information online, it will at least supply you with a list of what's available from it; you can then try a few different options to obtain the material, such as the aforementioned interlibrary loan. These options are covered later in this chapter.

Your local library

Your local library can be a source for secondary reference materials, especially if your family has lived in the area for a number of years. Local books of interest can include the following:

- Local histories
- Local biographies
- Microfilm records
- Indexes (such as marriage records or names in early histories)
- City and county directories
- Newspapers

Some local libraries maintain better genealogical reference materials than do others, although I've yet to visit a library where the librarians aren't helpful. Usually if they don't have the material on hand, they're willing to help with the research needed to find out how to go about getting it.

Interlibrary loan

One of the most-used means to obtain needed information, interlibrary loan (ILL) programs allow libraries to share materials with one another. For example, some of the materials you need might only be maintained by your state's historical or genealogical society. Other materials might be more widely available, but not in small libraries that cannot afford them. You might be able to access these materials through ILL.

If you're curious about the inner workings of the ILL process, visit the Online Community Library Center (OCLC) Web site (www.oclc.org). Different

Unofficially...
The National Genealogical Society maintains a lending library for its members. You can get more information on its Web site, at www. ngsgenealogy.org.

libraries use different consortiums (or intermediaries) to access OCLC ILL. For example, my local library belongs to Southeastern Ohio Regional Library Center (nic1.state.lib.oh.us/seoclient.html)—a consortium of 34 public library systems.

In some cases you won't be able to check the availability of a library's holdings yourself. In all cases, you won't be able to arrange to borrow the materials; the ILL itself must be arranged by a member library. Your librarian will be able to do the research to determine whether you can request the desired material through ILL; if you can't get the materials through ILL, the librarian will be able to find out if photocopies are available (and at what cost) or if you need to visit the appropriate site yourself. Some depositories have access restrictions; that is, their holdings are available only for authorized academic research.

Another shared information resource is the Research Libraries Information Network (RLIN), whose site is at www.rlg.org/rlin.html. Most major university libraries subscribe to this international service. Most also help patrons use the service for a search, but you might have to pay a charge. Records indexed include institutional holdings, notes on contents and notable illustrations, author/owner annotations, and the availability of microfilm service copies, plans for preservation microfilming, or the existence of an electronic version of the material.

You can search RLIN indexes on conference titles, corporate names, personal names, subject phrases and words, title words in any order, and more than 40 specialized access points such as form and genre, recordings publishers and numbers, ISBN, ISSN, and record status. Searches can be

> **"**
> You can search online catalogs for the titles you need, but you'll have to have a librarian arrange the actual interlibrary loan for you."
> —Mary Jo Stillwell, public library librarian and author
> **"**

Timesaver
The Genealogical
Library Master
Catalog is a
three-volume CD
set that provides
a multilibrary
bibliography of
genealogical
books, micro-
films, and manu-
scripts. You can
get more
information at
www.onelibrary.
com.

refined using logical operators (that is, and, or, not) and by limiting search results by record information. You can also search RLIN in Japanese, Arabic, Chinese, Korean, Persian, Hebrew, Yiddish, and Cyrillic.

Accessing a card catalog via Telnet

You can use Telnet to access hundreds of library card catalogs (and, in some cases, government databases, too). If you can't search a particular library catalog through the Web, chances are excellent that you'll find it accessible through a Telnet address.

Telnet allows your computer to act like it's in the library you're contacting—whether it's your local university library or a public library halfway around the world. Telnet turns the computer into a dumb terminal; for every keystroke, the computer just transmits that information to some other computer. The Telnet software that performs the commands is running on the remote machine and not on your computer.

Windows comes with a basic Telnet program, which you can access by clicking on the Start menu, selecting Run, and typing *telnet* in the box. Sometimes an ISP will include a Telnet client in its Internet startup kit, so check your documentation or call your ISP's help desk. If you don't have a Telnet client, you can find one by following the software links at www.genealogytips.com, on the Chapter 13 page.

When you run a Telnet application, you won't be able to edit and move text around as you do in a word processor—remember that your machine has been temporarily dumbed down. You'll be limited to correcting just the line you are working on. Also, some Telnet programs don't save anything that appears on your screen; once information scrolls off, it's gone. If you want a record of what's happening onscreen, you have to open a log file. Check with your Telnet program's help files to see if it will allow you to establish a log of your visit; in such instances, what you view on the site is saved as a simple text file. In other programs, you can highlight text and paste it elsewhere. In the Telnet program included with Windows, you must select the Copy command from the Edit menu; the traditional Control + C keyboard shortcut won't work.

If you remember the days of the old computer bulletin board systems, you will feel a sense of déjà vu when using Telnet. After you spend time on state-of-the-art Web sites, Telnet navigation will seem clunky. However, for viewing library card catalogs and indexes of other library holdings, a basic text interface is all you really need. Telnet provides access to some catalogs that wouldn't otherwise be available to you online.

Some popular Telnet sites

Because older materials may not have been entered into Web-based catalogs, using Telnet to search library catalogs is usually still the best approach to hunting for resources. The following are some good places to start:

- *TradeWave Corporation's Galaxy Telnet Search Site* www.einet.net/hytelnet/HYTELNET.html

- *Hytel Directory*   www.cam.ac.uk/ Hytelnet/index.html

- *New York Public Library*   Telnet address nyplgate.nypl.org 23 (login: nypl)

- *Telnet Sites—Genealogy Resources on the Internet* www.personal.umich.edu/~cgaunt/ gen_tel.html

- *United States Public Libraries*   www.cam.ac.uk/ Hytelnet/us0/us000pub.html

Bright Idea
If you don't like the Telnet program supplied by your ISP, check the Chapter 12 page at www. genealogytips. com for shareware Telnet products that offer more and different features. But beware—you may have to learn more commands to get the features you want.

Branching out

If your local library maintains a Web site, you may be able to conduct some additional searches from there—besides searching the library's card catalog. For example, when I type my library card number in the appropriate spot, my local library's site (St. Marys Community Public Library—library.norweld.lib. oh.us/stmarys) lets me access the databases available through the Ohio Public Library Information Network (OPLIN), which includes the following resources (check with your local librarian to see if you can access resources the same as or similar to those offered through OPLIN):

- *Archives USA*   Primary source materials from nearly 4,800 U.S. manuscript repositories, including records, complete with detailed indexes, of nearly 109,000 manuscript and other special collections.

- *EBSCOhost MasterFILE Premiere*   A daily-updated archive that maintains full-text documents from nearly 1,800 general reference, business, consumer, health, general science, and multi-cultural periodicals; indexing and abstracts for more than 2,700 periodicals; full-text files as far back as January 1990; and indexing and abstracts files as far back as January 1984.

- *Electric Library*   A full-text database of more than 800 newspapers and magazines (for example, *USA Today, Consumers Digest, Journal of the National Cancer Institute*), additional reference books (for example, *Colliers Encyclopaedia* CD-ROM, *World Almanac and Book of Facts*), as well as pictures, maps, television and radio transcripts, and classic books.

- *Encyclopaedia Britannica Online*   A site that offers all text from the print edition of *Encyclopaedia Britannica,* plus thousands of additional articles, digital images, Internet links tied to the articles, statistics for more than 190 nations, *Merriam-Webster's 10th Collegiate Dictionary* (including pronunciation guides and word histories), and special multimedia databases.

- *NetWellness*   A large base of medical experts providing online consumer health information, developed at the University of Cincinnati Medical Center.

- *SIRS Discoverer*   A database of full-text articles designed to help children do research that contains thousands of full-text articles selected from more than 450 magazines and newspapers, chosen for their educational content, interest, and level of readability.

- *SIRS Knowledge Source*   The online version of SIRS's most popular general reference database, which provides thousands of full-text articles on social, scientific, historic, economic, political, and global issues, selected from more than 1,200 newspapers, magazines, journals, and government publications; some articles include graphics, such as charts, maps, diagrams, and drawings.

The old college try

Even when they're not specifically genealogy related, the libraries at colleges and universities house personal papers and other collections that can be of historical assistance to the genealogist. Although you're unlikely to find entire collections online,

Timesaver
You can often find references to books and periodicals in the specialized online catalogs of genealogical libraries (which you'll learn about later in this chapter), and then use the citation to search for the works in nearby general collections.

many sites list guides and bibliographies for such collections.

It doesn't hurt to spend a few moments checking to see whether a particular library has collections on a particular surname. A friend uncovered a trove of information left to a college by her great-grandfather. I also learned that a great-uncle had left his personal papers to the university where he'd taught in the 1950s, as had his father.

College and university manuscript and historical collections can be of value, too, if you're curious about digging up more facts about such things as how your ancestors helped drain the Black Swamp in northwestern Ohio or formed one of the early settlements following the Louisiana Purchase. The librarians won't do your research for you, but they will answer questions about what collections are available for research. Keep in mind that knowing that a library has a collection isn't always enough; some libraries restrict access to fragile or valuable records for scholarly research only, so check in advance before you physically make a trip.

Most colleges and universities provide links to their libraries on their home pages. Check the pages for such institutions in your area. You may be pleasantly surprised at some of the information you're able to uncover using this route.

University of Cincinnati Archives & Rare Books Department
www.archives.uc.edu
The Archives & Rare Books Department of the University of Cincinnati Libraries houses the Rare Book Collection of the University Libraries (noted for its North American Indians collection), the German/Americana Collection (one of the nation's largest collections of books, pamphlets, documents,

journals, newspapers and manuscripts pertaining to German-American history), and other archival collections, such as the Urban Studies Collection and the Ohio Network Collection.

These collections include early documents and contemporary archival materials. The formats range from early and medieval manuscripts, books printed before 1501 (known as *incunabula*), modern printed works, photographs, and microfilm to audiovisual and electronic media. The collection records available online are a work in progress; currently, print inventories are available, along with some guides and bibliographies for collections.

Because it is not a genealogy library, the staff members aren't available for general genealogical research, although they will search their specially prepared indexes of public records important for genealogical research. (They ask that if you plan to visit the library for genealogical research, you call or write the department in advance.)

You can search the university's card catalog online at ucolk2.olk.uc.edu/screens/opacmenu. html. The Web site can tell you the current price of the library's services, such as that for obtaining a copy of a record. You'll be asked to send a check with a self-addressed, stamped envelope, and you'll be responsible for the cost of photocopying extra pages, so be sure to find out what the current limits are.

The Yale University Research Workstation
www.library.yale.edu/pubstation/libcats.html
The Yale University Research Workstation site provides links to the Yale Library online catalogs and other card catalog information. It is also a portal (that is, a gateway or a more highly developed links page) to other library catalogs around the world.

Bright Idea
Don't overlook original material, such as diaries, loose papers, letters, photographs, and other papers, which you can often find in a library's manuscript section.

Genealogical and historical collections

A number of libraries across the United States are specifically devoted to genealogical research. There you can access such staples to genealogy investigations as census, immigration, and other records. The holdings at these libraries vary. Depending on the budget, some may be more helpful than others, but they all provide a useful service. Many of them can be accessed online; the following are just a few of the ones that are available.

Allen County Public Library, Fort Wayne, Indiana
www.acpl.lib.in.us/genealogy/genealogy.html

The Allen County Public Library in Fort Wayne, Indiana, holds the largest public library collection of genealogical materials in the world. Its Family Histories collection includes more than 38,000 volumes of compiled genealogies on American and European families—from brief typescripts to well-documented multivolume works—almost 5,000 genealogies on microfiche, and numerous family newsletters. Other holdings include the following:

- *Historical publications*   Approximately 100,000 printed U.S. genealogy and local history publications, including biographical indexes, county and town histories, and various records, accessible through the catalog or on microfilm.

- *Miscellaneous U.S. records*   Microtext manuscript collections and reprint series of regional and national scope, including maps, manuscripts, and a selection of newspapers.

- *Native American records*   The Bibliography of Sources for Native American Family History details the print and microtext holdings by state and by tribe, which include Indian census schedules, Claims Commission decisions, and other items of Native American interest.

■ *African-American records*   The Bibliography of Sources for African-American Family History details print and microtext holdings by state, which include census slave schedules, Freedmen's Bureau records, and other African-American resources.

■ *Census records*   Records including federal, state, passenger list, and other census information.

■ *Military records*   Records including service and pension records, state archives, and various printed references.

■ *Audiocassettes and videos*   A selection of lectures and interviews, including taped genealogy lectures.

■ *Complementary collection*   Collections of biographical sources, government documents, legal references, firsthand accounts from Native Americans, and early American travel and exploration accounts.

American Antiquarian Society
www.americanantiquarian.org
The American Antiquarian Society (AAS) is an independent research library on American history, literature, and culture through 1876. The library contains more than three million books, pamphlets, newspapers, periodicals, and manuscripts.

Plans are under way to put AAS's five catalogs (books, serials, manuscripts, lithographs, and American engravings) online. At this point, there is no estimate given as to when that will occur.

Bright Idea
Heritage Books, publisher of the *Genealogical Periodical Annual Index* and other genealogy books, offers an online library at www.heritagebooks.com/library. Use of the site for other than browsing the card catalog requires a $30 annual subscription fee.

The Family History Library
www.lds.org/site_main_menu/
frameset-global-fam_his.html

Established in 1894, the Family History Library in Salt Lake City, Utah, has become the largest private genealogical collection in the world. Because not everyone can visit Salt Lake City to use the Family History Library, you can access most of its holdings at a Family History Center. (You can find a listing of the Family History Centers worldwide at www.lds. org/fam_his/how_do_i_beg/4_Where_is.html.)

The library houses millions of microfilms, thousands of microfiche and books, and many other records. Copies of microfilms and other materials are available for use at the Family History Library and at Family History Centers. They include the following:

■ *Special publications:*

Research outlines　Outlines that describe records of genealogical value, where they are located, and how they can be used; each outline also describes how to find the most important records in the Family History Library Catalog

Library Services and Resources (4 pages, free)　An annual overview of the Family History Library and the local Family History Centers

Where Do I Start? (4 pages, free)　Introduces the five-step process of genealogy research

A Guide to Research (24 pages; $0.40 U.S.)　A simple explanation of the research process

Using the Family History Library Catalog (44 pages; $0.75 U.S.)　A booklet that explains the Family History Library Catalog, including a listing of the worldwide resources available to each center

- *Microfilm Collection (items sometimes involve a postage and handling fee to ship to your local Family History Center):*

  Government birth and death records

  Church registers

  Census schedules

  Military files

  Immigration lists

- *Microfiche collections:*

  Accelerated Indexing Systems (U.S. census indexes, primarily 1790–1850)

  Periodical Source Index (PERSI), 1846–1990

  Reference Collection (books for getting started in various countries)

  Computer resources

- *FamilySearch computerized system of information:*

  Ancestral File

  Scottish church records

  Family History Library Catalog

  Social Security Death Index

  International Genealogical Index

  Military Index

  Shared Information

The Family History Center welcomes volunteers. Patrons are encouraged to share their time and efforts with the rest of the family history community by doing the following:

- Contributing to the Ancestral File, a computer file of linked families

- Correcting information already in the Ancestral File

Unofficially...
The Library of Congress acts as a repository of archived U.S. government records, many of which are of value to the genealogist. You can search the Library of Congress catalog at www.loc.gov/ catalog, search the site at www.loc.gov/ harvest/ query-lc.html, and find answers to frequently asked questions at www.loc.gov/ help.

- Indexing records (ask about the local Family Record Extraction program)

FamilySearch
www.familysearch.org

The FamilySearch Internet Genealogy Service is an outgrowth of the Church of Jesus Christ of Latter-day Saints Family History Library in Salt Lake City, Utah, and Family History Centers worldwide. The Internet site offers four types of searches:

1. *Ancestor Search includes the following:*

   - The Ancestral File of 35 million names organized into families and pedigrees

   - The International Genealogical Index, containing more than 600 million names extracted from worldwide vital records

   - Web sites, reviewed by volunteers and categorized to help researchers quickly find relevant family history information

2. *Keyword Search searches the following:*

   - The SourceGuide collection of more than 150 publications from the Family History Library

   - Web sites categorized by volunteers for the site

3. *Custom Search allows you to limit your search to one of the following categories:*

   - The Ancestral File

   - The International Genealogical Index

   - SourceGuide

   - The Family History Library Catalog

   - Web sites

   - The Pedigree Resource File

4. *Browse Categories includes the following:*

   - A topic search that you can refine by typing keywords in a designated area at the bottom of the screen

Upon first opening the FamilySearch page, you see the ancestor search screen, which includes tips to help refine a search. The ancestor search is a basic search by name. You can enter information in a number of other fields, including first and last name, father's or mother's name, and spouse's name. A new feature lets you search for a specific event that took place in a specific year or in a year range. You can also select a country and/or a state to aid in your query. If you're looking for an exact spelling, you can choose the option to check for an exact match; this does not check the parents' or spouses' names for exact spelling.

The keyword search is a broad search. Unless you want to explore lots of Web page links, you'll want to refine your search to weed out unwanted pages.

Although an online custom search can show you which vital records are available at a Family History Center, you'll need to find the one nearest you to retrieve that document in person; because of limited staffing, Family History Centers do not respond to mail requests.

At the custom search page, you can also browse through a number of genealogical indexes and books on the how-to guides link, including several online guides and sources listed by country and state. You'll also find definitions for many of the terms found in the how-to guides. The catalog helper can help answer your research goal questions; for example, if you ask about someone of a specific

Watch Out!
Don't phone a library and expect the staff to call you back with answers to all your questions. Most libraries operate on a tight budget. If you are unable to visit the library yourself, a librarian will probably tell you how to order the materials you need (for a fee).

age from Ohio, the catalog helper suggests looking first in the census records, vital records, or cemeteries. It then gives several more ideas to try if these do not help, such as military records or obituaries. With this search, FamilySearch also suggests more how-to guides that will aid in the search.

An index of thousands of Web sites categorized by the volunteers at FamilySearch is another way to search genealogical history here. This is a basic search engine to search for Web pages with content containing specific words. Finally, in the custom search, you'll find mailing lists in the collaboration lists link.

The Newberry Library
www.newberry.org

The Web site for Chicago's Newberry Library is primarily an informational site about the library, with one page showing as last updated using October 1996 library statistics; the records themselves aren't online.

The Newberry Library Bibliographies for Genealogy housed at the library include the following:

- U.S. states and localities
- Ethnic and national groups
- Canada
- Military
- Passenger lists
- Biographical resources
- Noble and royal lineages

Of interest to those who want to visit the library are the following:

- More than 17,000 genealogies, which cover colonial America, particularly New England, and also rare titles about gentry and noble families of the British Isles

- A local history collection that includes county, city, town, church, and other local histories

- Census holdings for the entire country from 1790 to 1850; complete holdings for all Midwestern states through 1880; 1870 holdings complete for all Southern and Border states, 1860 and 1880 holdings complete for many of these states; 20th century federal census microfilm for Illinois for 1900, 1910, and 1920

- Genealogical source material records of birth, death, and marriage, as well as probate, deed, court, tax, and cemetery records, primarily from the area of the Mississippi Valley to the eastern seaboard, as well as from Canada and the British Isles

- Military roster and pension reference works covering the colonial wars through the Civil War, plus information for a few states for the Spanish-American War and World War I; the Newberry's collection of Civil War unit histories is purported to be one of the country's best

- State historical and genealogical journals, as well as important regional and national journals such as *The New England Genealogical and Historical Register, The American Genealogist, The National Genealogical Society Quarterly*, and others, indexed in PERSI

- Collections including those on passenger lists, Revolutionary War veterans, and particular states and ethnic groups

Timesaver
If you'd like to organize a historical society in your area, The Field Services Alliance (FSA)—www.aaslh.org/Fsaindex.htm—provides guidance, technical services, training opportunities, and other forms of assistance to local historical societies, archives, libraries, and museums in their respective states or regions.

For a description of the library's limited correspondence services, mail a request, using the contact information on the Web site.

Historical societies

Historical societies are associations that not only dedicate themselves to preserving historical treasures, but provide resources to assist others in genealogical research. The kinds of available information differ greatly from society to society.

You can find out more about historical societies at www.genealogytips.com, on the Chapter 12 page. The Local History Services Department of the Indiana Historical Society also maintains a page called Historical Societies on the Internet, at www.indianahistory.org/lhsdir.htm. There you can find links to historical societies in every state, plus for Canada and other foreign countries. There are also links to such sites as The U.S. Air Force Historical Research Agency and other helpful information.

Just the facts

- You can take advantage of interlibrary loan services to access material that's not available at your local library.

- You can access library card catalogs through Telnet or the Web.

- When in doubt, ask a librarian.

- Don't overlook published family histories, but verify any information that you find in them.

- Some library catalogs allow you to search other book collections.

Bright Idea
Check out Jeffry A. Harris and John M. Harris's pamphlet "Some Basic Issues Involved in Organizing a Historical Society," available online at www.indianahistory.org/legal3.htm.

GET THE SCOOP ON...
The importance of census data ▪ Consulting city
directories and courthouse records ▪ The low-
down on military records ▪ Obtaining records
in person ▪ The benefits of land records

Finding the Records You Need

Chapter 13

I n the early days of the United States, when land parcels were being distributed to settlers, the settlers probably didn't imagine that they were creating a source of information when they signed the land transfer agreements.

Similarly, census records were intended to be used by the government for demographic purposes; when the census began, the enumerators probably didn't realize that people would be consulting their work for years to come; if they had, many of them would probably have tried to improve their hand-writing. Fortunately, however, we have these resources at our disposal.

In this chapter you'll learn how you can consult government records such as census data and how doing so will benefit your research. You'll also learn about other unlikely sources of genealogical information, such as city directories, land titles, and courthouse records.

U.S. census background

Census records are considered to be both primary and secondary sources. They are primary because they are an enumeration of the population for the years in which each census was taken and, as such, can be a record of where a family lived in that particular year. They are secondary in the sense that the accuracy of this data depends on an informant providing correct information and the enumerator (that is, the person recording the census data) accurately recording it. Early on, census takers often had to copy the day's work onto other forms, making additional copies for other jurisdictions. This not only required that all information be copied correctly, it also meant that the handwriting had to be legible to ensure accuracy.

The U.S. federal census is conducted each decade in order to provide a demographic picture of the nation. It began in 1790 as an enumeration of inhabitants, as stated in the Constitution. Over the years, the federal census has been expanded to include information such as language, place of origin, and other questions of interest to genealogists. Individual census records are sealed for 72 years to respect individual privacy; after that time, the records are transferred to microfiche and released.

Some states have also conducted censuses, usually for taxation purposes. Whereas the federal census is conducted on years ending in zero, state censuses were conducted during the time between federal censuses. The state censuses (the years for which vary from state to state) can be an excellent resource for cross-checking data.

As is the danger with any set of records, some census records have been destroyed. Alternative sources are sometimes available, such as tax lists, which you might be able to consult to fill in some blanks.

There is little consistency to the way the census was taken. Census records were gathered by local residents. Sometimes, information was obtained from the head of the household; other times, information was obtained from children or neighbors. In other instances, information was estimated by the enumerators themselves. Seasoned genealogists usually confirm information by comparing census data with that in a later or previous census. If your or someone else's citation is based solely on a census record, you need to make a judgment about whether the information is valid.

The enumerators were able to choose their own route throughout the area, so there is little consistency in the recording of information. Some enumerators worked in a zigzag pattern, crossing the road between dwellings, and others circled the block before proceeding to the next dwelling. As a result, families in close proximity might be listed at a different time, and they may not appear close together in the census records. Therefore, when you use census records for your research, take a few moments to scan other listings. You may come across familiar names, such as maternal parents or grandparents. Even if you already have information on those people, cross-checking can bring new information to light, such as information on aunts or uncles you haven't come across before.

Entire books (such as *The American Census: A Social History* by Margo J. Anderson [Yale University Press, 1990] and *The Census Book: A Genealogist's Guide to Federal Census Facts, Schedules and Indexes* by

Moneysaver
Before you invest in a census microfilm or CD, find out whether that information is available online.

William Dollarhide [Heritage Quest, 1999]) have been written about how to use census data. Some of the important points to keep in mind include the following:

- Census records are filed according to geographic location; you must know a family's geographic location in a census year to locate past census records about them.

- Ages recorded are based on the official date of each census, usually June 1 for those done in the late 1800s.

- Some early records were lost during the War of 1812 fires.

- Heads of household only were named in the 1790 through 1840 censuses; other family members were grouped by age and sex.

- The 1850 census was the first census to include the names and ages of all people in a household, as well as sex, color, occupation, birthplace, and value of real estate and personal property.

- The 1870 census gave the month of birth for those born during the year and the month of marriage for those married within the year, and it listed whether the father or mother of each individual was foreign born.

- In 1880 the census added information on the relationship of each person to the head of the household and the birthplace of the father and mother of each person.

- In 1921 fire destroyed much of the 1890 census.

- The 1900 census added the month and year of birth of each individual; the number of years a couple was married; the number of children

Bright Idea
When researching names in a census or elsewhere, consider the possibility that the surname was spelled phonetically or misspelled entirely. Check alternate spellings, and use the Soundex system (described later in this chapter) to help you.

borne by each woman and number still alive in 1900; whether the family rented or owned its residence, the residence type (home or farm), and whether the residence was mortgaged; and the year of immigration for foreign-born residents and whether they were naturalized or had filed first papers.

■ The 1910 census added whether a marriage was the first one or, if not, what number it was; the language spoken; employment status; and whether anyone in the household served in the Union or Confederate armies or navies.

■ Census records remain confidential for 72 years; therefore, the 1930 census will be released in 2002.

Like so many other resources for genealogists, the census isn't without some problems. The following are some of the drawbacks to using the federal census as a source of information:

■ Some of the census records have been destroyed.

■ No federal census records were taken before 1790; however, in many areas military censuses were taken before that date.

■ Records are inconsistent, as questions were added from census to census; fewer questions were asked in earlier censuses, so less information is available for them.

■ Some families were missed or overlooked (this is especially true in rural areas, where houses may have been off the beaten path, but it was also common in cities, where apartments above shops could be mistaken for offices).

■ Some records were provided by children or estimated by the enumerator.

Bright Idea
Check with historical societies in the geographical areas you need to research to see which documents they archive. Some even maintain old phonebooks.

- Some records do not transfer well to micro-fiche and can be hard to decipher.

- Large cities are broken down by district, so you may have to consult more than one area if you are unable to pinpoint an address.

- Some enumerators were not diligent, leaving some questions with no recorded answers.

- Communication problems sometimes caused confusion that resulted in incorrect answers to the census questions.

Links to sources for census data appear at www.genealogytips.com, on the Chapter 13 page.

Making sense of Soundex

The 1880, 1900, and most of the 1910 censuses have *Soundex* indexes on microfilm, which are coded surname indexes based on the way a surname *sounds,* rather than how it is spelled. Soundex is a code that gives numeric value to most consonants in a surname. The code consists of the first letter of the last name, followed by three digits. Consecutive consonants in a name are coded as one letter, so one d would be used for Reddy, as an example. As you can see by the following list, all vowels and some consonants are disregarded:

SOUNDEX NUMERIC ASSIGNMENT CHART

Soundex Numeric Code	Soundex Alphabetic Code
1	B P F V
2	C S K G J Q X Z
3	D T
4	L
5	M N
6	R
Disregard	A E I O U W Y H

During Franklin Roosevelt's presidential administration, U.S. Works Progress Administration
(WPA) workers began with the 1900 census, and
transferred information about each household to a
file card, using the Soundex system. The Soundex
system enables you to look at one surname and find
the exact location of all persons in a state with that
surname. Then, you can isolate the person you want
to check, go to the census records for the appropriate county, find the page listed in the Soundex file,
and view most of the information collected by the
enumerator.

For example, if I break down my last name
according to the Soundex rules, I have to disregard
most of the letters! My last name starts with an H, so
it gets listed first. I disregard the A and the next H,
which leaves me with only an N that has a Soundex
value. The number associated with N is 5, which
gives me H5. Soundex code. Soundex codes must
have three numerals, though, so I plug in zeros after
the five, giving me H500 as my Soundex code.

Some Web pages calculate Soundex codes for
you. All you have to do is input the name, and the
site gives you the code. You can find links to
Soundex sites at www.genealogytips.com, on the
Chapter 13 page.

Searching a surname in the 1990 census

In the mood for some trivia? Then take a break and
go to this page at the U.S. Census Bureau Web site:
www.census.gov/ftp/pub/genealogy/www/
namesearch.html. This page lets you do searches on
a surname. You can't consult any of the current
records (at least not until sometime after 2060, so
you'll have to be patient and maintain your health!),

Unofficially...
Smith is the most common surname in the United States, Jones is fourth, and Miller is seventh. I'll leave the search for the second most common up to you.

but you can learn some interesting statistics about your surname. For example, when I searched on my last name, Hahn, I learned that it ranks 925th in frequency in the United States, so 924 surnames are more common than mine.

Taking advantage of census transcripts

Census transcriptions (that is, typed or scanned copies of the original enumerator's handwritten records, which can be found on various sites online and at Family History Centers) are another great resource for genealogists. To get an idea about how searching these records can help, follow along as I do a search for information on Mary Hutson. First, gather together any lead information you have on the person on whom you're conducting a search. In this case, Mary Hutson is believed to have been born around 1810, possibly lived in Henry County, Alabama, in the late 1840s and early 1850s, and had a son named John.

Because you have the possible whereabouts during a census year (1850), one option would be to follow these steps:

1. Go to the USGenWeb Census Project pages, at www.rootsweb.com/~usgwcens.

2. Choose Alabama, Henry, and 1850. The directory listing will show pages containing name indexes and the actual transcriptions. Choose the directory file containing the index for the letter H.

3. After the text file loads, scroll down to the area where Hutson should appear. Seven Hutsons appear in the 1850 Henry County, Alabama, census; note that they are all listed on page pg0439a.

4. Press the Back button on your browser, and select the link to pg0439a.txt. When the page loads, look for the surname Hutson in the transcription. Sure enough, Mary is there:

9	923	937	Hutson	Rete	40	M	Farmer	3,000	NC
10	923	937	Hutson	Mary	40	F			GA
11	923	937	Hutson	John	12	M			GA
12	923	937	Hutson	Elenusor	6	M			AL
13	923	937	Hutson	Leanoler	5	F			AL
14	923	937	Hutson	Victory A. V.	3	F			AL

As you can see, the enumerator had a pretty hard time with some of the given names in this family. This will lead you to more questions, such as Was Mary's husband named Rete, Pete, or something else? What were Mary and Rete thinking when they named the second-oldest son? Or was this actually a girl? The questions are endless sometimes. But that's part of the fun of it.

As you can also see, Mary was most likely born in Georgia around 1810. She and Rete moved from Georgia sometime after John was born, around 1838. Another interesting clue is the gap in years between John and Elenusor. This very well could indicate another child that died young, or possibly two or three children. You should look for these clues in censuses: One of them could eventually send you to a correct place for more information or persons.

The problem with finding female relatives before 1850 is that the 1790–1840 censuses only showed the head of household's name. So, with Mary, you are now stuck trying to find her parents' wills, her birth and marriage records, or information from online family histories, to get information on her from earlier years.

> 66
> During the four years that we lived in the Washington, D.C. area, we tried to take full advantage of government resources . . . When we moved back to the Midwest, . . . we looked for ways to research them from the comfort of our own home—online.
> —Matthew L. Helm, author of *Genealogy Online For Dummies*, 2nd Edition (IDG Books)
> 99

Sometimes gaps between children are found to have logical explanations when you note the dates. One reason for this is during wartime when the husband is serving in the military; another is infant mortality rates. As you conduct such searches on your own, your detective skills will evolve, and soon you'll be able to intuit how one lead can lead to another—only in your case, you'll be solving a puzzle instead of a crime.

City directories

City directories have been around in the United States almost as long as there's been a country; directories for New York were published as early as 1786. The directories were created by commercial firms and sold to businesses and the public; they were usually published more frequently than every 10 years, so they are a good source for information in the years between censuses. Also, unlike the census, city directory information was gathered with the intention of publishing that data and releasing it to the public as soon as possible. Most contain the following:

- Advertisements for local products and services
- An alphabetical listing of surnames, by heads of households
- A business directory
- Local government information, including the names of those in office
- Occupations of those listed, sometimes with business addresses
- Public transportation information for the area
- A register that lists local charitable, educational, fraternal, and religious organizations, asylums,

banks, cemeteries, government offices, hospitals, and orphanages

- A street directory

The more recent city directories (generally since the 1950s or 1960s) also list children's and tenants' names. Some even mention the year of birth for those on the lists and give the year of marriage for the head of household.

The downside of city directories

Many city directories, especially very old ones, aren't perfect. Some of their shortcomings include the following:

- They only list adults.

- They're prone to list only permanent male employees in company information.

- The focus on heads of household means that more emphasis was placed on correct information on the husband than on the wife and children, if they are mentioned at all.

Of course you should confirm any information you find in a city directory. Unlike in the census, respondents weren't required by law to provide information. You'll often see "information refused" or "data unavailable" entries in city directories. Those are usually there only after the person doing the city directory survey was unable to gather information from the neighbors or city records.

Primary source media: City Directories Online

City Directories Online (www.citydirectories. psmedia.com) is a commercial, for-a-fee site that bills itself as City Directories of the United States. It is one of many sources for online city directory information; it is an especially good site because it

Unofficially...
City directories can give you a feel for the demographics of an area. You'll get a sense of the type of workers who populated a neighborhood, industries in the area, and other historic factors that lend a feel to what life was like at the time your ancestors lived there.

Unofficially...
City directory information is being added online daily. In addition to that found on Primary Source Media: City Directories Online, you can find city directory transcripts at such sites as Ancestry.com and RootsWeb. See the Chapter 13 page at www.genealogytips.com for up-to-date links to more information.

has lots of data gathered at one location. Its content is primarily for larger cities, but it allows for focused searches on any word or phrase, and across one or several directories simultaneously.

The site covers 9 major cities for the period of 1860 to 1865: Boston, Chicago, Cleveland, Detroit, New Orleans, New York, Philadelphia, St. Louis, and San Francisco. In addition to these 9 cities, the site has expanded to cover 99 cities, and is adding more. Its microfilm collection supports research in the following genealogy and social history areas:

- Case reports on the poor
- Church registers
- Employee records
- London marriage certificates
- Medieval manorial records
- Reports on German refugees from U.K. relief agencies
- Wills of German Jews who fled Nazi Germany

In the Essays section of this site, you'll find several case study examples about how city directories have been used to help locate ancestors.

Take it to court

At some point in your quest for information, you'll probably need to do some research onsite at a courthouse. Records in courthouse archives can tell you about ways in which your relatives conducted their day-to-day business.

The records you can find at a courthouse include those for the following:

- Court proceedings
- Deed and other property matters (such as variances and zoning)

- Divorce
- Marriage
- Probate
- Taxes
- Wills

You can find a wealth of information in the written judgments for cases. Court proceedings can give you interesting glimpses into the lives of your ancestors, and the judgments given by the judge usually contain interesting facts. Many judgments are published in collections in law libraries or court libraries; the librarian there can help you conduct searches.

Most of your court-related research, however, will revolve around the documents and information listed previously. Before you can conduct a courthouse expedition, you must uncover the names of the county or counties in which the ancestors you want to research conducted their business. Remember that it never hurts to research surrounding counties, too. Boundaries can change over time, and area residents who ended up in a neighboring county's jurisdiction may not have noted such a change on any of their personal papers on which you're basing your research.

After you determine the jurisdiction, study the local history of that area. Get some basic information about the land survey system—the method used to divide the land into the identifiable parcels described in deed records, the two most common of which are the *rectangular survey system* and the *metes and bounds system*—and the court system in that area. This information will help you understand the answers you find.

Bright Idea
The DISABLED-GENIES mailing list is for those who have disabilities that can make researching difficult. You can subscribe to this list by sending the word *subscribe* as the only text in the body of a message, to disabled-genies-l-request@rootsweb.com.

Learning all you can about an area prior to traveling there to do your research can also tip you off to any special things you might want to look for while you're there in person.

Next, set a clear objective for what you want to obtain when you make the trip. Study your family group sheets to verify what information you've already gathered from all sources. Make a note of any holes in that research.

Scheduling a courthouse visit

Courthouses seem like they'd be official, well-oiled, smooth-running machines. The buildings are usually impressive in appearance. There's something about them that inspires awe and conveys a certain amount of authority. Unfortunately, in many cases, that's where the inspiration ends.

Those in charge of the records kept at a courthouse are part of the local political machine. In my area of Ohio, for example, the person in charge of the records is the clerk of courts, an elected official. When a new clerk of courts is elected, he or she sometimes brings in a new office staff as well, so even if you've been to a given courthouse before, call ahead to ask about the accessibility of the records you want to consult. If the office is in transition, the staff member with whom you speak may need to do some research to find out where to direct you to find those records. You want this person on your side. Don't antagonize the clerk's office employee or put that person under pressure, which is what can happen when you show up unannounced. If you can't get the answer you need during your initial phone call, ask something like this: "I plan to be in the area to do my research on *<date>*. Would it be convenient for you if I check back on *<name a day several days*

Unofficially...
When you're trying to access records, whether from a courthouse, a church archive, or anywhere else, be nice to the staff. Even if a clerk is rude, try to get on his or her good side. Employees are human, and the clerk could be having a bad day; a confrontation will only delay your research.

before you plan to make your trip> to verify that those records will be available for me at that time?"

Be courteous, considerate, and up front when you're ascertaining appointment information. If your schedule is flexible, volunteer that information. Use the salesperson's trick of giving the staff person a choice: "The last thing I want to do is be a disruption to your routine, so if you know you have a meeting or another event that either of these dates would disrupt, please let me know. At this time, I'm thinking I can either plan my visit for *<date and time>* or *<date and time>*. Which one works best for you?" If the staff person tells you that both of those times are bad, accept that, and revisit your schedule to see if you can suggest another time.

On the other hand, if your schedule isn't very flexible—for example, because of fixed vacation days off from your job—use a different approach: "I only have a couple of days available when I can make the trip. It'd really help me out if I could schedule my visit for either *<date and time>* or *<date and time>*. Which of those dates works best for you?"

In any event, if you're told that either time is okay, don't procrastinate. Go with the earliest appointment date and time. That way, if unforeseen circumstances cause you or the clerk to reschedule your meeting, you're able to go at another time that's convenient for you.

Other things you'll want to confirm when you phone are the office's hours, the cost of photocopies, and dates or times when you should avoid visiting. In general, you should not plan a visit at the same time as a local election or primary. You'll also want to avoid courthouse offices a few days before or after an election or a primary.

Timesaver
Many municipalities are now placing information—including the locations where records are held—about their record collections on Web sites. Before you call, see if the information is listed on the Web; you'll save yourself time and the cost of a phone call.

Before setting out on a trip, verify your appointment by phone. The person with whom you scheduled your appointment may be ill that day or have a family emergency that prevents him or her from being there to help you.

What to expect from courthouse research

A degree of serendipity will always play a role in any genealogical research you do—those pleasant (and sometimes unpleasant) surprises when you find information when and where you least expect it.

My friend's Aunt Hazel, who was trying to do some research on her family, is a good example of serendipity's role. Aunt Hazel had amassed a great deal of information but was unable to find information about a distant uncle. On a trip to the courthouse, which yielded no records, she met a clerk who worked there. As it turns out, the clerk's sister had recently purchased a collection of books at an auction, and among them was Aunt Hazel's family Bible!

Your trip to the courthouse may not be as fortuitous as Hazel's, but you can still find a great deal of information. Some of the things, in no particular order of importance, that you can check for during your courthouse expedition include the following:

- *Marriage records, which can provide you with such things as*

   Age of the couple

   Maiden name verification

   Names of the couple's parents

   Religion of the minister performing the ceremony

   Residence information for all parties

   Names of witnesses or bondsmen

Bright Idea
Check university Web sites for details on genealogical information available online. The University of Michigan maintains a Genealogy Resources On The Internet index page, at www-personal.umich.edu/~cgaunt/gen_web.html, that includes alphabetically arranged links to states and territories in the United States, Canada, and most other countries.

- *Deed records, which can show*

  Date of purchase

  Land parcel descriptions (exact location verification)

  Heirs who benefited from an estate land division

  Names of buyers, sellers, or adjoining landowners

  Name of wife

  Proof that a person was in a geographic area at a particular time

- *Wills, which have information on*

  Division of the estate

  Heirs (names, addresses, and more)

  Other property

- *Probate records, which show*

  Children's names

  Names of other family members, such as in-laws and other relatives

  Disbursement of a will

  Estate divisions for those who died intestate (that is, without a will)

- *Tax records, which can be used to verify the*

  Exact locations of land parcels

  Location of a person at a point in time

  Value of the land

  Value of personal property and information about possessions

- *Civil lawsuits*

- *Criminal records*

Watch Out!
Many of the military records kept in the St. Louis Center were destroyed by fire in 1973.

The advantage of visiting a courthouse

Some courthouse records are available at other locations besides the local courthouse, such as through a Family History Center, but in many cases the packets or loose papers are only available at the court. Offsite records usually only duplicate what is maintained in the archives of the clerk's office books, which are handwritten summaries of the papers that were filed in the clerk's office. The signatures in those books are not the signatures appearing on the original documents themselves; they are the handwritten copies of the information transcribed or transferred to the books by the clerk. After the originals were copied into the books, they were returned to the appropriate person or filed at the courthouse. Documents for civil or criminal court cases, probate court cases, or chancery (if the state had chancery courts) cases were usually filed in paper jackets called *packets*. Therefore, to see the full documentation, you must ask to view the case file packets or loose papers.

Also, although most of the record books have some sort of index, you should use it as a guide, but you should not rely on it. Records you need may not necessarily be indexed under a name where you expect them to be. As you make your way, you'll probably encounter variations in the way names were spelled.

As you locate the records you need, be certain to also make a note of anyone else mentioned in them. Witnesses to legal documents also often served as estate administrators, guardians, and partners in real estate transactions. Treat every name you encounter as a lead or a clue to other information. Knowing those names may help you track down the verification you're after in census or ship passenger list records, for example.

Family members and friends often immigrated from the same village and then settled in the same area in the new country. Because of the spelling variations or downright misspelled surnames that are common in so many records, a name may elude you. Finding a hit on one of those other names associated in one instance with your ancestor may help you know where to begin to find the additional information you want.

Citing courthouse information

When you cite the information you gather at the courthouse, be sure to record the following:

- The accurate, exact title of the record
- The form used (original or microfilm)
- The location of the record
- The significant dates

Land records

If your ancestor bought land directly from the federal government in one of the 30 public land states (basically from Ohio west), you can request a search of the National Archives records. If you're having trouble finding land records, consider consulting tax records, which usually point you in the right direction by giving you an idea of when the land transferred hands.

You can search The Official Federal Land Patent Records Site at www.glorecords.blm.gov. It provides image access to more than two million federal land title records issued between 1820 and 1908 for the eastern public land states. The site is also in the process of adding images of serial patents (that is,

Timesaver
You can find vital records information for all states and territories of the United States, as well as guidelines about how to go about obtaining them, at vitalrec. com/index.html. You can find that site's foreign vital records information links at vitalrec. com/links2.html.

land permits) issued between 1908 and the mid-1960s. You can find links to sources to help find land permits at www.genealogytips.com, on the Chapter 13 Web page.

Military records

Most genealogists first research census and county records. Then, following the pattern of working from known information to unknown, from present to past, they begin to identify ancestors who would have been of an age to serve in one of the wars.

War records list age, birthplace, and physical description; however, military records primarily consist of the serviceman's rank, military unit, dates of service, payroll and muster rolls, and discharge, desertion, or death, and they are therefore mainly used to prove military service. Genealogists most often use the compiled service record and the pension application record to find information about people serving in the military because they're more complete. Some more recent war records list age, birthplace, and physical description; but again, military records are mainly used only to prove military service.

Military pension records often contain a lot of useful genealogical data. For example, a Revolutionary War pension file can include pages of narrative describing the service in the war, from the time the person enlisted until his discharge. Such narratives sometimes even contain information about the wife and children. Other details can include the soldier's birthday, physical description, place of residence, medical ailments, and how much money he made per year.

The National Archives has military service records, beginning with the Revolutionary War, listed in a microfilm catalog. Major libraries with genealogical collections maintain copies of those microfilm publications.

Until World War I, there were different kinds of soldiers—regular soldiers and volunteers. Today we would consider regular soldiers as career service people. Volunteers were civilians called into military service to meet an emergency, much like today's Reservists; even when the "volunteers" were drafted, they were still considered volunteers. Career soldier records are filed separately from volunteer records.

At least some members of your family probably served in the military. To obtain copies of their records, you usually need to know their names, ages, places of residence, and spouses' names.

You can find links at www.genealogytips.com to places online that can provide you with the specific information you'll need (and the costs) to order military records.

Obtaining records online

Even when you can't find the records themselves online, you can save yourself considerable time by consulting online guides that instruct you on how to go about obtaining specific records. For example, the U.S. Department of Health and Human Services publishes a booklet called "Where to Write for Vital Records: Births, Deaths, Marriages and Divorces" that lists the name and address of each state's vital records agency, the current cost of ordering a record from that state, and the dates for which these records are available. (The entire catalog is online at www.pueblo.gsa.gov.) You can place an order and have the booklet mailed to you, or you can immediately link to this document by state or download the entire document in .pdf format, at

Watch Out!
The National Archives and Records Administration recently changed how you go about ordering copies of military records, so verify the procedure before you order. You can find more information at www.genealogytips.com.

www.pueblo.gsa.gov/cic_text/misc/vital-records/
w2welcom.htm.

The National Center for Health Statistics (NCHS)
provides guidelines for ordering state documents, at
www.cdc.gov/nchs/howto/w2w/guidelin.htm.

Another option is to call the Social Security
Administration's toll-free telephone number and
ask a representative about the fees and addresses for
obtaining vital records. (Check your telephone
directory under U.S. Government, Social Security
Administration, for the number.) Help is also available through the Federal Information Center, at
800-688-9889 (toll free) or 800-326-2996 (toll free
TTY).

When you have to leave the house

As we've discussed throughout this book, not all
your research will take place from the comfort of
your computer chair. There will be times when you
have to leave the house, sometimes for trips farther
away than the post office.

Finding maps online

Whether your research takes you to a local city, to an
obscure rural location, or across the country, you
can find a map, complete with driving directions
directly to your site, at any of these locations:

- www.maps.com

- www.altavista.com

- www.yahoo.com

AAA members can obtain information online by
entering their zip codes at www.aaa.com. Another
option is to visit such sites as About.com and Suite101,
both of which maintain sections with regional and
city information, such as the one on the South-
western United States at gosouthwest.about.com.

Online travel assistance

For times when your research requires more than a day trip, you can save money on travel and accommodations arrangements at a number of commercial Web sites, including the following:

- www.priceline.com
- www.cheaptickets.com
- www.lowestfare.com

Just the facts

- Census data is made public 72 years after the census is taken.
- City directories can provide helpful name and demographic information, as can courthouse documents.
- Land records can help you pinpoint your ancestors in a particular geographic area.
- Copies of most early military records can be obtained through the National Archives.
- When your search for records of your ancestors takes you away from home, you can use your computer to make travel planning easier.

Other Online Considerations

PART VI

Chapter 14

GET THE SCOOP ON...
Putting together a good Web site ▪ What to
avoid putting on a Web page ▪ Free hosts for
your Web site ▪ How to attract visitors

Creating Personal Web Pages

Y ou might decide to place your family tree research on a Web site. Doing so will not only allow you to be generous about sharing your data, but it will also allow you to amaze your friends and family with all the work you have done.

From my experience, most personal Web sites are established out of necessity. Quite often, the contacts you make will keep requesting information, until you realize it's easier just to put everything up on a site and let people take what they want. It's much easier to give people a URL telling them where they can access the information than to spend half your day sending email attachments in response to requests. After you've had a site for a while, you might even decide to register a domain name.

Planning is a very important part of Web site design. In this chapter, I will show you how to do it all, from planning to putting it online. I'll also show you what to avoid, so that when family members and

Bright Idea
The Save a Page option described in Chapter 4 lets you preserve a Web page so that you can study its design and HTML code in an HTML editor. (But remember that you can't use this feature to copy a page for your site unless you have permission from the page owner.)

friends visit, they'll be able to appreciate your work fully.

Planning your site

To get off to a good start with your site, you as the author (Webmaster) should decide the following:

- What information you want to include
- How much time you'll have to devote to maintaining the site
- How many pages will be included in the site
- What pages you've seen that you'd like to borrow from because they represent your vision of the type of site you want to create
- How to incorporate any other ideas you already have about your site's design and appearance
- Where the site will be located

Determining content

In determining what you will place on your site, you need to temporarily revert to the dark ages of record keeping. Get a clean sheet of paper and a pen or pencil. With these, you will begin mapping your site to best suit your needs; you'll also end up with a handy reference to what your site's folder layout will look like when finished.

At the top of the paper, write the site's name and Web address. (This will get you acquainted with this information early on in the life of your site. If you don't have a site yet, you can just use a generic placeholder for now.) Next, write the purpose of your site in one or two sentences, such as "This site is designed to give people the opportunity to view my family's genealogical history. Also, it will give family members I don't know the chance to contact me for more information and to be included in this site."

You now have a defined purpose for your site. If you adhere to it, you will save a lot of time in the process of determining what to include on your pages. Say you just had a roll of film developed with pictures of your family dog and would love to have scans of him on your site. Sure, Spot may be cute, fluffy, and photogenic, but he probably wouldn't be best suited for your genealogy site. It doesn't matter that he is a member of your family; someone in your extended family may be put off by this canine intrusion into the bloodline. Save Spot for another site devoted to your immediate family's activities outside its ancestors. Or, at the very least, devote a personal section of your Web site to non-genealogy-related information.

All sites should have these two pages: an index—often referred to as a *home page*—and a links page. The index page should have a link to all pages contained in the Web site. If the site is very large, you can use the index page to link to the subsections of the site, and then create an index page for each subsection with links to all pages contained in that subsection and to the main index page.

The links page is where you can share Web addresses to other sites or pages that don't necessarily deal with the topic of your Web site. Put a link to those adorable pictures of Spot on the links page. That's the purpose of a links page; you may recall that these interconnected links are what make the World Wide Web a web.

Now, all you need to do is complete the map of your site by choosing subsections, pages, and links to guide you in efficiently building your site. This

Bright Idea
The *site map* is the comprehensive index of the pages on your Web site. You should make it prominent enough so visitors can find it (that eases their navigation through the pages on your site) and unobtrusive enough to complement your page design.

may seem like an intimidating task at this point because you may not yet know exactly what you'll end up putting on your site. That's okay. You can revise your Web site even after you get it online; however, your job will be easier in the long run if you have to make only a few changes later. Having a grasp on what you believe will be important for your site navigation will also make it easier for you to determine how you want to design your site. But at this point you're still in the brainstorming stage. Nothing is chiseled in stone. You can adapt and change your site map as your plans, and later as your Web pages, evolve.

Getting ideas

If you're stuck on what you'd like to include, taking a peek at sites similar to the one you want to build can give you some ideas. This can be valuable because it helps you discover ways you can get the job done and what problems to avoid.

This section includes some examples of genealogy sites. It's a good idea to study a variety of such pages to remember that not everyone has the same vision for a Web site. You probably have a pretty good idea of the way you'd like your site to look and feel; you've probably gotten some ideas from the Web sites you've already visited. If you see something you want to add to your site while you're viewing these pages, remember to go back to the design map you're initially keeping on paper and take some notes. The following are but a few such sites, chosen at random as some good examples of what's out there:

■ *Family Histories of Giddeon*Powell*Lacy*Watson (www.giddeon.com/gen)* This site has a clean design appearance, with an unobtrusive background. It also includes a members-only area: a password-protected portion of the site where the site owner posts information for members of his family.

- *Hennekes Genealogy Page (www.hennekes.com/ cadwolf)* This site was built using FrontPage and offers a search tool.

- *Oaks and Acorns (www.isp.on.ca/genealogy)* This is a well-designed site with a nice set of links.

- *Rory's Stories—Genealogy and Family History (free.prohosting.com/~roryc/main.html)* This is a nicely built site with helpful tips, charts, and information, even though it uses frames.

- *Self Family Newsletter (www.self-family.com)* This is an example of a site on its own domain, designed with a nice layout.

Watch Out!
Don't place con-fidential family information on your Web site where others can see it. If you must have this info online for other relatives to access, research the possibility of incorporating a password protec-tion scheme onto your site.

Things to avoid on your site

You can find many ways to spice up a Web site, but just because you can doesn't mean you should. You may not agree with all these points. My personal pet peeve is when a site plays music without providing me the option of turning off the sound on the page. Others despise animated link buttons. Some prefer text-only pages. In other words, you'll need to weigh your personal tastes against the features that will make your site the most pleasing and accessible to the most people. The following are some of the things you should watch out for:

- *Document weight* No page, including its images, should exceed 50KB–60KB. This will ensure that your page loads in a timely fash-ion. If a page takes too long to load, the visitor will not likely come back for a while; he or she may not even stick around to wait for the page

Unofficially...
A GEDCOM file submitted to WorldConnect's GEDCOM database (wc. rootsweb.com) can serve as a complete backup because it preserves your entire genealogy file, according to *RootsWeb Review*, Vol. 3, No. 10. Also, the WorldConnect database is set up to exclude living persons from what it displays, so it does some of your work for you.

to appear the first time. If there is no way around it, be kind and place an indicator of the page's size next to the link (for example: <u>Link Name (124KB)</u>). Or place a "please be patient" notice at the top of your page, indicating that it may take some extra time to open.

- *Use of living people's information* When you place genealogy data online, be sure to delete the information related to living persons unless you have their permission to display it.

- *Animated graphics* Stay away from large animated graphics. These tend to distract visitors from the information contained on your pages. Small buttons are okay.

- *The use of <blink>* Never use the <blink> HTML tag in your pages. It's distracting and makes your page difficult to read, especially for those who have eye problems.

- *"Under construction" pages* Do not use pages that state they are under construction unless they're an announcement of features you expect to have on your site by a specific date. Then it's okay to announce them. Otherwise, wait to place a page on your Web site until it is completed. (Most pages continue to evolve; considering a page completed today doesn't mean that you can't change or update it tomorrow.)

- *Sites with frames* You can tell a site has frames when only a portion of the screen refreshes when you click on a site link. Frames are especially frustrating when links are not directed offsite; this is known as having a page from another Web site "trapped in a frame." There have been some ongoing copyright arguments regarding the trapped-in-a-frame issue, because it gives the appearance that the frames site is providing the content on the linked page.

- *Scrolling status bar messages*   Scrolling status bar messages are distracting, and they prevent the link information from displaying on the status bar.

- *Large background images*   A distinctive picture in the background can add beauty and character to your Web site, but if you're not careful about the image size you use, it can also increase the time it takes your page to load. (I check these things out. I was once at a site that had a background image of 80KB behind about 12KB of data. Your first priority should always be how best to display your information.)

- *Inappropriate text colors*   Make your page as easy as possible for others to read. Your favorite colors may be emerald and lime green; however, using one as your background color and the other as your text color is going to make your page almost impossible to read. There have been times when I've been forced to copy what I wanted to read and paste it into a word processing program as ordinary text in order to see it. It's usually best to save fancy colors for use in buttons and other (small) graphics on your page.

- *Music*   If you insist on having musical accompaniment for your page, only do so if you provide the means for a visitor to turn the music off if that's what he or she desires. (For the reasons mentioned earlier in this chapter, I never take the time to read a Web site that doesn't offer me that option.)

This old home page: Building a site

After you've determined the content of your page, you need to put it into HTML coding. If you use one of the large free Web space providers discussed later in the chapter, you'll actually be able to use the site's built-in home page design program to put your page together right on the site. These programs tend to be fairly easy to use and have lots of options to make your page unique.

Unofficially...
HTML stands for hypertext markup language—the language or code used to create pages so they can be displayed on the World Wide Web. HTML allows for *hyper-links* (that is, links to other pages on the Web) and *markup* for text attri-butes, graphics insertion, and other formatting features.

Even though there are programs that create HTML code for you, you should have a basic under-standing of how HTML works. It's very hard to debug a Web page if you don't understand what the raw HTML is doing; if you're looking at it through a WYSIWYG (that is, what you see is what you get) editor, you're getting a view of how that program interprets the tags (the individual pieces of HTML code that appear between angle brackets when you view the code in a text editor)—not the tags them-selves (such as <p> for a new paragraph or <br> for a line break). In order to troubleshoot properly, you need to learn a few things about HTML.

If you know HTML or how to use an HTML editor already, you might want to just skip ahead to look over the hints and help in finding problems with your site. If you don't know HTML, you can fol-low the links provided in this chapter to find help in getting started. The scope of this book does not allow for a course on HTML; for that you'd need to read a book like *HTML 4 For Dummies* by Natanya Pitts and Ed Tittel (IDG Books) or *Creating Web Pages For Dummies* by Bud E. Smith (IDG Books); however, if you follow the advice in this chapter, you'll be well on your way to mastering your site quickly.

HTML tools and tutorials

A multitude of sites are available to help you learn how to build a Web site. Some sites that offer instructions for the beginner, advice for advanced HTML programmers, and tips for everyone's Web sites follow:

- *Guides to HTML*   www.hypernews.org/ HyperNews/get/www/html/guides.html

- *HTML: An Interactive Tutorial for Beginners* www.davesite.com/webstation/html

- *HTML Goodies*   www.htmlgoodies.com

- *MyComputer.com Webmaster Tools: Guestbooks, Hit Counters, Polls, Search Engines, and More* www.mycomputer.com

The World Wide Web Consortium (W3C) is the authority on HTML. That organization approves the code that becomes the official part of the language. Important pages to visit at the W3C site include the following:

- *Hypertext Terms*   www.w3.org/Terms.html

- *Index of HTML Elements*   www.w3.org/TR/ REC-html40/index/elements.html

- *W3C HyperText Markup Language Home Page* www.w3.org/MarkUp

Both Netscape and Microsoft provide basic HTML editors with their Web browsers. Netscape includes Composer, and Internet Explorer includes FrontPage Express. Both meet basic needs; for more advanced uses, a commercial program may be more appropriate. The following are two of the most popular commercial programs you can use to generate HTML code:

Timesaver
When you're looking for ideas from other Web pages, try some genealogy-specific search sites. That will give you an idea of the way other people present genealogy information without having to wade through a bunch of sites that don't show genealogy information.

- *Microsoft FrontPage 2000   (www.microsoft.com/ insider/frontpage2000)*   FrontPage is a WYSI-WYG program and HTML editor that allows you to build a Web page with the same ease as using your favorite word processor. FrontPage comes with some versions of Microsoft Office 2000, or can be purchased separately.

- *Adobe PageMill (www.adobe.com/products/pagemill)* Another WYSIWYG HTML editor, PageMill is on level with FrontPage in quality. Just like FrontPage, PageMill is easily integrated with your current office applications.

You can find links to software sites at www. genealogytips.com, on the Chapter 14 page.

Troubleshooting your site

After you go live with your site on the World Wide Web, have someone else load and check the pages for you on his or her computer. Another person will not only notice things you've overlooked, but he or she will experience problems you weren't even aware existed, such as those caused when your HTML code directs the browser to go to your hard drive to retrieve an image or a font. The picture may load for you, but it won't for anyone viewing your page online. Links to some of the most popular troubleshooting utilities are available on the Chapter 14 page at www.genealogytips.com.

Although such problems can be frustrating, many errors that occur in Web sites are simple ones. Some common HTML coding problems include the following:

- *Broken images*   An incorrect file path in the image tag is usually the cause of images that

Bright Idea
Validation is the term used to describe the process of checking an HTML-coded page to verify that it is in compliance with established HTML standards and ensure that the page will display properly in a browser. The W3C free validation service site is at validator. w3.org.

won't load with the page; this is known as having *broken images*. This problem occurs most often if you use an older WYSIWYG HTML editor. The most recent updates to the ones mentioned earlier in this chapter have pretty much corrected that problem. Check to make sure your image tags do not include a file path to your hard drive.

- *Broken hyperlinks*   A broken hyperlink is one that doesn't properly direct a visitor to the link intended. Make sure you have used the proper URL. There are times (such as with some active server pages [*.asp]) when it's safest to direct your link to the home page for a site and indicate that your visitor must follow certain instructions on that site to arrive at the information you intend him or her to see. Oftentimes a broken link is the result of a Web page that's no longer online.

- *Images appearing too small or large*   Check the width and height attributes in the image tag.

- *HTML code appearing in the browser*   This is most likely the result of a tag not being closed with a right angle bracket (>).

- *Fonts appearing in the wrong color, size, or style* This is the result of a <font> tag being omitted or placed incorrectly.

Going with Plan B

If you prefer to be a little more creative, and you have a basic understanding of HTML, you might want to design your pages on your computer before uploading them to your Web site. For that you will need some basic tools:

Timesaver
Once you've built your site, test it. A variety of Web sites can test your links for you and tell you about links that don't work. You'll find links to these pages at www. genealogytips. com, on the Chapter 14 page.

- An HTML editor (unless you're the type who likes to use a text editor to write your code yourself)
- An FTP program
- An image-editing program

HTML editors

For the purpose of this demonstration I will assume that you want to be able to see your page's layout as it's being created. For this you need a WYSIWYG editor. I mentioned two commercial editors earlier in this chapter. Other common examples that may already exist on your computer as part of your browser options are Netscape's Composer and Microsoft's FrontPage Express. Both are quite easy to learn as they do much of the work for you and allow novice users the ability to make professional-looking pages in little time.

FTP programs

FTP stands for File Transfer Protocol, and is the most common method of transferring files from computers onto a Web server. Netscape Communicator and Internet Explorer have built-in FTP programs for uploading files from Composer and FrontPage Express; most Web page designers, however, find that using a separate FTP program is simpler.

If you use a free Web space provider, when you open your FTP program, you will have to follow the instructions given in the email from that provider about what address to connect to (for example, ftp.XOOM.com). You input your username and password to log in. When you are connected via FTP to your Web site, you will see two windows in the FTP

> 66
> I use Microsoft FrontPage 2000 to create my Web pages; I find that the import and publish features in that program are sometimes easier than using an FTP program to upload or download information to and from my site.
> —R.J. Corradino, college student and poet
> 99

program. One shows the contents on your computer and the other the contents of your Web site. If your free Web space provider has a Java interface, you may be able to access the file space right from the Web, without using FTP.

Transferring files is as simple as finding the correct file path on your computer, highlighting the file you want to move, and clicking a button.

You can also use the FTP program to rename or delete files from your Web site. You'll learn more about FTP programs in Chapter 15.

Image editors

Images, be they backgrounds or photos of your family, can really bring life to your site. But you need to be careful to control the size of the objects. You can control how large the image is displayed by adjusting the HTML code in your page, but the size of the image file itself has a great effect on how fast your page loads. Image editors allow you to change the size, color, and format of the image. You can also crop unwanted areas from a photo, merge several pictures into one, or even create animated images.

What you can do is limited only by your willingness to learn your way around the program, as programs vary widely in their capabilities. This, incidentally, is one of the most amusing parts of creating a Web site. (I often use some of my relaxation time to alter or create images; I refer to this as my "coloring time.") When the boss has been giving you a hard time all week at work, you can come home, open up your image editor, and with little work, his head can be placed on the body of a mule. (It's best not to put that on your Web site, though.)

Bright Idea
When you're updating your site, include New! icons beside the link to the page that's being updated. This calls attention to the updates, so that frequent users can quickly see what's been changed.

Extras for your site

Now that you have your site coming together nicely, it's time to explore some possibilities for a few finishing touches.

Counters

A counter is an enhancement that tracks the number of visitors to your site. Every time someone lands on your page, the counter adds another digit to your tally. This is a good way to indicate how popular your site is, and with certain counters, you can tell where your visitors came from and how long they stayed.

After you've mastered the basics of HTML, placing a counter on your site is a very simple process. First of all, find a site that gives away free counters, such as the following:

- *Free Counter and Statistics Tracker*
  www.sitemeter.com

- *HTML Goodies*   www.htmlgoodies.com

- *MyComputer.com Webmaster Tools*
  www.mycomputer.com

Most of these sites require a simple sign-up process, after which you can access the HTML code necessary to have a working counter on your page. Some sites offer free downloads that include any graphics that accompany the counter. Other sites, such as XOOM.com, have all-in-one counters and guestbooks bundled together that are available to both their own and non-XOOM customers.

Guestbooks

A guestbook on a Web site is exactly the same as those in the real world—a way for visitors to leave their comments, suggestions, and compliments, or just say hello. To obtain a free guestbook, go to one of the same sites mentioned earlier for finding free counters, or check out Miatrade Free Guestbooks (www.miatrade.com). Placing a guestbook on your site is as easy as adding a counter: You simply include the code in your page.

Mailing lists

If you would like to establish a lasting relationship with your Web site guests, why not give them the option of talking back to you? A mailing list allows a group of people to send messages to the rest of the group without having to email each one individually. eGroups (www.egroups.com) and ListBot (www.listbot.com) both offer free and easy-to-manage mailing lists that you can add to your Web site.

There are two types of mailing lists to choose from: a regular list where all members can post messages and an announcement list to which only selected persons can post messages. The latter version is good for people who want to use it only as a means for informing subscribers when there is new information posted on the Web site—an excellent way of boosting return traffic. A person can join either type of list by typing an email address into a box on your Web page and clicking a button.

Getting your Web site up and running

Your choices regarding where to put your Web site include the following:

- *Getting a personal domain*   Although it costs a bit of money, you can get a personal domain of your own, such as mine, at www.ricehahn.com. You can find more information about creating an Internet domain on the Chapter 14 page at www.genealogytips.com.

- *Using personal or free Web space*   Unless you plan on creating a site with hundreds of pages, or

Unofficially...
When you build a Web site, make sure you put an email link or other contact information on the page. This way, people can send you comments, suggestions, or offers to donate material.

you simply prefer a domain of your own, using personal or free Web space may be your best choice. Most likely, you have free personal space provided by your Internet provider just sitting there doing nothing. (In Chapter 2, I recommended that you consider this option when searching for an ISP.) Your Web site address will look something like this: www.*yourisp*.com/~*yourusername*. An alternative is to choose one of several free space providers. (You will learn some of the steps and pitfalls of this option later in this chapter.)

Timesaver
I've made it easy for you to search for a domain name or find a hosting site by providing a special link for that on www. genealogytips. com.

Having a personal domain name gives you an easy address to give to people. Most people start out with free pages and graduate to a personal domain; unless you're sure you want to incur the expense of having a site, you'll probably want to stay with the free pages for a while. If you want to register your own domain name, see the Chapter 14 page at www.genealogytips.com, where you'll find links and instructions for registering your own domain.

After you've chosen a domain name, you need to find a Web host on which to park your domain. The cost can range from about $10 to $50 or more per month. Part of the fee is determined by your needs for your personal site; for example, do you prefer to have somebody else design your pages and do the site maintenance, or will you be doing that work yourself? In addition to the ongoing monthly fees, there's also a charge of $35 per year for the domain name, with the first two years payable within 4 to 6 weeks of your domain's activation, which means that it's going to cost $70 off the bat.

You can find information and step-by-step instructions about what to do to get a domain, plus links to several companies that provide domain hosting on the Chapter 14 page at www.genealogytips.com.

If you're using free space, you might end up with a very long URL. A practical way around it is to use a redirect URL. Some companies give you a free redirect URL that will automatically send visitors to your site via a much shorter and easier-to-remember URL. An example of a redirect would be like the www.surf.to/*yourname* or www.welcome.to/*yourname*, choices available from V3; the V3 redirects are free, in exchange for a popup ad that appears during the redirection. If you'd like to use one, see the links to redirect service providers at www.genealogytips.com, on the Chapter 14 page.

An upside to using one of the redirect services is that you can change where the URL redirects. This allows you to change your host without having to change the URL people already know. You simply change the information at the free redirect provider's site that tells which site the URL should redirect to.

Free sites

Free Web site hosts are an excellent way to get your position established on the World Wide Web. Most of the free hosts offer an onsite page builder to help even someone with no HTML experience set up his or her first page in minutes. In the following sections you will find information on four providers that all offer these services, in slightly different variations. The one you ultimately choose will depend on your needs, level of experience, and what you think will appear attractive to your Web site visitors.

The word *free* on the Internet does come with a catch. It would be nice to think that hosts all give

Watch Out!
Don't move your Web site to a new location without leaving information behind on how to find you. Otherwise, a visitor who bookmarked the old site won't be able to get to your new location. You can find the HTML code for a Web page redirect or refresh on the Chapter 14 page at www.genealogytips.com.

away space on their servers just because they're so darned nice, but in reality you are worth a great deal of money to them, whether you spend a penny or not. Visitors to your site will click on advertisements, join up for services, and leave detailed information about their online habits by completing surveys or selecting options that use *cookies*, or small text files placed on a user's hard disk that are read by servers all over the Internet to determine where people are going when they're online. You will be offered a chance to buy many products and services, but none of these providers will insist that you purchase anything in exchange for their services—only that you read their offers.

GeoCities
GeoCities.yahoo.com

Oldest of the free Web space providers, GeoCities is also one of the most crowded. Millions of sites are sorted into 41 "neighborhoods" that attempt to present the content in fairly manageable categories.

Navigation on the site itself is easy. The home page has links at the top that take you to information on how to get a free home page, build a page, edit pages, and upload files. The home page is also a mini site map that lists some of the neighborhoods, such as Heartland, which is the home of most genealogy pages.

GeoCities also supports FrontPage server extensions and has wizards available that can help you customize your site based on your input to questions.

Though unique in providing free hosting at its inception, GeoCities has suffered image problems due to its complicated URL structure, popup advertisements on every page, cookies, and JavaScript. All

Unofficially... Microsoft FrontPage requires components, called FrontPage server extensions, that perform certain functions, like the hit counter, site search form, and other special Web page features. If you plan to use these, make sure your host supports them, or the components won't work.

these make site navigation difficult and at times rather annoying. Things have improved somewhat since the site's takeover by directory giant Yahoo!; however, because of its enormous size, reorganization of GeoCities is a daunting task. On the upside, because of its affiliation with Yahoo!, GeoCities now lets its users integrate more online services into one package. You can access Yahoo! Pager, Yahoo!, GeoCities Mail, and Personalized Yahoo! all with a single login, rather than separately. Affiliate programs also allow GeoCities members to sell approved goods on their sites and earn commissions from all sales. Members also each have 15MB of storage space, which is plenty for most users.

One other challenge that continues to face anyone who tries to access a site on GeoCities is the amount of bandwidth necessary to maintain those millions of sites; inadequate bandwidth means that pages load slowly.

XOOM.com
xoom.com/home

XOOM is another of the original free hosting companies recently gobbled up by a corporate giant. In this case, the NBC television network has taken XOOM and its millions of users into its fold. Despite its size, XOOM manages to be rather unobtrusive and easy to surf. There are no popup advertisements, the URLs are straightforward, and its high-speed servers mean fast page loading.

One of the advantages of XOOM is its member programs and services. Using XOOM's in-house, ready-made services, you can install chat rooms and shopping centers, stream classic movies, and even get free Internet access if you live within a service area. The catches are few. You will get email from

XOOM offering to sell you products, but this is limited to about two emails per week.

Rather than place ads on your page, XOOM places a XOOMbar across the top of your site that links visitors to its products and services. This is much less annoying than a popup, and you hardly notice this after a while. XOOM lists the allotted storage space as 500MB per member, but your Web site space is unlimited, as long as it is legal content and is all accessible from your Web page. Using this space for archival storage of your files is a no-no.

Lycos Network
www.tripod.lycos.com and angelfire.lycos.com

The Lycos network offers two options, Tripod and Angelfire, which give a similar service somewhere in between the levels offered by GeoCities and XOOM. Using either banner or popup advertisements, they are not as easy to navigate as XOOM, but their pages are still far less cumbersome than those at GeoCities. Both were originally independent hosts that have improved much since their affiliation with the Lycos Network, and despite their considerable size, they manage to give a good level of personal service. Offering basic affiliate programs such as commission sales and an online game room, these sites appear to be focused more on basic hosting than on becoming major shopping centers, like XOOM. Storage limits begin at 5MB per member, and can be increased up to 30MB.

Spaceports
www.spaceports.com

Spaceports, an upstart free provider, offers users control over how their sites are administered; the levels of personal service to each customer are high, and page-loading time is not a problem. Rather than dictate the type of advertisements placed on the pages, Spaceports offers a member a choice of voluntarily placing small banner ads from which the member will receive a commission for every click-through, or having a popup ad placed by Spaceports that pays no commission.

The good points about Spaceports are obvious, but the downside is that it's not as easy as some of the other sites for a novice to use. There is at present no built-in page-building program like the ones available at the more established sites; but if you already can create your own pages offline, this may be an attractive alternative to the megahosts. Web space is unlimited, although you are required to apply for extra space after 10MB.

Signing up for a free site

When you've decided which provider will best suit your needs, go to the home page for that provider and click on the sign-up or join now link. You will be required to give varying degrees of information, such as your name, address, and a valid email address; you're also sometimes expected to complete survey information that asks for such things as your household income and hobbies.

When you finish the initial signup, you should check your email, as all the sites will send you a confirmation email. You have to reply to it in order to activate your account. You'll also receive a password that protects the information on your site; the pages there can't be altered without first logging in using that password.

That's all there is to it. You now have your own Web site, empty as it may be. But you'll soon change that. I'll give you some suggestions on how.

Watch Out!
Carefully read the terms of service at any "free" Web site space provider; this agreement should cover how much control you retain over the data on your site. Make sure you don't lose the copyright on your content or have any other restrictions on the rights to distribute the site content.

Getting your page up on a free site

As mentioned earlier in the chapter, if you use one of the large free Web space providers, you will find a built-in home page design program that will let you put your page together right on the site. Most also offer an easy-to-use interface for uploading files from your computer, as well as large libraries of images and backgrounds to further enhance your pages.

To design your page and access any of the available extras, you will need to follow these steps:

1. Go to the home page of your Web provider's site.

2. Click on the members login button.

3. Follow the prompts to enter your username and password.

4. Choose the option to edit your site.

You should have little problem in getting started as these onsite editors are designed specifically for those with no HTML or Web page design experience.

Promoting your site

When your site is built and online, you want others to be able to find it. After all, that's the whole point, right? The following are some of the ways to promote your site:

■ Search engines and portals

■ Link exchanges with other sites or banner networks and Web rings

■ Email announcements

The following sections explain how you use these options.

Timesaver
When you visit HTML tutorial sites or read the suggested HTML books, research how you can use <meta> tags with some search engines to help increase the traffic to your site.

Registering your site

There are thousands of search engines on the Web. However, most people generally use the most popular 10 or so on a frequent basis.

Before you begin surfing to search engines, there are a few items you need to prepare. Open your text editor, Notepad, or word processor, and type the following information to make it easier when you register with multiple sites. That way you'll be able to switch between windows to copy and paste this information when you need it into each site with which you register:

- *Keywords*   Do some brainstorming, and come up with 20 to 30 words that you think people will type in a search engine in order to find a site similar to yours.

- *Web site description*   This is a sentence or two that describes what purpose your Web site serves.

- *Web site name*   Your Web site name is generally what you have (or should have) as the title of the main page.

- *Web site URL*   This is the address others will use to find your site, such as www. genealogytips.com.

The folks at WEBalley have a free tool that will submit your site's information to 72 search engines at once. All you need do is go to www.weballey.net/webannouncer and follow the instructions, using the information you have jotted down.

Using link exchanges and Web rings

Link exchanges do exactly what the name implies. You host banners on your site that users can click, and in turn, your banner is shown on others' sites so

Timesaver
Even if you use WEBalley or another multiple-search-engine registration site, you still need to go to Yahoo! to register separately. Yahoo! does not allow remote registration of URLs.

that their users may click to your site. Similar to a link exchange, a Web ring is a circle of Web sites with a similar theme or subject.

One or both of these services may be of help to you in promoting your site. Take a look at some of the following, and choose for yourself:

- *LinkBuddies (www.linkbuddies.com)*
  LinkBuddies provides a link exchange and a lot of other services for its members.

- *Microsoft bCentral (www.bcentral.com/?leindex)*
  Formerly LinkExchange, this oldest and most well known of link exchanges, is now owned by Microsoft.

- *WebRing (www.webring.org)*   At WebRing you can browse the subjects and find a ring or rings to which you want to subscribe.

Another way to exchange links is manually, by contacting the Webmaster of sites with a similar subject as yours and informing them that you are linking to them and would like a reciprocal link in return. Most Webmasters will be happy to comply with your request.

Using email signatures

At the end of every email message you send, in your signature, place the address to your site below your name. This is a good way to get your site address out there, especially when people forward your emails to others and leave your signature in place at the end of your message. Additionally, people have come to rely on signature files as a source of contact information. If someone can't remember your site address, he or she can open your email and find it at the end of your message. For more information on email signatures, see Chapter 5.

Just the facts

- A Web site can be a great way for you to share information with others.

- You can use HTML editors to create Web pages.

- You can get free counters, guestbooks, and other services online.

- Registering your site with search engines and directories can increase traffic to your site.

- Email updates about added content are a great way to keep visitors informed and encourage repeat visits.

GET THE SCOOP ON...
Performing an online virus check ▪ Separating
email fact from fiction ▪ Easy ways to share
files with others ▪ Organizing an online family
reunion ▪ Family ancestor myths and
genealogy scams

Online Extras

Chapter 15

A t this point, you've accomplished a lot.
You've determined the scope of your
personal genealogical journey, you've
chosen a way to organize all your research and
materials, and you've learned the methods that will
work best as you conduct your research.

As you've discovered, researching your family
tree can be an adventure. It involves a lot of work,
but that doesn't mean you can't have fun along the
way. Nor does it mean that streamlining that work
makes you lazy. It just makes you more efficient!

The online extras included in this chapter will
give you ideas on some enjoyable ways to adopt
some additional, effective, online work habits. You'll
learn how to gather the family for an online family
reunion that you'll host in a chat channel. I'll take
you through the steps of finding and installing chat
software, and give other suggestions on how to go
about planning your reunion. You'll learn about the
urban legends sites that help you determine which
are the made-up stories people sometimes circulate
by email as if they're the truth. To get you started,

I first tip you off about the nasty curse of being online: the dreaded virus.

Online virus checking

Timesaver
You can find up-to-date virus news on the ICSA Virus Lab News and Alerts Web site, at www.icsa.net/ services/ consortia/ anti-virus/ news.shtml.

During your time online, you'll receive a large number of files: programs and information you download from Web sites, word processing files sent to you by new-found family members via email, digital photographs, and more. You've probably heard the adage that it's impossible to make something foolproof because fools are so ingenious. That's sadly the case when it comes to deviant computer hackers. New and improved computer viruses are an everyday reality of the online world.

Viruses come in all shapes and forms. Some are just a nuisance, such as one that flashes an annoying message or causes your cursor to jump around the screen. Some viruses sit in memory and use up resources, making your system run more slowly. Others can attack the files on your hard drive— renaming the files and then deleting your originals. Some attack your email client while they're worming their way on their path of destruction, sending themselves to everybody in your address book. (This type of virus uses up enough bandwidth that it's shut down entire corporate email servers.)

No one is safe from viruses. Treat every file you receive online as if it's candy from a stranger. It doesn't matter how well you know and respect the people who send viruses to you. It doesn't matter if they are running a virus detection program, such as the ones listed at www.genealogytips.com, on the Chapter 15 page. If they haven't downloaded and installed the most recent virus patterns, they could unknowingly be housing a number of viruses on their system and inadvertently spreading them to others in the process.

The same applies to you. If you choose to run an antivirus program, keep your virus patterns up to date. The patterns are what your antivirus program uses to detect whether any of the files you receive contain a known virus. Many commercial program manufacturers notify you immediately when the patterns change. If you opt not to be on the email notification list or have the automatic online update option, you should at the very least check for new virus patterns weekly. (Recently, new patterns have been added daily.)

If you have a hard time remembering to update your virus patterns, you can use an online virus scanner that makes free house calls each time you receive a new file. Visit Trend Micro's free HouseCall site (housecall.antivirus.com/pc_housecall). Complete the registration form, submit your email address, and then follow the simple instructions. You can choose to scan the entire or partial contents of any drive installed on your system. If HouseCall detects a virus, you're given the option of letting HouseCall see if it can clean the file. Otherwise, you receive a congratulatory message each time your drive or files pass the test.

Uncovering urban legends and myths

When you've been online for any length of time, you'll start to shudder each time a member of the family gets his or her first Internet account. It's not that you're not grateful for the chance to visit with the person via email or chat, but you're now a part of one more person's email list! Every joke is new to him or her. That's not so bad, but every email chain letter is new to him or her, too.

Moneysaver
You can find trial versions of antivirus and other commercial, shareware, and freeware programs at Tucows (www.tucows.com).

Do yourself and your new online friends a favor, and visit The AFU and Urban Legend Web site, at www.urbanlegends.com. (*AFU* stands for the newsgroup, alt.folklore.urban.) There you'll find explanations on all kinds of hoaxes making the email rounds, in addition to other interesting hoaxes. It's a free site, but be forewarned: The site does contain some adult content.

Family legends and outright genealogy scams

Family legends are similar to urban legends—they're wrong assumptions or stories—but they're usually about someone who is purported to be your ancestor. These stories are usually passed down from one generation to the next and are therefore assumed to be true. Your job as a genealogist is to track down the information to prove or disprove the relationship.

Genealogy scams are falsehoods passed on to you by someone outside your family, usually in the hopes of getting you to make an investment or a purchase. No matter what some advertisers will have you believe, no one magic potion (or mail-in offer or Web site) is going to reveal all the secrets of your ancestral universe to you.

You can learn about scams perpetrated against those in the genealogy community and the truths about some pilgrim legends at the Web sites described in the following sections.

Genealogy Frauds

www.linkline.com/personal/xymox/fraud/fraud.htm

Part of the 1600s Ancestors Database Web site, the Genealogy Frauds page provides links to fraud reports, including one about a publisher who invented parishes in Europe and used them for the forged wills and birth and marriage certificates he sold.

The National Genealogical Society Consumer Protection Committee

www.ngsgenealogy.org/about/content/committees/consumer.html

The National Genealogical Society (NGS) Consumer Protection Committee was formed to research the large number of surname and coats of arms books that usually consist primarily of lists of surnames, but are marketed as family histories.

Pilgrim Myths and Realities

www.plimoth.org/Library/pilmyth.htm

The Pilgrim Myths and Realities site describes Plimoth Plantation's pilgrim myths and realities. The purpose of the site is to dispel the romantic notions about the pilgrims and pass along the true story about them. This site falls within the family legends category, rather than the genealogy frauds category.

As with other things in life, if it seems too good to be true, it probably is. Before you purchase any goods or services from an online retailer, check the consumer protection links provided at www.genealogytips.com, on the Chapter 15 page. You may be glad you did.

Exchanging files the easy way

You will probably have digital photographs, photocopies (or electronic photocopies—documents you've scanned as graphics or text files), and other things you want to share with others. Read on to learn how to make these file-sharing chores as easy as possible.

> **66**
> The wrongful assumption of arms in Scotland is punishable by fine and imprisonment.
> —Society of Genealogists *The Right of Arms* Web page, www.sog.org.uk/leaflets/arms.html
> **99**

The ups and downs of email research

Email is great for almost instantaneous communications. Its advantages for streamlining your research are enormous. For example, university librarians are some of the most generous people in the world. I've written to them to receive such information as the following:

- The contact name and email address for the university alumni association (Most universities now post this information on their Web sites.)

- Confirmation on a quote and bibliography information from an out-of-print book I knew had been authored by someone affiliated with that college

- The date of a local street name change

Keep in mind that although the librarians are generous, you don't want to take advantage of them. Only send email queries for answers you are unable to find or confirm through your own searches.

Occasionally in response to your requests, or as information from friends or associates, you'll receive an email attachment (for more about attachments, see Chapter 5). These are a mixed blessing, especially for those who use the Internet for work while performing genealogical research on the side. At some point during your time online, while waiting for an important message to arrive from a client, you'll receive a huge unrelated email attachment, likely during one of the slowest, most bogged-down periods of the day, so the email ties up your email client for a long time. When the message finally downloads, you discover it's a video animation, music file, or cutesy animated musical greeting card (in the form of a multimegabyte executable [.exe] file) from your Aunt Bertha. Although you might appreciate the sentiment, the manner in which the file was sent can really be frustrating.

You can't always avoid this problem. Some acquaintances just don't understand the inconvenience of being on the receiving end of such mailings. You can set a file size limitation within your email program options, but this won't solve the problem if you conduct business on your home computer and you're expecting a large attachment from a client. In addition to a polite note to the offender requesting that he or she check with you before sending large files, you can also learn and then teach others the suggestions described in the following sections.

Zip 'em up

A file-compression program is worth its hard drive space in gold. Such programs allow you to compress and decompress files so that they take up much less archival space. The reduced file size also makes the files much more convenient to send as email attachments or downloads, as discussed later in this section. Plus, compressing is easy to do.

WinZip (www.winzip.com) is one of the most popular archival tools for Windows users. It's easy to use and it's free for noncommercial use. Once you've downloaded the program and followed the onsite instructions on installing it, compressing a file is simple:

1. From within Windows Explorer (or the Open dialog box within any other program you're currently working in), locate the file you want to compress.

2. Place your mouse pointed over the name of the file you want to compress and right-click

Watch Out! Some people want their email address kept secret. Use the bcc (blind carbon copy) option in your email program for bulk email messages. This hides all the email addresses. The recipient still knows whom the email is from; he or she just won't know who else received a copy of it.

Bright Idea
If you're using a
file compression
program other
than WinZip and
that program
doesn't allow for
the right-click
menu options,
you should be
able to double-
click (with the
left mouse but-
ton) to unzip a
file. In this case,
the program will
let the computer
know that it's
the one to
use with all
.zip files.

on the filename (that is, use the right mouse button rather than clicking on the left button like you usually do).

3. From the resulting menu, select the option Add to *filename*.zip (where *filename* is the name of your chosen file).

4. Follow the screen prompts. The zipped file will appear in the same directory location as your original file.

To save the zipped file to another location on your hard drive, choose the Add to Zip menu option, and follow the prompts. Likewise, if you want to zip several files together (such as an assortment of scanned or digital family photographs), select the Add to Zip option and then follow the screen prompts to assign a zip filename for the archive of multiple files and the hard drive location for that archive.

Free online hard drive space

Getting free online hard drive space is a simple way to share large files with others. Some Web sites will give you free hard drive space; links to some of them are listed at www.genealogytips.com, on the Chapter 15 page. When you sign up with one of these sites, you can access the free space just as you would access a hard drive on your home computer. This is a great option for high-speed connections, which are discussed in Chapter 2. Because the files transfer so fast, it can be like having another hard drive in your computer.

Intranets

An *intranet* is a Web-style site that's usually maintained by a company or an organization on its networked computers. An intranet can be connected to the Internet, but its primary function is to provide the employees within that organization the means to communicate and share files.

Think of your family as a private company. You, too, have proprietary information. Therefore, for privacy reasons, your "company" has information, such as the following, that is inappropriate to post on a public Web site:

- Any GEDCOM files that include personal information on living persons

- Family members' contact information, including home addresses and phone numbers

- Recent family photos that include citation information

- Personal announcements, such as births, marriages, family reunion locations and times, and related items

If you know how to create and maintain a Web site (see Chapter 14) and have the time to maintain a special site for the convenience of your family, you can create an intranet and house it on an intranet host site. I've provided links to free intranet hosts at www.genealogytips.com, on the Chapter 15 page.

Most intranet host sites offer storage space so that you can develop a password-protected intranet community. Useful features to watch for are address books and calendars. That way, you'll have databases that store contact information, such as phone numbers, snail mail addresses (Internet slang for mail delivered by a postal service), and email addresses. What an easy way to ensure that no one loses the phone number for a distant relative! Everybody's Christmas card list can remain up to date, too.

FTP

File Transfer Protocol (FTP) is an easy way to transfer files to and from your computer to another computer or server over the Internet. At first, it can seem difficult to use, but with the use of an FTP program, it proves to be very easy. When you get the hang of it, you'll find that it is much like transferring files from one directory to another on your own computer's hard drive.

I've included links to FTP programs at www.genealogytips.com, on the Chapter 15 page. The steps for transferring a file vary slightly from program to program. But after a quick review of the Help file, you'll be FTPing in no time at all.

Planning an online family reunion

You can get everyone in the family together for a reunion without the inconvenience of long-distance travel or the hassles of booking a location and planning the meal. Do it online!

Conference calls are expensive. Some Internet options, such as Internet phones, NetMeeting, and Web cams, require the newest, fastest computer equipment, plus a huge amount of resources (RAM). AOL offers Instant Messenger, but the interface can get clumsy with a large group of people. That isn't the case with Internet Relay Chat (IRC).

IRC is a free and easy way for you to get together with family members in an online chat room, known as a *chat channel.* One of the most popular locations to do so is on the Undernet IRC network. As long as everyone in the family downloads and installs an IRC client (you'll learn about this in a minute), everyone can meet online and chat by typing real-time messages to one another, no matter the type or speed of the computer. You can create a personal chat channel or join a large number of channels in existence already.

For example, my frequent writing partner Keith Giddeon and I have yet to meet in real life (r/l, in IRC acronym jargon). Keith lives in Florida, and I live in Ohio. We do most of our work together on the Undernet in a chat channel that's kept secret most of the time. We maintain another channel called #Authors (www.blueroses.com/authors) that we use for what we call our "virtual water cooler breaks." But we only open our other channel, #AuthorsCafe, for special occasions, such as author interviews. Otherwise, it remains password protected and hidden so that we can work there in private. Both #Authors and #AuthorsCafe are official Undernet channels, registered with CService (www.undernet.org). Unless your family plans to get together frequently, chances are you won't need to do anything that formal, as you'll see when I discuss actually planning and setting up your reunion later in this section.

Before you plan your reunion, you can go online to familiarize yourself with exactly how a chat channel operates. For example, as I write this, I'm connected to the Dallas, Texas, server (dallas.tx.us. undernet.org, ports 6661 through 6669).

With more than 18,000 channels in existence already, it's easy to find someone to chat with at almost any time of day or night. Channels can be any combination of letters and numbers, and are always prefaced by a number sign (#). Channels such as #help, #ircnewbies, #new2irc, and #mIRC are there specifically to answer any questions you might have. Channels range from those for people who want to pursue adult (that is, X-rated) conversation to those geared toward standard interests, such as #genealogy, #politics, #Bible, #cooking, and #gardening.

It only takes three easy steps to get online to chat:

1. Install what is known as a chat client.

2. Configure that program to connect to IRC.

3. Join or create a channel after you're connected to the Undernet.

Chat software choices

The following are the chat clients used most often with the Windows 95 and 98 operating systems:

- *mIRC* This is the most popular IRC software for Windows. It is constantly being updated with new features. The program comes with an excellent FAQ for IRC beginners.

- *pIRCh* This is another popular IRC client for Windows. Although it is rarely updated, many people still like it. You can find download and installation instructions for this program at www.bcpl.lib.md.us/~frappa/pirch.html.

- *IRCle* This is one of the clients that can be used with a Mac. The Web site for this program is at www.xs4all.nl/~ircle.

Connecting to IRC

For these instructions, I'm going to assume you have installed mIRC, which is the easiest client to use with Windows. If you're not using mIRC, the basic instructions will be just about the same. Follow these steps to get started:

1. Upon launching mIRC for the first time, some-where on your screen you will see a window

Unofficially...
On arrival on IRC, you're usually greeted with a welcome message in your Status window that informs you of current user status, such as "there are 15519 users and 19486 invisible on 43 servers . . . 67 operator(s) online . . . 18307 channels formed."

called the mIRC Setup dialog box. From within the mIRC Setup dialog box, fill in the following:

- *Choose a Server* In the pull-down menu below the Add, Edit, Delete, and Sort buttons, choose any server that begins with *Undernet:*. (Note to AOL users: You must use one of the Undernet: Washington, DC, servers.)

- *Full Name* Put anything here. It doesn't have to be your real name, and in fact it is best *not* to place your real name here. Most people choose a nickname they intend to use online and place that in this box.

- *E-mail Address* For the sake of safety and privacy, it's best to use alternative information here. You can type in anything, as long as it takes the standard e-mail address form (for example, nickname@whatever.com).

- *Nickname* Place the name by which you want to be known in the chat room here. Some people choose to use a combination real name and initials, and others prefer to mask their identity or create an online identity completely different from their real name. You can change this information later. For example, you may want to use a fictitious nickname while you're online for casual chats and then, so others will know for sure who you are, switch to a nickname closer to your real name for your family reunions. I sometimes use PamRH. To avoid unwanted messages from others outside your channel, it's best not to use a distinctly female name (such as Pamela). (See further details under Invisible Mode, below.)

- *Alternative*   Place a second nickname here in case someone else online is currently using the first. It's best to use a nickname similar to the one you regularly use. It's a good idea to make your alternative your first nickname choice with a typographic symbol at the end, such as ^ (caret) or - (hyphen) added. This will make you more easily recognizable to your online friends should your regular nickname be currently in use by someone else.

- *Invisible Mode*   Place a check here. This will save you a lot of annoyance in the future. Invisible means that unless someone knows your nickname, he or she can't see if you're online by doing a simple /who search on any of your user parameters. IRC programs have what is known as a *notify list,* which is similar to a buddy list on AOL. The difference on IRC is that you can change your nickname at any time. When you're invisible, unless someone is in a channel with you or knows the specific nickname you're using at the moment, they can't find you. Sadly, this is important because some "adult" users keep a list of common female or male names in their notify lists, depending on their preferences.

2. Click on the Identd tab on the mIRC Setup dialog box, and fill in the following:

- *Enable IDENTD Server*   Check this.

- *User ID* Look at what you used as your email address. On this line place what comes before the @ sign. Using the example above, it would be *nickname.*

3. Make sure you're online—that is, connected through your Internet service provider. Then click on the IRC Servers tab. Select any of the Undernet servers.

4. Click Connect to IRC Server. Within moments, you are connected to IRC.

5. After you've connected, you'll see a flashing cursor on the bottom line of your status window. To join a channel, on that line type /join #Authors (or any other channel name), and then press the Enter key.

Joining a chat channel

If you join a channel and there is no one talking, type in something like, "Hello, I'm new here," and press the Enter key. Your sentence will then appear in the channel window. You don't need to type in your nickname; the program places that before your sentence automatically. Chances are someone will talk with you, although some people who are logged on to the channel may be away working in other windows or programs. They aren't ignoring you on purpose, so be patient. Eventually someone will click over to see if anyone has joined the channel and will reply to your message.

For public channels, the best times for chatting can vary. For example, in #Authors we sometimes have a chat crowd around EDT lunchtime hours, there's sometimes a dinner crowd, and our evening regulars seem to begin arriving at around 8 p.m., with our busiest times usually between 10 p.m. and midnight.

Watch Out!
Use caution when you chat on IRC. You wouldn't divulge your home address to a stranger you met on the street. The same logic applies online. When people ask me, "Where are you from?" I tell them Ohio; I live in a small town, so I don't name the city.

You may feel uncomfortable upon your initial visits to the IRC world. If you do, sit back and watch the conversation to get a feel for the channel. It's okay to lurk until you feel comfortable enough to join in. There's no rule that says you have to chat before you feel like doing so. You can even join more than one chat channel at a time if you want, and click between them to observe the conversation. Eventually you'll find a person with some spare time who is willing to carry on a friendly conversation or help tutor you on how to use the special features of the program if you feel you need them.

Special instructions for AOL users

If you're connected online through AOL, you need to follow these steps in order to chat:

1. Make sure you're using AOL 3.0 or higher. If you don't have AOL 3.0 or above, use the keyword UPGRADE.

2. Download an IRC client, as described earlier in the chapter.

3. After you download the program, install it. You should find the file mirc541s.exe in the download directory under your AOL directory. Go offline and close all other programs. Find and run the mIRC installation program to install it on your computer.

4. Now, you can use mIRC. Make sure you're logged in to AOL (log back on if you followed the recommended instructions and logged off for the installation). Then run the mIRC program. (You should find mirc.exe in C:\mirc.) You'll see a welcome screen, and then the setup screen.

Bright Idea
In IRC you're limited to nine characters when you choose a nickname. For your own protection, use a nickname that doesn't identify you as male or female, but choose something neutral, like BlueRose or SciFiFan. Special characters at the beginning or end of a nickname help you avoid duplicating someone else's.

5. To complete the setup and connect to IRC, go to the Connect page.

Online family reunion dress rehearsal

Even if some of your family members aren't online, the ones who are can get together. Before you decide on a date for your family's online reunion and send out the email invitations, you might want to create a chat channel so that you're familiar with the process. First, you need to settle on a name. As pointed out earlier, at any given time there are more than 18,000 channels in existence on the Undernet. Your chat program has an option that allows you to retrieve all those channel names, but reading through such a list would be time-consuming. There's an easier way to check to see if a channel name is available: Use the /who command. This shows you information on the channel, if one exists, and any users not invisible in that channel. For example, when I checked both #family and #reunion, the server returned this information as part of the reply:

#family X H@d cservice@undernet.org :2

For help type: /msg X help

#reunion X H@d cservice@undernet.org :2

For help type: /msg X help

X and sometimes W are *bots*, online robots that CService assigns to most registered channels to preserve the channel settings. So the returned information above tells us that permanent channels already use those channel names.

Because family members need to know the channel name before the reunion (so they'll know where to join you), it's best to select a name not likely to be in use as a permanent or temporary channel. Unlike nicknames, which are limited to nine characters, channel names can be any length. For this demonstration, I'll use #ourfamilyreunion (all one word, without spaces) as the channel name and make Hahn the password. Note that the password is case-sensitive.

Creating a channel is easy. In the status window or from within another channel, type "/join #ourfamilyreunion" (without the quotation marks) and press Enter. It's that easy. You now have your own chat channel.

Next you need to set the channel parameters. To do so, follow these steps:

1. Double-click anywhere in the channel window. (That's the area to the left of your nickname and above the cursor line.) This opens the mIRC Channel Control dialog box.

2. Starting from the top, and working your way down, first type in a message in the Topic line, such as, "Welcome to our Family Reunion channel!"

3. Place a checkmark beside Secret. This makes your channel invisible to anyone who isn't in the channel. Your channel won't show up on anyone's channel list, thereby preventing any unwanted visitors from dropping by.

4. Next you want to set the password. Put a check mark beside the word Key, and type your password. Make it a word that will be easy for others to remember.

5. Put a check mark beside No external messages. This prevents users from outside your chat room from sending advertisement-style messages to your channel.

6. Put a check mark beside Only ops change Topic. (You may have noticed the @ beside your nickname. That means you're the channel operator, or *op*.) By only allowing the ops to change the topic, you create a safety precaution that keeps the kids (or unruly adults) in line and prevents anyone from placing an unsuitable line as the topic. This may seem like a petty detail, but sometimes family members engage in passionate disagreements. The last thing you want is a topic such as "Drop Dead, Uncle Fred" starting an argument and ruining all your hard work.

You enter all IRC commands at the cursor in either the status window or a channel, and press Enter after typing the command. The following are some common IRC commands:

- */join* #channelname   The command to enter a channel

- */join* #channelname password   The command to enter a secret channel—for example, the command to enter the one we created would be /join #ourfamilyreunion hahn

- */part*   The command to exit a channel but remain on IRC

- */quit*   The command to exit the channel and the IRC server

Conducting an online reunion

Okay. Now you're ready to send out your email invitations. It's up to you whether you want to contact some of your other relatives to choose a date or if you simply want to pick one that's convenient for you for the initial meeting. You probably won't get much productive work done during your initial outing anyhow. Some prefer to schedule an informal meeting for the first outing and have the formal online family reunion sometime after that. You can save the family discussions chosen for your family reunion agenda for the actual date of the reunion; it's probably better that you do that anyhow, because those who already know how to chat online may not attend this initial meeting. Call it a tutorial session, if you like. People will need to get past the introductions to one another and to learn how to chat.

Chatting itself is simple. You type comments into the area below the window in which the chat comments appear. Remember that your chat program will automatically preface your comments with your nickname, so you only have to type the comments.

It's up to you whether you want to establish chat rules. Some prefer to have a chat moderator. In this situation, a member of the channel notifies the moderator that he or she would like to ask a question by typing a question mark (?); the person then waits to ask the question until the moderator acknowledges him or her. Such acknowledgement is usually something like "Fawnn GA." In this case, Fawnn would be the online nickname, and GA stands for "go ahead." In a moderated chat, GA goes at the end of any comment or question to signify that the speaker is finished. An exclamation point (!) is used to signify that a person wants to make a comment.

Even if you don't intend to have a moderated chat, when it comes time for your actual family reunion, it's a good idea to have some questions already prepared to use as ice breakers. You can get people to start chatting by first telling them that there's no reason to feel embarrassed about word spellings or grammar. Everyone realizes that unedited conversation is hitting the channel window. After you do that and establish any rules for the reunion (such as no profanity or gossip), you can start things off by asking questions like "Who would like to share something about the genealogy program you've found to be most helpful to you and why?" or "Has anyone been having any specific problems tracking down some of the information you need to find?" Other topics could include discussing the specifics about recent births, marriages, or deaths in the family. Online family reunions give you the chance to meet with other family members to keep up on what's going on in one another's lives, without the expense of traveling somewhere or incurring long-distance phone charges to do so.

When you send out your invitation, feel free to send people to the chat instructions at www. genealogy.com. You can link there from the Chapter 15 Web page. That makes it easy for others to know how to go about getting an IRC program and installing it. Your invitation should include other things about your online family reunion meeting, such as the following:

- The date
- The time
- The place (the channel name)
- Your contact information, in case anyone has any questions or agenda suggestions
- Any other instructions that you believe will add to the reunion's success, such as listing the agenda, if you've prepared one

> **66**
> My daughter gets home from work at midnight. That's too late for me to phone her because I'd wake the other members of her family. We often get together on IRC for late-night chats. It's a convenient way for us to spend some extra time together.
> —Kay Frank, mother, grandmother
> **99**

The journey continues

You never know when you'll pass your genealogy research on to someone else, or even if you'll be around to do so. For the same reason you have a will, you should also have some sort of guidelines established so that the next person to use the research you've gathered will be able to make sense of it all. You should keep these guidelines in your main notebook or another easily accessible place.

You should make your guidelines as easy to follow as possible. Now isn't the time for overly sensitive feelings or thin skin. Although your genealogy project is for your own enjoyment, it's also a part of preserving your family's history. Therefore, it's in your best interest to occasionally have other family members or friends read over your guidelines to make sure they understand them. Note any ambiguities. Ask for suggestions on how you can make the information clearer. You aren't obligated to follow everyone's suggestion to the letter. This project is your vision; suggestions are only the opinions of others. But keep in mind that those opinions can shed valuable light on how others perceive your work, and use that knowledge to filter the things others tell you as you establish and continue to refine those guidelines.

I hope you've enjoyed learning about the online genealogy world as much as I've enjoyed telling you about it. Your journey is just beginning; I'm sure you'll be referring to this book a lot in the years to come. Take advantage of the links at www.genealogytips.com—I've put them there to make your life easier. You're at the end of this book, but at the beginning of an exciting adventure. Here's hoping that every family record source and reference you find is a correct one!

Just the facts

- No computer files are safe from viruses; you can ensure the safety of yours by installing an antivirus program and keeping the virus patterns up to date or by performing an online virus check.

- Learn to spot myths spread by email and help those who are new to the email community do the same.

- One of the easiest ways to share files with others is by taking advantage of free online hard drive space.

- You can get everyone in the family together for an online family reunion in IRC chat.

Glossary

a femme sole   Early probate term for an unmarried woman.

abstract   A summary of the main points in a document or Web site.

abstract company   A private company that maintains and compiles abstracts of title.

abstract of title   The legal history of the ownership and possession of land.

access control   The ability to control who can get at or manipulate information in, for example, a Web server.

accessibility   The efforts to ensure that Web access is available to people with impairments.

ACSS (audio cascading style sheet)   The language that tells a computer how to read a Web page aloud. This is now part of the most recent conventions for Cascading Style Sheets (CSS2). The CSS home page is at www.w3.org/Style/css.

administration   The handling of a decedent's estate without a will.

337

administrator A person appointed by the court to handle the estate of a deceased person or the affairs of an incompetent person. A female administrator is called an *administratrix*.

affidavit A written statement made under oath in the presence of a notary public or another authorized official.

age of majority The legal age for adulthood. This age varies from area to area.

agricultural schedule A part of the federal census that lists farmers and statistical information about their farms and crops, available for 1850–1880.

ahnentafel system A century-old genealogical numbering system, so named because the word means "ancestor table" in German; also sometimes called the Sosa-Stradonitz System.

allied and associated families Other families who are associated with the family being researched, by church attendance, intermarriage, travel, and witnessing of legal documents.

ancestor A person from whom another is descended; this term generally refers to those before your grandparents.

ancestor chart A chart starting with one individual and moving backward through all the generations of his or her ancestors.

Ancestral File A database created and maintained by the Church of Jesus Christ of Latter-day Saints.

ancestral numbering system A method of assigning a number to yourself and others in your lineage. The number assignment is based on which numbering system you use.

anonymous FTP   A means of connecting to a remote computer as a guest or an anonymous user in order to transfer files to or from a computer.

antebellum   Occurring before the U.S. Civil War.

Archie   An Internet program (now made obsolete by Internet search engines and directories) that provided a means to search for files available via anonymous FTP.

archive   A repository of official records of public or private agencies or historical documents.

attachment   A file sent within the body of an email message or a newsgroup posting.

backbone   The infrastructure of the Internet and the high-speed data lines that support it.

bandwidth   The amount of information that can be transferred at a given time.

banns   *See* marriage banns.

baseline   The survey lines in public domain states, running in an east–west direction.

baud   A speed measurement for data transmission that in simple terms is a variable rate of 1 bit per second (bps).

BBS (bulletin board system)   Popular between 1980 and 1995, these systems were primarily run by single users known as SYSOPs (system operators) who allowed others to dial in to their personal (usually, home) computers to access or exchange data. These cyberspace pioneers let others log in to their computers and leave or respond to messages. Early SIGs (special interest groups) have almost all evolved to the forums now on the Internet. (Some organizations still operate campuswide bulletin boards; they are now usually referred to as bboards, rather than BBs.)

bells and whistles Enhancements to a computer system or program.

beneficiary Somebody who benefits from a provision made by another, such as in a will.

bequest Property transferred to a beneficiary in a will.

Bible record Family record pages of a Bible, containing vital information.

bibliography A list of reference materials cited within a book or an article.

biographical sketch A short history of a person's life.

biography A detailed history of a person's life.

birth certificate A government-issued record and form of identification, recording the date, place, and time of birth, in addition to other vital statistics.

BITNET (because it's time network) A cooperative computer network that connected academic and research institutions over the Internet. The system allowed for email, mailing lists, and file transfers; however, although it has been almost obsolete since 1995 because of the growth of the Internet, some universities still have some aspects in place that restrict access to other BITNET computers.

BMP (bitmap) An image saved in pixilated format wherein each pixel determines the color to display; the collection of tiny dots or squares (pixels) are then arranged on the screen to form the pattern. *Bitmap* can mean the image file itself or the data file for the image.

bookmark A Web link stored on a computer to allow you to retrieve Web sites you have already visited to avoid having to search for them again.

bounce When an email message gets returned to the sender without reaching its recipient.

bounty land Land received by a veteran, his family, or an assignee, for military service, awarded by the state or federal government.

browser A computer program that allows you to view World Wide Web pages; Netscape Navigator and Internet Explorer are the most popular.

Bureau of Refugees, Freedmen, and Abandoned Lands *See* Freedman's Bureau.

burned county A county whose courthouse records have been lost or destroyed.

cache The documents retrieved from Web sites for display in a browser and stored on a local hard drive.

CD-R (compact disc–recordable) A drive that reads or runs CDs as well as records data to a CD; however, unlike a CD-RW or hard drive, once data is saved to a CD-R disc, it's permanent and cannot be overwritten.

CD-ROM (compact disc–read-only memory) A read-only disk, sometimes referred to as a CD, that is used in a computer's CD-ROM drive. A CD-ROM can hold more than 650MB of data.

CD-RW (compact disc–recordable rewritable) A read-write CD drive used to burn data onto a CD. The CD-RW format holds more data than a floppy disk; however, a standard has not yet been established, so not all such drives write in similar formats, which means there may be some incompatibility problems in sharing such discs.

census The enumeration of inhabitants of a region, done by a census enumerator, for the federal or a state government.

chancery court A court of equity distinct from a court of common law, usually dealing with divorce or family matters. Now abolished in most states.

channel An IRC chat room.

charter A list of the goals and objectives of a mailing list or newsgroup.

chat The means of "talking" in real-time via typed messages sent across a network such as the Undernet or in a browser chat (sometimes referred to as Internet Relay Chat).

chat room A site on the Internet that allows people to be involved in real-time group discussion.

chattel *See* personal property.

Christian name The first and middle names given to a child at birth or baptism.

Church of Jesus Christ of Latter-day Saints A religious denomination, commonly know as Mormons, that conducts genealogical research for their own religious purposes and that they also make available to the public through their Family History Centers, library, and Web sites.

citation A formal notation documenting the source of information.

cite A notation calling attention to the proof or source of the information (citation).

city directory An alphabetical listing of all residents and businesses in a community that usually includes basic address and other information about those listed on its pages.

civil code Laws of a state or federal government, often including the regulation of what civil records can be obtained and by whom.

civil lawsuit A legal case between two or more private parties in a private action, distinct from a criminal lawsuit.

civil records Records maintained by any level of government, including municipal, state, or federal.

civil registration The act of recording information in civil records as required by law.

Civil War census A special federal census of Union veterans of the Civil War, conducted in 1890.

clerk of courts *See* county clerk.

click-stream Information collected about which sites a Web user has been to.

client A program that uses the service of another program and provides an interface to retrieve data from a server, such as a Web client that serves as a browser, and runs on the computer requesting the information, or an email client.

codicil An addition to a will that modifies or revokes the distribution of the estate.

collateral relative A person who shares a common ancestor with another, but not a direct line.

compiled service record A collection of military records taken from various original documents and compiled into one record, filed alphabetically by the soldier's name.

compiled source Information collected from various original sources into one record.

compress To decrease the size of a file so that it takes less time to transmit or uses less storage space, using a program such as WinZip.

conflicting information Information that comes from different sources and contains inconsistencies or directly conflicting accounts of events, usually requiring additional research to determine validity.

conservator *See* guardian.

consideration The reason to enter into a contractual exchange, including sale of property, that may or may not be monetary. In land transactions, the seller receives money as consideration, and the buyer receives the land.

consolidated index An index combining the indexes of a number of sources.

cookies Files created by a Web browser that contain information relating to a particular site. They can be used to store information such as the frequency of visits or user preferences in interactive sites.

copyright The right of ownership over original works or information.

county clerk The person handling designated documents and transactions in a courthouse.

county court A local government office that administers the affairs of its jurisdiction, including birth, death, and marriage registration.

county formation date The date of incorporation of a new county, either as a secession from an existing territory or as the creation of a new one.

county seat The administrative center for a county.

coverture An early probate term for a married woman.

criminal lawsuit Legal proceedings brought by the state against one or more parties who have been accused of breaking a criminal law.

CSS (cascading style sheet)   A part of an HTML document with details letting the browser know how to display a particular presentation (using fonts, colors, spacing, and so on) on the screen or in print. For further information, see the W3C CSS home page, at www.w3.org/Style/css. *See also* style sheet.

d'Aboville System   A genealogical numbering system.

database   A computer program used to manage data by providing the means to store, retrieve, and sort the information. Also, information organized for optimal search and retrieval.

de Villiers/Pama System   A genealogical numbering system.

death certificate   The official document issued by the government recording the date, time, and place of death, in addition to other vital statistics.

death notice   The mention of a person's death in a list of recent decedents, differentiated from an obituary by its short length and selective information.

decedent   A deceased person.

declaration of intention   A sworn statement made regarding an alien's intention to become a citizen.

deed   A legal document that transfers title to property.

descendant   A person with a direct familial link to an ancestor (for example, grandson, great-granddaughter).

descendant chart   A chart that starts with a person of your choice in your lineage and comes down the generations, listing that person's descendants.

descendant numbering system   A method of numbering the descendants of an ancestor for cross-referencing purposes.

dial-up connection   A connection to the Internet established over telephone lines via an Internet service provider.

digest   A version of a mailing list that contains all messages for a given period; those who subscribe to a digest periodically receive the list with all messages in one digest email instead of getting them as individual email messages.

digital camera   A camera that processes images digitally for upload onto a computer, bypassing the need for film developing and scanning.

digital signature   A means to authenticate a computer user, comprised of a numeric sequence that can be authenticated using a secret key, intended to provide security and proof of origin; something you can do with PKC. W3C addresses the digital signature of XML documents at www.w3.org/People/Berners-Lee/Weaving.

direct connection   A direct link to the Internet, not using a dial-up account, such as a cable modem or T1 line.

directory   Unlike a search engine that searches the Web for content, a directory (such as Yahoo!) performs the search to find matches within those Web pages it contains in its catalog. Also, the level in a hierarchical filing system (that is, embedded folders within a directory for a hard drive partition).

DNS (Domain Name System)   A database system that translates an IP address (for example, 168.144.30.223) into a domain name (for example, www.ricehahn.com).

DOM (Document Object Model)   An Internet protocol that allows programs to access a document as a set of objects. The W3C DOM home page is at www.w3.org/DOM.

domain name A name for a Web site, such as www.ricehahn.com or www.blueroses.com. Common names include .com to designate a commercial site, .org for an organization, .edu for a university site, .gov for a government site, and .net for a network. Outside the United States, country designations are used (for example, .uk indicates a site in the United Kingdom). The Internet Corporation for Assigned Names and Numbers is at www.icann.org.

double dating A practice that shows two separate year dates because of calendar changes in the 1700s.

dower Rights to a portion of an estate that's allotted to a widow.

download To retrieve information (such as a file or an email message) from a remote computer to your own; can also be used to refer to the file being downloaded.

drop chart A depiction of a connection between two people, one from an earlier generation and the other from a later one, that shows their link generation by generation.

EDI (electronic data interchange) A standard of the electronic exchange of commercial documents, established before the creation of the Web.

email (electronic mail) Messages, text, or data sent from one computer to another.

email attachment *See* attachment.

emigrant A person who leaves a country to establish residence in another one, considered in terms of his or her relationship to his or her old country.

emigration The act of becoming an emigrant.

emoticon A graphical representation of emotion using typographic symbols, including :) for a happy face, ;) for a wink, and :(for a sad face.

endnotes Notes containing citations and additional information for the ideas expressed in an article that appear at the end of an article.

enumeration district An area assigned to a census taker.

enumeration order The order in which census entries were obtained and recorded (for example, house by house down a given street).

enumerator Someone who makes a list, usually for a census or for tax purposes.

estate The property held and the debts left by a person at the time of his or her death.

evidence Facts that indicate whether something is true, offered as proof of a lineage.

executor The person who is named in a will to handle the affairs of an estate after the death of the devisor. A female executor is referred to as an executrix.

extract To copy a portion or an entire record verbatim from a source.

family association Those descended from an ancestor or a group of ancestors.

family group sheet A page (often a preprinted form) listing a family unit, including the father, mother, and children of that union. The page also includes the dates and places of birth, death and burial for each individual, and other information and source documentation. Also called a family group record.

family history   A study of a family, including historical information on events and circumstances in the lives of ancestors, rather than only a compilation of dates, places, and lineage.

Family History Center   A local branch of the Family History Library.

Family History Library   The genealogical library operated in Salt Lake City, Utah, by the Church of Jesus Christ of Latter-day Saints, where visitors can research church records compiled on church members and their ancestors.

Family History Library Catalog   The database maintained by the Church of Jesus Christ of Latter-day Saints, accessible at www.familysearch.org/Search/searchcatalog.asp.

family outline report   A list beginning with an ancestor and listing his or her descendants.

family traditions   Family stories or customs, handed down from one generation to the next.

FamilySearch   The Web site operated by the Church of Jesus Christ of Latter-day Saints (www.familysearch.com).

FAQ (frequently asked questions)   A collection of questions and answers that frequently arise for a given topic.

federal land grant   *See* land grant.

filter   A rule used to manage incoming and stored email by performing actions that automatically route messages to various folders based on the sender's address, send prewritten replies, or delete messages that contain specific headers or addresses. Also known as a sorting rule.

flame An insulting or argumentative email message.

flamer Someone who posts insulting or argumentative messages.

flash ROM A chip that can be used to upgrade a modem by installing a new program that rewrites the ROM in the modem with new technology standards.

footnote A note at the bottom of a page containing citations or additional information about information appearing within the text of the article. Sometimes this same data appears at the end of an article, rather than on every page. *See* endnotes.

forum An area on the Internet used for posting messages; messages are related to a specific topic and are hosted by a newsgroup, a mailing list, or another online service.

fraternal order A nonprofit association formed for the benefit of its members.

Freedman's Bureau The bureau established in the War Department by an act of March 3, 1865, that supervised all relief and educational activities relating to refugees and freedmen, including issuing rations, clothing, and medicine, and assumed custody of confiscated lands or property in the former Confederate States, border states, District of Columbia, and Indian Territory.

FTM (Family Tree Maker) A popular genealogy computer program distributed by Broderbund.

FTP (File Transfer Protocol) The means to connect to an FTP site (another computer) using a Web browser to download files; a computer program used for this purpose.

gateway A computer or computer software that connects two computers that use different protocols.

gatewayed Connected via a gateway.

gazetteer A geographical dictionary.

GEDCOM (genealogical data communication) A file format designed for transferring genealogical data between different programs.

GenCount An email report generated by the GenServ system that indicates the number of times the selected surname appears.

genealogical society An organization interested in the genealogical history of the families in a regional area or an ethnic group and dedicated to the preservation of documents and history. Many *genealogical societies* also assist members with genealogical research.

genealogy The record or history of a person's descent, or the study of a person's family.

GenSample A list of people with a given surname who have posted records in the GenServ system.

GenServ A database that is in GEDCOM format and stored on a central computer.

GIF (Graphics Interchange Format) A file format, created by CompuServe, used to compress digital images.

given name *See* Christian name.

grantee A buyer.

grantor A seller.

graphic A computer image, typically a drawing or photograph.

guardian A person who oversees the affairs and interests of a minor or of an incompetent person, including a parent, a person designated by the parents, or a court-appointed trustee.

GUI (graphical user interface) The portion of a computer's operating system that uses icons to initiate commands, rather than relying on typed command-line instructions.

head of household The person whose name appears first in the census enumeration of a household. Before 1850 this was the only information recorded in census enumeration.

heir The recipient of the property of a decedent, designated by a will or by the court.

heirloom An object passed down from generation to generation, generally within the family, by gift or bequest.

Henry System A genealogical numbering system assigning a particular sequence of numbers to the descendants of an ancestor.

hierarchy The structure of messages and replies in a newsgroup, based on the subject of a message, usually organized by date. Commonly referred to as a thread.

historical society An organization dedicated to preserving the history of a geographic area.

home guard Historically, a regional group of men prepared for a call to arms in an emergency. A lay army.

home page A site on the World Wide Web that is either for personal or corporate users.

Homestead Act of 1862 A federal law setting the terms for land acquisition by settlers.

host A central computer to which others are connected in a network that performs a function such as data storage, file transfer, or data processing.

HTML (hypertext markup language) A set of instructions, using regular text, that is added to text documents interpreted by a Web browser to affect the display in that browser.

HTTP (Hypertext Transfer Protocol) A method for transferring documents and information across the Web, using HTML.

hybrid A Web site that contains both a directory and a search engine, such as Lycos, at www.lycos.com.

hyperlink *See* link.

hypermedia An advanced form of hypertext, incorporating text, images, video, and sound.

hypertext Text that has hyperlinks.

ILL (interlibrary loan) The transfer of a book or other materials from one library to another for a patron's use.

immigrant A person who moves to a new country, considered in terms of his new country.

immigration The act of moving into one country from another.

in-law A person related through marriage.

indentured servant One who entered into a contract binding that person to a specified term of service to another, often in exchange for passage.

index A cross-referenced list of a collection of records, available on computer database or index cards. Also used in terms of the Web. *See also* directory.

industry schedule   A part of the federal census listing those enumerated; also called products of industry.

International Genealogical Index   A list of births and marriages of deceased individuals reflected in records collected by the Church of Jesus Christ of Latter-day Saints. It is part of the FamilySearch collection of CD-ROMs that is accessible at Family History Centers.

Internet   The worldwide network of computers, interconnected for the transfer of information.

InterNIC (Internet Network Information Center)   The company that administers domain name registration and assigns IP addresses. It is a group of three organizations: General Atomics handles information services, AT&T handles directory and database services, and Network Solutions (NSI) handles registration services. For more information, see the FAQ at www.internic.net/faq.html.

intestate   Dying without leaving a valid will.

intranet   A computer network within a company, sometimes connected to the Internet, maintained by an administrator who controls access of the local network.

inventory   A list of a decedent's property, compiled near the time of death, often by court-appointed representatives.

IP (Internet Protocol)   The means by which computers route packets of information across the Internet. IP sometimes also refers to intellectual property, but in those instances, it is usually referred to as IPR, for intellectual property rights.

IP address   The numeric routing address given to a domain name.

IRC (Internet Relay Chat)   An Internet protocol that allows users to interface with other users in real-time. *See also* chat.

irregular unit   An armed group of men gathered for a specific purpose.

ISP (Internet service provider)   An intermediary company that provides connections to the Internet for a fee.

JP (justice of the peace)   An elected official with powers enacted by statute, often able to perform marriages and witness legal documents.

JPEG or JPG (Joint Photographic Experts Group) A group that defined a means for encoding photographs and other graphics containing a large number of colors into a format that uses fewer bytes than the pixel-by-pixel approaches used by GIF and PNG, with little visible degradation in quality. The format JFIF is now commonly referred to as JPEG. W3C has JPEG pointers at www.w3.org/Graphics/JPEG.

jurisdiction   The legal boundary of a geographic area, controlled by a central authority, such as a county.

kinship report   A list describing the relationship of a person to the other entries in a database.

kith and kin   Friends and close family of an individual.

land grant   A parcel of land, commonly given by a government to new citizens or as a reward for service (such as in the army).

land patent   A document conveying a land grant.

land record A document listing the transfer of land title for a given parcel of land. *See also* abstract of title.

land warrant A certificate issued by the United States government authorizing the conveyance of land.

LDS *See* Church of Jesus Christ of Latter-day Saints.

legal notice A notice, meeting the requirements of the law, for a specific purpose.

Library of Congress The library of the U.S. government, accessible by the public, that acts as a repository of archived government records, many of which are of value to the genealogist.

line mode Specific instructions, typed manually, for a computer program without a graphical user interface (such as that used by Microsoft Windows).

lineage society A formal group whose members are direct descendants from specific ancestors.

link A portion of a Web page, usually indicated with a colored border or colored text, that links to another page anywhere on the Internet. It uses HTML to direct computers to the linking site. Short for hyperlink.

list *See* mailing list.

listowner The person who maintains a mailing list.

local history The history and stories of a local area, which may include family histories.

loose papers The original legal documents of legal proceedings, filed in packets, stored at a courthouse.

lurk To participate in a list by only reading the messages rather than posting messages.

maiden name The original surname of a woman before marriage.

mailing list An email discussion forum whereby participants subscribe to the list, receive copies of messages sent by other members, and can email their own comments. Some mailing lists are moderated or have a moderator who receives all mail, screens it, and decides which messages to pass on. Unmoderated lists simply redirect all mail received to the list of recipients. Also called simply list.

Manumission Papers Documents granting freedom to a slave.

manuscript collection An assortment of an individual's writings and letters, sometimes in the possession of a library or an archive.

marriage banns A proclamation indicating intent to marry, usually made in front of a church congregation. Also called simply *banns*.

marriage certificate A legal document certifying a marriage.

marriage license A document issued by an ecclesiastical or a civil authority that grants permission to marry.

maternal ancestor An ancestor from the mother's side of the family.

matriculated Enrolled in a college or university.

memorabilia Items with sentimental or collectable significance to a family.

meridian A north–south survey line.

metes and bounds Land measurements using geographic landmarks to define the boundaries of a parcel of land.

microfiche   A system for storing document images on photographic cards that are displayed on a microfiche reader, which enlarges and projects the image on a screen.

microfilm   Similar to microfiche, but stored on rolls of photographic film.

micropublication   Records on microfilm or microfiche.

militia   A group of local lay soldiers, organized for call to duty in cases of emergency. *See also* home guard.

modem   A computer used for transferring information over telephone lines; the name is derived from modulator-demodulator, to describe the device's action.

moderator   The person entrusted with the maintenance of a moderated newsgroup, frequently monitoring posts before distribution.

mortality schedule   An additional part of the federal census, detailing the deaths in each family within the preceding 12-month period, usually from June 1 of the previous year to May 31 of the current year.

mortgage   A document recording the pledge to repay money borrowed, usually placing conditions on the sale of property and recorded at the county level.

mug book   Slang term for a local history, which often contains biographies, photographs, and line drawings.

muster roll   A listing of all personnel in a military unit.

NATF-80 form A government form used to request information from the National Archives, usually regarding military service.

National Archives Archives operated by the U.S. government that contain information relating to the history of the country and its citizens.

naturalization The legal process by which someone of foreign birth becomes a U.S. citizen.

necrology A collection of obituaries or a list of those who died within a specified time frame.

negative research A search that provides no results but still provides guidance (for example, discovering that two decades are missing from the records), thus assisting in subsequent searches.

neighbors People living in proximity to the person being researched who may provide additional avenues for the search. *See also* allied and associated families.

Netiquette Acceptable behavior on the Internet.

newbie A person who is new to or unfamiliar with computers or the Internet.

news server A computer that stores newsgroup postings, accessed by a Web browser or newsreader.

newsgroup An organized distribution list, dedicated to a specific topic, that does not require subscription but can be accessed via a Web browser or newsreader.

newsgroup posting attachment *See* attachment.

newsreader A computer program that allows you to read newsgroup postings.

NGSQ (National Genealogical Society Quarterly) numbering A modification of the Register System that assigns an Arabic numeral to each child and uses a + in front of each child carried forward.

nickname A common name for a person, different from the birth name and usually not legally recognized. On the Internet, a name used to refer to a user, not necessarily corresponding to the person's given name.

node Any equipment physically connected to the Internet that relays information.

obituary A death announcement, usually published in a newspaper, often including family information and used as a primary or secondary research source.

offline Disconnected from the Internet.

one-name study A Web site devoted to the research of one particular surname.

online Connected to the Internet.

OPAC (Online Public Access Catalog) A computerized library catalog.

oral history The unwritten stories told by family members, passed down from generation to generation.

orphan Currently, a child for whom both parents are deceased; earlier, a child with one or both parents deceased.

orphaned A computer model or software package no longer supported by a manufacturer.

OSI (Open Systems Interconnection or Open Systems Interconnect) A standard developed by the International Organization for Standardization to allow computer systems made by different vendors to communicate with each other.

packet A unit into which information is divided for transmission across the Internet.

PAF (Personal Ancestral File) A computer program for genealogy storage, available through LDS.

parent county The county from which another county was formed, or the county from which land was taken to create a new county or part of a new county.

passenger list The list of passengers on a ship, often consulted when researching immigration.

paternal ancestor An ancestor from the father's side of the family.

patronymic A name derived from a father's name.

pedigree chart A chart that shows lines of direct ancestors.

Pedigree Resource File A lineage-linked pedigree file that contains pedigrees and family group sheet data in electronic form. This expanded form of the Ancestral File can contain notes and source documentation.

pension Money paid on a regular basis to a retired or disabled person, due to military service or a government program.

periodical A magazine or another publication, produced at regular intervals, often quarterly or monthly.

personal property Possessions owned by a person, often referred to as chattel, including everything but land. *See also* real property.

personal Web page A Web site maintained by an individual who posts the content of the site.

petition A document, signed by supporters, requesting specific action, usually of a government.

petition for land An application filed for a land grant.

PGP (pretty good privacy) An e-mail security system that uses PKC.

PICS (Platform for Internet Content Selection)   A method for controlling access to information used by parents wishing to control sites accessed by children. The PICS home page is at www.w3.org/PICS.

PKC (public key cryptography)   A mathematics-based security system used to authenticate information.

PKI (public key infrastructure)   A network of authorities who lend assistance to electronic commerce by verifying information with the use of cryptography keys supplied by registered members.

plantation account   Records regarding a plantation's business activities, kept in narrative or tabular format.

plat map   A map of a tract of land, showing the lots within that tract as well as the tract owners' names.

PNG (Portable Network Graphics)   A file format for compressing digital images. W3C recommendations regarding this format can be found at www.w3.org/Graphics/PNG.

political boundary   The jurisdiction of a particular level of government.

POP (point of presence)   The closest site where a user can connect to an Internet server or other remote server; in most cases it is the telephone number from which a user can connect without incurring long distance phone charges.

population schedule   The main part of the federal census, listing the inhabitants (the free inhabitants, before 1870) of an area, with varying degrees of other personal data.

portal   A Web site that provides visitors with the ability to access many sites on a particular subject.

power of attorney A legal document that grants permission for someone to act on another's behalf.

PPP (Point-to-Point Protocol) A means by which computers communicate using TCP/IP over standard telephone lines, ISDN, and other high-speed connections.

primary source A record that can be used as proof of an event's occurrence, often maintained by a church or government. *See also* secondary source.

probate The legal process for carrying out instructions in a will.

probate record A record indicating the proceedings of the distribution of an estate.

professional researcher Someone who performs research for a fee.

progenitor The earliest identifiable ancestor of a family line.

protocol A set of rules that allow computers to communicate or interact, such as FTP and HTTP.

query A request for information or data exchange.

RAM (random-access memory) The working memory of a computer, used for storing data temporarily while the computer runs programs and performs other chores. *Random access* refers to the fact that any area of RAM can be accessed directly and immediately, unlike the time it can take the computer to retrieve information from a hard drive or floppy disk. RAM is volatile memory because information in RAM disappears (that is, you lose your data) if the power is switched off before being saved to disk.

real property Land, as opposed to personal possessions. *See also* personal property.

reapportionment   The redistribution of electoral districts due to population changes.

Record System   A formal genealogical numbering system that assigns an Arabic numeral to each member of a family.

rectangular survey system   The method used to divide land into the surveyed, identifiable parcels described in deed records.

Register System   A formal genealogical numbering system that uses an Arabic numeral preceding each child that is carried forward in the compilation, developed by the New England Historic Genealogical Society for its publication, the *Register.*

regular soldier   A member of the military, serving duty and receiving pay. *See also* volunteer soldier.

repository   The location where items are kept, such as a museum, a library, an archives, or a courthouse.

research calendar   A chronological list of research conducted, showing sources, surnames, and results.

reunion   An organized meeting of descendants or people with a common tie.

Revolutionary War   The U.S. War of Independence, 1776–1783.

ROM (read-only memory)   Nonvolatile storage that can be read but not changed; it holds its contents even when the power is turned off. When data is placed in ROM, it stays there permanently. ROM chips contain the essential software of the computer, called firmware.

RSL (Roots Surname List)   A list of surname searches, dates, and locations, listing contact information for the researcher.

SASE (self-addressed, stamped envelope)   An envelope, usually sent to an organization to facilitate the return of information, used to reduce the organization's expenses.

scanner   A device that converts pictures and documents into digital images for use on a computer.

search engine   An Internet program that gives users the means to search for Web pages based on search criteria, such as by topic or keywords.

secondary source   A record that cannot be relied on as proof but provides background information. *See also* primary source.

server   A program that provides a service (typically information) to the requesting program, called the client. A Web server holds Web pages and allows client programs to retrieve and display them.

service record   A form of record that chronicles someone's military career.

sexton   The caretaker who maintains a cemetery and is responsible for burials.

shareware   Software available on a trial basis before the user purchases it.

signature   Lines of (preferably) text placed at the end of an email message.

site   An informal way of referring to a Web site.

site map   An index of all pages available on a Web site.

slave   A person considered to be the property of another person, capable of being bought and sold.

slave schedule   A part of the federal census (1850, 1860) that lists a description of all slaves owned by a slave owner, without listing names.

snail An informal way of referring to mail hand-delivered by a postal service.

sorting rule *See* filter.

Sosa-Stradonitz System *See* ahnentafel system.

sound card A computer device that allows digital sound files to be played via speakers or headsets.

Soundex An indexing system developed for use with a census and based on the phonetic sound of the consonants in a surname.

source Any reference consulted for research, usually written, but including information obtained from individuals.

source citation An acknowledgment in a note, a footnote, or an endnote providing bibliographic information for the origin of information.

source code The information used by a Web browser to display Web documents. Also, the input sent to a compiler to derive machine or object code.

spam Unsolicited commercial email, usually mass distributed and always unwelcome.

spider A program that searches (or crawls) the Web, looking for pages and categorizing them, usually for a search engine. Sometimes referred to as a robot or bot.

sponsor Someone who vouches for a person's suitability for membership in a lineage society. Also, someone who stands up for a child at a baptism.

SSDI (Social Security Death Index) An index of persons for whom Social Security death claims have been filed with the U.S. government. It is available online, at www.ancestry.com/search/rectype/vital/ssdi/main.htm, and it is also a part of the

FamilySearch collection of CD-ROMs available at Family History Centers.

superior court A court capable of overruling the decisions of a lower court.

surname The last name of a person, given at birth or assumed after marriage.

survey A legal description and detailed illustration of the boundaries of a parcel of land.

survey system A method of defining land boundaries to facilitate sales and transfers.

syntax The terms and characters used to conduct online searches.

tally A record of quantity, usually indicated by marks under categories.

tax record A list of taxpayers within a jurisdiction, also containing an inventory of property.

TCP (Transmission Control Protocol) An Internet protocol used in networks that follow U.S. Department of Defense standards. TCP is connection and stream oriented; it provides reliable communication over packet-switched networks. (*TCP/IP* stands for Transmission Control Protocol/Internet Protocol.)

Telnet A method for connecting to remote computers through a terminal window, often used by libraries to provide access to their databases.

testator The person making a will. A female testator is referred to as a testatrix.

thread Forum messages that refer to the same topic.

topographic map A map indicating the physical contours of a geographic area.

tract book   A book listing the lots or parcels of land within a geographic area.

transcribe   To accurately duplicate all aspects of an original document.

transcribed record   A written or typed copy duplicating the exact words used.

transcript   A word-for-word copy of the text in a document.

TT (tiny tafel)   A family database standard with set field lengths (except for surnames and optional fields) that allows for easy visual or computer scanning.

upload   To transmit files to another computer.

URI (uniform resource identifier)   The string (often starting with http:) that is used to identify a Web site address.

URL (uniform resource locator)   A term used sometimes for certain URIs, once used to indicate that they might change, but now assumed to be synonymous with URI and actually the more commonly used term.

U.S. Colored Troops database   A database of information on 235,000 troops of African descent, maintained by the Fifty-fourth Massachusetts Infantry Web site and in conjunction with the dedication of the African American Civil War Memorial. Available online at www.itd.nps.gov/cwss/usct.html.

Usenet   A worldwide network of thousands of UNIX systems with a decentralized administration that exists to transmit postings to special interest newsgroups, sometimes referred to as SIGs.

video-capture card   A device allowing digital video images to be stored, played, and edited on a computer.

vital record   A record that relates to birth, marriage, and death.

vital statistic   A record that relates to birth, marriage, and death. *See also* vital record.

volunteer soldier   A layperson, not enlisted, performing the duties of a soldier.

W3C (World Wide Web Consortium)   An organization of Web designers committed to defining new standards for HTML and other facets of the Internet.

WAI (Web Accessibility Initiative)   An initiative devoted to promoting the accessibility of the Internet.

War Between the States   Another name for the U.S. Civil War, 1861–1865.

warrant   A certificate ordering an action or the payment of a sum of money. *See also* land warrant.

Web browser   *See* browser.

Web site   A Web page or group of pages on the World Wide Web.

Webmaster   The person who maintains a Web site (sometimes referred to as the Webmeister or Webmistress).

widow's pension   A pension paid to the wife of a deceased man.

will   A legal document indicating a testator's intentions in the division of his property after death.

witness   A person who attests to the validity of information, guaranteeing it in writing.

World Wide Web The common name for the area of the Internet that allows people to access information via HTML.

Zip disk A storage device that can hold 100MB or 250MB, which is more information than conventional forms such as floppy disks.

Resource Guide

Resources appear on the companion Web site for this book, www.genealogytips.com. Each chapter in the book has a companion page made up of links related to the topics covered in that chapter. On the companion Web site, you'll find resources on the following genealogy-related topics:

- Adoption
- African Americans
- Cemeteries
- Church records
- Land
- Maps
- Military records tutorials
- Miscellaneous genealogical studies
- Newspaper and ephemera dealers
- Online newspaper resources

- Paper preservation
- Professional (genealogy) researchers
- Publishers
- Social Security Death Index
- State resources
- U.S. state libraries and archives
- Worldwide genealogical resources
- Vital records

Recommended Reading

This appendix lists a number of books that may help you expand your knowledge of genealogical research and other genealogy topics. You can find links to more information on these titles at www.genealogytips.com, on the Appendix C page.

General genealogy publications

Bentley, Elizabeth Petty. *The Genealogist's Address Book.* Baltimore, MD: Genealogical Publishing Company, 1998.

Carangelo, Lori. *The Ultimate Search Book 2000 Edition: Worldwide Adoption, Genealogy and Other Search Secrets.* Palm Desert, CA: Access Press, 1999.

Coran, Pierre. *Family Tree.* Minneapolis, MN: Lerner Publishing Group, 1999.

Doane, Gilbert H., and James B. Bell. *Searching for Your Ancestors: The How and Why of Genealogy.* Minneapolis, MN: University of Minnesota Press, 1992.

Eichholz, Alice (editor). *Ancestry's Red Book: American State, County and Town Sources*. Salt Lake City, UT: Ancestry, 1992.

Everton, Lee. *The Handybook for Genealogists* (8th edition). Logan, UT: Everton Publishers, 1992.

Gilmer, Lois C. *Genealogical Research and Resources: A Guide for Library Use*. Chicago, IL: American Library Association Editions, 1988.

Meyerink, Kory L. *Printed Sources: A Guide to Published Genealogical Records*. Salt Lake City, UT: Ancestry, 1998.

Neagles, James C. *The Library of Congress: A Guide to Genealogical and Historical Research*. Salt Lake City, UT: Ancestry, 1990.

Sperry, Kip. *Abbreviations & Acronyms; A Guide for Family Historians*. Orem, UT: Ancestry, 2000.

Szucs, Loretto Dennis, and Sandra Hargreaves Luebking (editors). *The Source* (revised edition). Salt Lake City, UT: Ancestry, 1997.

Association publications

Encyclopedia of Associations. Detroit: Gale Research, Annual.

Citations and evidence publications

Jacobus, Donald Lines. *Genealogy as Pastime and Profession*. Baltimore, MD: Genealogical Publishing Company, 1968.

Lackey, Richard S. *Cite Your Sources: A Manual for Documenting Family Histories and Genealogical Records*. Jackson, MS: University Press of Mississippi, 1986.

Mills, Elizabeth Shown. *Evidence! Citation & Analysis for the Family Historian (Item 3846)*. Baltimore, MD: Genealogical Publishing Company, 1997.

Rose, Christine. *What IS the Preponderance of the Evidence?* San Jose, CA: Rose Family Association, 1996.

Stevenson, Noel C. *Genealogical Evidence: A Guide to the Standard of Proof Relating to Pedigrees, Ancestry, Heirship and Family History* (revised edition). Laguna Hills, CA: Aegean Park Press, 1989.

Ethnic publications

Brockman, Terra Castiglia, and Terry C. Brockman. *A Student's Guide to Italian American Genealogy* (Oryx American Family Tree Series). Phoenix, AZ: Oryx Press, 1996.

Danky, James Philip, Maureen E. Hady, and Henry Louis Gates, Jr. (editors). *African-American Newspapers and Periodicals: A National Bibliography* (Harvard University Press Reference Library). Cambridge, MA: Harvard University Press, 1999.

Johnson, Anne E. *A Student's Guide to British American Genealogy* (Oryx American Family Tree Series). Phoenix, AZ: Oryx Press, 1996.

Johnson, Anne E., and Adam Merton Cooper. *A Student's Guide to African American Genealogy* (Oryx American Family Tree Series). Phoenix: Oryx Press, 1996.

McKenna, Erin, and Charles T. Galbraith. *A Student's Guide to Irish American Genealogy* (Oryx American Family Tree Series). Phoenix, AZ: Oryx Press, 1996.

Paddock, Lisa Olson, and Carl Sokolnicki Rollyson. *A Student's Guide to Scandinavian American Genealogy* (Oryx American Family Tree Series). Phoenix, AZ: Oryx Press, 1996.

Records of Ethnic Fraternal Benefit Associations in the United States: Essays and Inventories. St. Paul, MN: Immigration History Research Center, University of Minnesota, 1981.

Robl, Gregory. *A Student's Guide to German American Genealogy* (Oryx American Family Tree Series). Phoenix, AZ: Oryx Press, 1996.

Rollyson, Carl Sokolnicki, and Lisa Olson Paddock. *A Student's Guide to Polish American Genealogy* (Oryx American Family Tree Series). Phoenix, AZ: Oryx Press, 1996.

Ryskamp, George R., and Peggy Ryskamp. *A Student's Guide to Mexican American Genealogy* (Oryx American Family Tree Series). Phoenix, AZ: Oryx Press, 1996.

She, Colleen. *A Student's Guide to Chinese American Genealogy* (Oryx American Family Tree Series). Phoenix, AZ: Oryx Press, 1996.

Wynar, Lubomyr R. *Encyclopedic Directory of Ethnic Organizations in the United States.* Littleton, CO: Libraries Unlimited, 1975.

Family history publications

Hatcher, Patricia Law. *Producing a Quality Family History.* Salt Lake City, UT: Ancestry, 1966.

Wilson, Richard S. *Publishing Your Family History on the Internet.* Cincinnati: Betterway Books, 1999.

Historical society publications

Carson, Dina C. (Editor). *Directory of Historical Organizations in the United States and Canada.* Denver, CO: Iron Gate Publishing, 1994.

Immigrant publications

The Bristol Registers of Servants Sent to Foreign Plantations, 1654–1686. Baltimore, MD: Genealogical Publishing Company, 1988.

Coldham, Peter Wilson. *Child Apprentices in America from Christ's Hospital, London, 1617–1688.* Baltimore, MD: Genealogical Publishing Company, 1990.

Daniels, Roger. *Coming to America: A History of Immigration and Ethnicity in American Life.* New York: HarperCollins, 1990.

Filby, P. William. *Passenger and Immigration Lists Bibliography 1538–1900* (revised edition). Detroit, MI: Gale Research, 1988.

Kurzweil, Arthur. *From Generation to Generation: How to Trace Your Jewish Genealogy and Personal History.* New York: William Morrow, 1980.

Law, Hugh T. *How to Trace Your Ancestors to Europe.* Baton Rouge, LA: Cottonwood Books, 1987.

Newman, John J. *American Naturalization Processes and Procedures 1790–1985.* Indianapolis, IN: Indianapolis Historical Society, 1985.

Rose, James, and Alice Eichholz (editors). *Black Genesis.* Detroit, MI: Gale Research, 1978.

Shaefer, Christine. *Guide to Naturalization Records of the United States.* Baltimore, MD: Genealogical Publishing Company, 1997.

Smith, Jessie Carney. *Ethnic Genealogy: A Research Guide.* Westport, CT: Greenwood Press, 1983.

Tan, Thomas Tsu-wee. *Your Chinese Roots: The Overseas Chinese Story.* Singapore: Times Books International, 1986.

Wellauer, Maralyn Ann. *German Immigration to America in the Nineteenth Century: A Genealogist's Guide.* Milwaukee, WI: Roots International, 1985.

Books about library collections and published sources

Bentley, Elizabeth Petty. *The Genealogists's Address Book.* Baltimore, MD: Genealogical Publishing Company, 1991.

Filby, P. William (compiler). *Directory of American Libraries with Genealogy or Local History Collections.* Wilmington, DE: Scholarly Resources, 1988.

Herbert, Miranda C., and Barbara McNeil (editors). *Biography and Genealogy Master Index* (8 volumes, 5 volumes., 3 volumes, and annual supplements since 1990). Detroit, MI: Gale Research, 1980, 1985–present.

Kaminkow, Marion J. (editor). *Genealogies in the Library of Congress: A Bibliography* (volumes 1 and 2). Baltimore, MD: Magna Carta Book Company, 1987.

Kemp, Thomas Jay. *The 1997 Genealogy Annual: A Bibliography of Published Sources* (Genealogy Annual). Wilmington, DE: Scholarly Resources, 2000.

Military publications

Groene, Bertram Hawthorne. *Tracing Your Civil War Ancestor.* New York: Ballantine Books, 1989.

Ethnic newspaper bibliographies

Arndt, Karl J.R. *German-American Newspapers and Periodicals, 1732–1955.* New York: Johnson Reprint, 1985.

Brigham, Clarence S. *History and Bibliography of American Newspapers 1690–1820.* Westport, CT: Greenwood Publishing Group, 1976.

Harris, Ruth Ann M., and Donald M. Jacobs (editors). *The Search for Missing Friends: Irish Immigrant Advertisements Placed in the Boston Pilot 1831–1850.* Boston: New England Historic Genealogical Society, 1989.

Mallegg, Kristen B. (editor). *Gale Directory of Publications and Broadcast Media.* Detroit, MI: Gale Group, 1999.

Westly, Travis. *Checklist of American Eighteenth Century Newspapers in the Library of Congress.* Washington, DC: Library of Congress, 1996.

Wynar, Lubomyr R., and Anna T. Wynar. *Encyclopedic Directory of Ethnic Newspapers and Periodicals in the United States* (2nd edition). Littleton, CO: Libraries Unlimited, 1976.

Paper and manuscript preservation publications

Brown, Margaret R. *Boxes for the Protection of Rare Books: Their Design and Construction.* Washington, DC: Library of Congress, 1982.

Clapp, Anne F. *Curatorial Care of Works of Art on Paper.* New York: Nick Lyons Books, 1987.

Ritzenthaler, Mary Lynn, Gerald J. Munoff, and Margery S. Long. *Archives and Manuscripts: Administration of Photographic Collections.* Chicago: Society American Archivists, 1984.

Online guide publications

Crowe, Elizabeth Powell. *Genealogy Online: Millennium Edition*. New York: McGraw-Hill Computing, 1999.

Flinn, Cherri Melton. *Genealogy Basics Online*. Cincinnati, OH: Muska & Lipman Publishing, 2000.

Helm, Matthew L., and April Leigh Helm. *Genealogy Online For Dummies* (with CD-ROM). Foster City, CA: IDG Books Worldwide, 1999.

Kemp, Thomas Jay. *The Genealogist's Virtual Library: Full-Text Books on the World Wide Web*. Wilmington, DE: Scholarly Resources, 2000.

McClure, Rhonda R., and Shirley Langdon Wilcox. *The Complete Idiot's Guide to Online Genealogy*. Indianapolis, IN: Macmillan, 1999.

Publications that index periodicals

Bibliography of Genealogy and Local History Periodicals with Union List of Major U.S. Collections. Fort Wayne, IN: Allen County Public Library Foundation, 1990.

Periodical Source Index (PERSI). Fort Wayne, IN: Allen County Public Library, 1986–present.

Relationship publications

Arnold, Jackie Smith. *Kinship: It's All Relative*. Baltimore, MD: Clearfield Company, 1995.

Horowitz, Lois. *Dozens of Cousins: Blue Genes, Horse Thieves, and Other Relative Surprises in Your Family Tree*. Berkeley, CA: Ten Speed Press, 1999.

Oral history publications

Zimmerman, William. *How to Tape Instant Oral Biographies*. Cincinnati, OH: Betterway Books, 1999.

Photographs and photographic preservation publications

Coe, B., and M.A. Haworth-Booth. *A Guide to Early Photographic Processes*. London: Victoria and Albert Museum, 1983.

Eastman Kodak Company. *The Book of Film Care* (Kodak Publication H-23). Rochester, NY: Eastman Kodak Company, 1983.

Eaton, George. *Conservation of Photographs* (Kodak Publication F-40). Rochester, NY: Silver Pixel Press, 1985.

Hendriks, Klaus B., and Anne Whitehurst. *Conservation of Photographic Materials: A Basic Reading List*. Ottawa, Ontario: National Archives of Canada, 1988.

Keefe, Lawrence E., Jr., and Dennis Inch. *The Life of a Photograph: Archival Processing, Matting, Framing, and Storage*. Boston: Focal Press, 1984.

Nadeau, Luis. *Encyclopedia of Printing, Photographic and Photomechanical Processes*. New Brunswick, Canada: Mr. Luis R Nadeau, 1989.

National Research Council. *Preservation of Historical Records*. Washington, DC: National Academy Press, 1986.

Ostroff, Eugene (editor). *Pioneers of Photography, Their Achievements in Science and Technology*. Springfield, VA: Society for Imaging Science and Technology, 1987.

Porro, Jennifer (editor). *Photographic Preservation and the Research Library.* Mountain View, CA: Research Libraries Group, 1991.

Reilly, James M. *Care and Identification of 19th-Century Photographic Prints* (Kodak Publication G-2S). Rochester, NY: Eastman Kodak Company, 1998.

Rempel, Siegfried. *The Care of Photographs.* New York: Nick Lyons Books, 1987.

Ritzenthaler, Mary Lynn, Gerald J. Munoff, and Margery S. Long. *Archives and Manuscripts: Administration of Photographic Collections* (SAA Basic Manual Series). Chicago: Society of American Archivists, 1984.

Thomson, Garry. *The Museum Environment* (2nd edition). Boston: Butterworths, 1994.

Tuttle, Craig A. *An Ounce of Preservation: A Guide to the Care of Papers and Photographs.* Highland City, FL: Rainbow Books, 1995.

Wilhelm, Henry, and Carol Brower. *The Permanence and Care of Color Photographs: Traditional and Digital Color Prints, Color Negatives, Slides, and Motion Pictures.* Rochester, NY: Preservation Publishing Company, 1993.

Scanning Publications

Sullivan, Michael J. *Make Your Scanner A Great Design & Production Tool.* Cincinnati, OH: North Light Books, 1998.

Abbreviations and Acronyms Found in Genealogy

A s you research your family tree, you will come across dozens of abbreviations and acronyms, some of which may be difficult to decipher. Many of them point to foreign words or phrases, have a historical context with which you might not be familiar, can have a number of meanings, and can be capitalized and punctuated a variety of ways. To help you with your detective work, I've provided a long list of genealogy-, geography-, and computer-related abbreviations and acronyms at www.genealogytips.com, on the Appendix D page. The list is provided as a guideline only—not as a definitive reference.

To prevent confusion or misinterpretation in your own work, it's a good idea to avoid using abbreviations or acronyms in your citations. If you do use them, be sure to provide a key so that future generations and others using your work will know for sure what you intended.

The *Unofficial Guide* ™ Reader Questionnaire

If you would like to express your opinion about online genealogy or this guide, please complete this questionnaire and mail it to:

The *Unofficial Guide* ™ Reader Questionnaire
Lifestyle Guides
IDG Books Worldwide, Inc.
909 Third Avenue
New York, NY 10022

Gender: ___ M ___ F

Age: ___ Under 30 ___ 31–40
___ 41–50 ___ Over 50

Education: ___ High school ___ College
___ Graduate/Professional

What is your occupation?

_____

How did you hear about this guide?
___ Friend or relative
___ Newspaper, magazine, or Internet
___ Radio or TV
___ Recommended at bookstore
___ Recommended by librarian
___ Picked it up on my own
___ Familiar with the *Unofficial Guide* ™ travel series

Did you go to the bookstore specifically for a book on online genealogy? Yes ___ No ___

Have you used any other *Unofficial Guides* ™?
Yes ___ No ___

If "Yes," which ones?

_____
_____
_____

What other book(s) on online genealogy have you purchased?

_____

_____

_____

Was this book:
___ more helpful than other(s)
___ less helpful than other(s)

Do you think this book was worth its price?
Yes ___   No ___

Did this book cover all topics related to online genealogy adequately?   Yes ___   No ___

Please explain your answer:

_____

_____

_____

Were there any specific sections in this book that were of particular help to you?   Yes ___   No ___

Please explain your answer:

_____

_____

_____

On a scale of 1 to 10, with 10 being the best rating, how would you rate this guide?   ___

What other titles would you like to see published in the _Unofficial Guide_™ series?

_____

_____

_____

Are _Unofficial Guides_™ readily available in your area?   Yes ___   No ___

Other comments:

_____

_____

_____

Get the inside scoop...
with the *Unofficial Guides*™!

Health and Fitness

The Unofficial Guide to Alternative Medicine
ISBN: 0-02-862526-9

The Unofficial Guide to Coping with Menopause
ISBN: 0-02-862694-X

The Unofficial Guide to Dieting Safely
ISBN: 0-02-862521-8

The Unofficial Guide to Having a Baby
ISBN: 0-02-862695-8

The Unofficial Guide to Living with Diabetes
ISBN: 0-02-862919-1

The Unofficial Guide to Smart Nutrition
ISBN: 0-02-863589-2

The Unofficial Guide to Surviving Breast Cancer
ISBN: 0-02-863491-8

Career Planning

The Unofficial Guide to Acing the Interview
ISBN: 0-02-862924-8

The Unofficial Guide to Earning What You Deserve
ISBN: 0-02-862716-4

The Unofficial Guide to Hiring and Firing People
ISBN: 0-02-862523-4

Business and Personal Finance

The Unofficial Guide to Beating Debt
ISBN: 0-02-863337-7

The Unofficial Guide to Investing
ISBN: 0-02-862458-0

The Unofficial Guide to Investing in Mutual Funds
ISBN: 0-02-862920-5

The Unofficial Guide to Managing Your Personal Finances
ISBN: 0-02-862921-3

The Unofficial Guide to Marketing Your Business Online
ISBN: 0-7645-6268-1